PELICAN BOOKS

A325

THE PELICAN GUIDE TO ENGLISH LITERATURE

3

FROM DONNE TO MARVELL

From Donne to Marvell

VOLUME

3

THE PELICAN GUIDE TO ENGLISH LITERATURE

★

EDITED BY BORIS FORD

PENGUIN BOOKS

BALTIMORE · MARYLAND

Penguin Books Ltd, Harmondsworth, Middlesex
U.S.A.: Penguin Books Inc., 3300 Clipper Mill Road, Baltimore 11, Md
AUSTRALIA: Penguin Books Pty Ltd, 762 Whitehorse Road,
Mitcham, Victoria

—

First published 1956
Reprinted with revisions 1960, 1962

—

Made and printed in Great Britain
by Hazell Watson and Viney Ltd
Aylesbury and Slough
Set in Monotype Bembo

CONTENTS

GENERAL INTRODUCTION

IN introducing this *Guide to English Literature*, it is as well to remember that this is the age of the Digest and the Headline, of the Comic and the Tabloid, of the Bestseller and the Month's Masterpiece: an age when a 'deep-seated spiritual vulgarity ... lies at the heart of our civilization', in the words of the novelist L. H. Myers. Perhaps in response to this, the twentieth century has also been a period of unusually lively criticism, a time when a small number of writers and critics have made a determined effort to elicit from literature what is of living value to us today; to re-establish, that is, a sense of literary tradition and to define the high standards that this tradition implies. At the same time it is also important that this feeling for a *living* literature and for the values it embodies should be given as wide a currency as possible, and that literature – both today's literature and yesterday's – should have a real and not merely a nominal existence among a comparatively large number of general readers.

It is to meet this second need that the *Guide* has been planned and produced; and it is the general state of letters and reading today which has determined the shape that it has taken. For this *Guide* has been expressly designed for those thousands of people who might be described as something less than advanced and specialist students of literature, but who accept with genuine respect what is known as 'our literary heritage'. For many of them this amounts, in memory, to an unattractive amalgam of set texts and school prizes, and as a result they have come to read only current books – fiction and biography and travel. Though they are probably familiar with such names as Pope, George Eliot, Langland, Marvell, Yeats, Dr Johnson, Hopkins, D. H. Lawrence, they might hesitate to describe their work intimately, or to fit them into any larger pattern of growth and achievement. If this account is a fair one, it seems probable that very many people would be glad of guidance that would help them respond to what is living and contemporary in literature, for, like the other arts, it has the power to enrich the imagination and to clarify thought and feeling. Not that one is offering literature as a substitute religion or as providing a philosophy for life. Its satisfactions are of their own kind, though they are satisfactions intimately bound up with the life of each

individual reader, and therefore not without their bearing on his atti
tude to life.

At any rate, it is in this spirit that the *Guide* is offered to the gener.
reader. For this reason it does not set out to compete with the stan
dard Histories of Literature, which inevitably tend to have a take-it-or
leave-it attitude about them. This is not a *Bradshaw* or a *Whitaker'.
Almanack* of English literature. Nor is it a digest or potted-version
nor again a portrait-gallery of the Great. Works such as these already
abound and there is no need to add to the number. What this wor
sets out to offer is, by contrast, a guide to the history and traditions c
English literature, a contour-map of the literary scene. It attempts
that is, to draw up an ordered account of literature that is concerned
first and foremost, with value for the present, and this as a direct en
couragement to people to read widely in an informed way.

The *Guide* consists of seven volumes, as follows:

1. *The Age of Chaucer*
2. *The Age of Shakespeare*
3. *From Donne to Marvell*
4. *From Dryden to Johnson*
5. *From Blake to Byron*
6. *From Dickens to Hardy*
7. *The Modern Age*

The boundaries between the separate volumes cannot be sharply
drawn, and in some instances there is an overlap. Far from being
disadvantage, however, this should help to make the *Guide* a singl
work rather than seven distinct works. Each separate volume, with
the exception of the last, has been named after those writers who
dominate or stand conveniently at either end of the period, and who
also indicate between them the strength of the age in literature.

Though the *Guide* has been designed as a single work, in the sens
that it attempts to provide a coherent and developing account of the
tradition of English literature, each separate volume exists in its own
right. Thus each volume sets out to provide the reader with four kind
of related material:

(i) An account of the social context of literature in each period, at
tempting to answer such questions as 'Why did the literature of thi
period deal with *this* rather than *that* kind of problem?', 'What factor

tended to encourage the play rather than the novel, prose rather than verse, in this period?', 'What was the relationship between writer and public?', 'What was the reading public like in its tastes and make-up?' This section of each volume provides an account of contemporary society at its points of contact with literature.

(ii) A literary survey of the period, describing the general characteristics of the period's literature in such a way as to enable the reader to trace its growth and to keep his bearings. The aim of this section is to answer such questions as 'What *kind* of literature was written in this period?', 'Which authors matter most?', 'Where does the strength of the period lie?'

(iii) Detailed studies of some of the chief writers and works in the period. Coming after the general surveys, the aim of this section is to convey a sense of what it means to read closely and with perception, and also to suggest how the literature of a given period is most profitably read, i.e. with what assumptions and with what kind of attention. This section also includes an account of whichever one of the other arts particularly flourished at the time, as perhaps throwing a helpful if indirect light on the literature itself.

(iv) An appendix of essential facts for reference purposes, such as authors' biographies (in miniature), bibliographies, books for further study, and so on.

Thus each volume of the *Guide* has been planned as a whole, and the contributors have been chosen as people whose approach to literature is based on common assumptions; for it was essential that the *Guide* should have cohesion and should reveal some collaborative agreements (though inevitably, and quite rightly, it reveals disagreements as well). They agree on the need for rigorous standards, and thus they have felt it essential to take no reputations for granted, but rather to examine once again, and often in close detail, the strength and weakness of our literary heritage.

BORIS FORD

NOTES

Notes designated by an asterisk, etc., are given at the
foot of each page. Numbered notes are given
at the end of each chapter.

PART
I

THE BACKGROUND TO ENGLISH
LITERATURE: 1603–60

BY MARJORIE COX

Formerly Lecturer in Modern History, University of Manchester

Elizabethan and Seventeenth-Century

THE relationship between literature and the society in which it is
created eludes any easy definition or even description. In different
periods, different aspects of the life of society will constitute the relevant historical 'background' of literature. Economically, the period
1603–60 is not sharply divided from the reign of Elizabeth I, and
scarcely any significant date in economic development falls within it.
The age has no distinguishing economic characteristics of its own, unless it be colonial expansion, and much has still to be learned of its
economic activities. The price rise which had set the economic pace of
the later sixteenth century continued, though at a diminishing rate,
and brought, as before, opportunities for the adventurous and difficulties for the conservative all along the social scale. The most dynamic
point in the economy was still in foreign trade: it was here that the
greatest fortunes were made and the speediest. Profits were almost as
spectacular in certain branches of industry; the cloth industry remained, despite setbacks from James I's interference, the most widespread source of industrial wealth, but the chances for projectors lay
rather in heavier industries such as coal and metals, and in newer
enterprises such as alum and glass, where royal monopolies gave protection as they had done under Elizabeth. Industry as a whole revealed
the same mixture of traditional and new methods of organization
as had distinguished it in the later sixteenth century; only a small proportion was carried on by capitalist employers and workmen, the
bulk remaining in the hands of small masters.

Agriculture, which employed the overwhelming mass of the population, showed none of the striking features of the Tudor or Augustan
ages. Although enclosure seems to have continued, it had not the
dramatic quality of the Tudor movement, and only feeble echoes of
the great anti-enclosure risings were heard in the Midlands in 1607.

Improvements in technique were the theme of many books from Elizabeth's reign onwards, but despite the introduction of some new crops and more efficient farming for markets, especially in districts within range of London's expanding demand, there was no general change of methods. The most impressive innovation was the draining of fenlands in East Anglia, sponsored chiefly by the Earl of Bedford using Dutch engineers. For the most part cultivation was on traditional lines, even if estate management had to be tightened up to meet an inflationary situation.

Socially, English society showed its long-established fluidity; in spite of the cult of heraldry and genealogy, there was no aristocratic or even 'gentle' *caste*. By means of the acquisition of land, the *nouveau riche* was soon absorbed into the gentry, if not so easily into the aristocracy, as witness the objections to Lionel Cranfield's peerage. Landownership gave social status and political authority; birth was an added glory but not an essential. The dominant feature of the social structure of this period is generally held to be 'the rise of the gentry'[1]; this phrase summarizes the multiple movements of society over several generations, whereby many members of the gentry (landowners above yeomen and below the peerage) were gaining economically at the expense of the peerage. The comparison is a total one, and must not obscure the numbers of the gentry who failed, or those of the nobility whose wealth persisted into the Augustan age, but broadly, these years, together with the Elizabethan period, can be contrasted with the century after the Restoration, when the drift of land was away from the gentry towards the large magnates. This landowning gentry was constantly recruited from the more successful yeomen below and from city merchants and lawyers. Nothing like the urban patriciates of Italy or the Netherlands had developed in England, and the rigid contrasts of *rus* and *urbs* and of landowning and trade were absent. The working of primogeniture and the absence of the French rule of *dérogeance* sent the younger sons of the gentry as apprentices into trade; financial needs led to marriages with city heiresses; city men invested in land and landowners were involved in industrial and commercial enterprises. The Puritan squires and peers of the Providence and Massachusetts ventures, among them John Pym, can be paralleled by the Royalist Edmund Verney's investments in monopoly patents and drainage schemes or the Catholic Sir Thomas Tresham's highly commercialized agriculture.

It is in politics rather than in the social and economic spheres that the period has a distinctive character; a summary description, covering a highly complex development, is 'the winning of the initiative by the House of Commons'. Its climax was in civil war and an interregnum, followed by the restoration of a monarchy fundamentally modified though superficially the same. Many of those who lived through the early Stuart reigns contrasted them sadly with the glories of Elizabeth's; opposition M.P.s measured the royal foreign policy by an Elizabethan yardstick and found it wanting; conservative statesmen like Clarendon and Newcastle saw in the Civil War a judgement on departure from Elizabethan methods. Yet in many ways the change of sovereign in 1603 merely exacerbated difficulties already present during the nineties. The demands of continuous warfare for men and money had roused unwonted opposition among the country gentry, the pillars of the Tudor monarchy, and the Queen's grants of monopolies caused popular murmuring and a cooler welcome from her Commons in 1601. Corruption in politics grew with the rivalry between Essex and Cecil. Disillusion gripped the Queen, and only her peculiar skill could have produced from the situation of 1601 her 'Golden Speech' celebrating the mutual love of prince and subjects. In fact, she left to her successors a legacy of unsolved problems: the Crown's financial position, the meaning of the Commons' privilege of free speech, and the precise nature of the Church of England, of which the sovereign was head. In religion and in politics, questioning and the desire for definition grew with the century. These domestic problems had as their background the rising diplomatic tension on the Continent, culminating in the outbreak in 1618 of the politico-religious struggle of the Thirty Years' War. By 1635 all the major European powers were involved, with the exception of England. To James and Charles the interests of a daughter and a sister were at stake, but to numerous frustrated Englishmen the survival of Protestantism itself seemed in the balance, while England pursued a policy of non-intervention.

Whereas the Victorian habit was to see the decisive change in the history of thought in the Renaissance of the fifteenth and sixteenth centuries, contemporary historians find it rather in the seventeenth century.[2] Nothing is more difficult to plot than a change in habits of thinking, for its penetration can only be very gradual. In the early seventeenth century the old Aristotelian cosmology was undermined by particular observations, such as Galileo's, but not yet replaced by a satisfactory new synthesis, so that before Newton various old and new theories of the universe and ways of thinking about nature could co-exist. Nevertheless the gradual replacement of the assumptions of medieval scholasticism by those of modern experimental science begins in this period. Empirical observation became the ideal of advanced scholars, and enforced fundamental philosophical thinking, while curiosity marked the dilettanti of the upper classes. The 'new philosophy' was already a catchword at the beginning of the century, and by the Restoration scientific experiment was achieving a fashionable status. In some quarters the changes in philosophy made for modifications in traditional theology, but the main stream of religious thought carried on from the older sources of Calvin and Hooker. It was, indeed, the problems of religion, at various levels and often inextricably mingled with secular problems, which were the conscious concern of the age, whatever the shifting of the philosophical foundations.

The Milieu of Literature 1603–42

Literacy, and to some extent the habit of reading, seem to have been comparatively widespread through society in this period; romances, histories, sermons, handbooks on manners and on business, broadside ballads and the early beginnings of newspapers fed the general demand, and there was a considerable increase in the number of books printed annually.[3] But many of the works considered in later chapters circulated for a long time in manuscript among the author's friends and acquaintances; during their authors' lifetimes the poems of Donne and Herbert were read chiefly in manuscript, while Browne's *Religio Medici* was printed only through a friend's indiscretion. These facts are a reminder of the intimacy of the cultivated society within which much of the literature was produced. A surprising number of the well-known men of letters, of politics, and of religion were friends or at least habitual acquaintances. The 'tribe of Ben' formed a strong nucleus, and the circles were linked by a central figure like Sir Henry Wotton, ex-ambassador and Provost of Eton, a close friend of Donne, a friend of Izaak Walton, and an acquaintance of Milton. Clarendon's autobiography reveals the large London circle to which he belonged as a young man at the Middle Temple – Jonson, Selden, Sir Kenelm Digby, Thomas May, and Thomas Carew – and his links with the Great Tew circle and with Edmund Waller, cousin of John Hampden and frequenter of Penshurst, the home of the Sidneys.

Writers of this period, and not merely the most famous, reveal an astonishing versatility and range of knowledge. Versatility was, of course, an accepted social ideal, but what made possible the varied intellectual activities of Ralegh, Bacon, Selden, Burton, Browne, Sir Kenelm Digby, and many others was the relative compactness of their world of knowledge; politics, law, history, philosophy, poetry, and science could all be touched. But breadth of learning was matched by breadth of experience; most writers were not solely men of letters but had careers in the political, academic, or clerical worlds.

The concentration of cultivated society followed from the overwhelming and growing predominance of London. No other English town approached its population of approximately 300,000, and its increase was not materially checked by plague. To meet the increased demand for houses, mainly by nobility, gentry, courtiers, and professional men, London was expanding westwards towards Westminster. Though for the most part it remained the haphazard, overcrowded town described by Stow in 1598, the Italianizing of London's architecture began under the leadership of Inigo Jones. The bulk of England's foreign trade passed through the port of London; the great trading companies were based on the city; the hub of the major English industry – the cloth trade – was there, at Blackwell Hall; and also the chief market for raising loans and buying and selling land.

The reasons for the magnetic influence of London were not only economic, but political, social, and legal. Every session of Parliament at Westminster brought over 400 members, sometimes with their families, to London. More regularly the Common Law and Prerogative courts brought numerous suitors and their witnesses to town. Contemporaries were well aware of the significance for London shopkeepers of the legal terms. The Inns of Court, the city schools, and certain famous schoolmasters drew many, and finally there were those who came to the capital for pleasure. Judging by the complaints of contemporaries, this habit was on the increase; King James was only one among many who denounced 'those swarms of gentry, who through the instigation of their wives ... did neglect their country hospitality and cumber the city'. The beginnings of the London season can be found in the early seventeenth century; parks, pleasure gardens, theatres, and transport (hackney coaches and sedan chairs existed under Charles I) were developed to meet the demand. It is impossible to say what proportion of the nobility and gentry frequented London, but in 1632 some 250 were prosecuted in the Star Chamber for disobeying the King's proclamation to return to their estates. Perhaps Sir Humphrey Mildmay, a country gentleman of Essex with Court connexions, was unusual in spending between four and six months a year in London, but his diary gives a typical round of pleasures. Besides swimming and boating on the Thames, dicing and card-playing and going a-maying in Hyde Park, he went to wrestling matches and to the theatre (sometimes two or three times a week), seeing Shirley's *The Gamester*, Fletcher's *The Pastoral*, and in 1635 *Othello*. Like the citizens of London, he watched the spectacles of Court and city activity: the reception of an ambassador, the progress of a Knight of the Garter, and the Lord Mayor's Show.

London was an essential part of the *milieu* of literature; some writers were born there, Milton the son of a scrivener, Donne of a prosperous ironmonger, Herrick of a goldsmith; more were drawn there by its attraction as an economic, social, and intellectual centre. But London was only part of the background of cultivated society: most of the men of letters of this period, and many of their contemporaries of the 'political nation', shared with the Earl of Clare in 'all the ornaments the University, Inns of Court, Court, Camp, travel, and language could enrich him with'.[4] It is this common social and cultural ground which must be explored now.

No single modern institution provides an analogy to the Court of the early seventeenth century. The Court had still a central and magnetic position in society; contact with it could give power, office, and wealth. Royal favour alone raised George Villiers, of a minor Leicestershire family, to a dukedom and his relatives to wealth and influence. This was a spectacular demonstration of the ways of the Court, and it is small wonder that the ambitious and needy alike flocked to it. George Herbert, while Public Orator of the University of Cambridge, was haunted by 'Court-hopes', seldom looking 'towards Cambridge unless the King were there, but then he never fail'd'; Richard Baxter, the son of an obscure Shropshire freeholder, was urged 'to go to London and get acquaintance at Court and get some office as being the only rising way'.

The Court took its tone from the personal character and tastes of the sovereign. In this period, therefore, the machinery remained the same – the royal household with its increasing number of officials subsisting largely on perquisites from suitors and its waste and extravagance in catering – but with the change from James to Charles the atmosphere of the Court changed. 'Two sorts of men King James had never kindness for', wrote a contemporary, 'those whose hawks and dogs flew and run as well as his own, and those who were able to speak as much reason as himself'. Hunting and scholarship were his dominant interests. In many ways shrewd, good-humoured and approachable, he lacked Tudor dignity and political sense. His Queen's taste for luxury in dress and entertainment, and his own lavish gifts to favourites and general fecklessness in money matters, raised Court expenditure to unprecedented heights. In 1617 James travelled farther north than Elizabeth had ever done, but in general royal progresses declined. Moreover, Elizabeth had never submitted herself so abjectly to her favourites.

The accession of Charles, 'temperate, chaste, and serious', brought a change. Although Court expenditure remained such as to astonish Rubens, the sprawling lavishness of James disappeared; the Court and household were better ordered, and something more than the dignity of Elizabeth's Court was regained, though without its popular appeal. The decline of royal progresses continued, and there was increasingly a private or coterie quality in the Court; Van Dyck's portraits (confined almost entirely to the Court circle) reveal, if nothing more, the way in which Charles and his Court liked to be portrayed. The fashionable interest, led by the King, was now largely in the visual arts; the collecting of pictures, begun by Arundel, was continued by Charles with genuine taste, and at amazing expense in view of his financial straits. Living artists, too, especially Rubens and Van Dyck, were patronized. This dominant aesthetic interest formed a link between Charles and various continental Courts. The missions of papal representatives to Charles were accompanied or masked by gifts, including a Titian and a bust of Charles by Bernini. Courtiers like the dubious Balthazar Gerbier, the Roman Catholic Tobie Mathew, and Endymion Porter with his Romanist wife, were used as middle-men in transactions with Catholic states mingling diplomacy and art-collecting. These links with the Continent and with Rome were tightened by Henrietta Maria. Partly through her influence conversions to Rome became frequent in the Court circle, despite Charles's disapproval. The politics and taste of her own group, including Jermyn, Mathew, and Suckling, were influenced by her French origin, and her interests ran to drama and the masque. Court life under her influence seems to have been dignified if frivolous.

Behind this Court, at its zenith in the thirties, lay the 'personal rule' of Charles. It was made possible by some dubious fiscal expedients, and by others legally correct but politically unwise. Under this rule the integrity of the judges became suspect, and while its chief agents, Laud and Strafford, were of unimpeachable honesty, others, more intimately associated with the Court, made corrupt profits. When such a régime championed the social welfare of the lower classes, it could not but be suspected of using this as a pretext for action against its political opponents among the upper classes. This political bias and the Roman Catholic aura clinging to the Court tended to isolate it from many Englishmen.[5]

The two universities were at this period well within the orbit of Crown and government; both were within easy distance of London, and both owed to James their exemption from subsidies and their representation in Parliament. The reigns of the first two Stuarts saw an increase in royal interference not only in the universities, in the election of Chancellors (Buckingham and Holland at Cambridge, and Laud at Oxford), but in the colleges. Just as the pulpits were 'tuned', so the discipline and curriculum of the universities were matters of concern to the Crown; they were, in an age of religio-political crisis, 'the nurseries of our religion' and as such had to be safeguarded.

The university population in this period seems to have been somewhat over 5,000, and the average age of undergraduates entering the colleges about sixteen. The social origins of undergraduates remained diverse, the increasing number of sons of the nobility and gentry mingling with sons of yeomen and craftsmen. Severe criticisms of university life and education were made by many contemporaries. The denunciations of the curriculum by Bacon and Milton are well known. Others, Laud and the Puritans alike, were concerned about the morals of undergraduates. Evidence on both counts is difficult to assess. At Oxford, Sir Thomas Bodley's munificent foundation, together with the many subsequent gifts of books and manuscripts (Laud and Cromwell were both donors), gave the university a library second only to that of the Vatican. Chairs of Geometry, Astronomy, History, and Music, and lectures in Natural Philosophy were founded. A certain receptiveness to new ideas was shown at Cambridge in the teaching of Ramist logic.* But, by and large, the teaching of undergraduates was still cast in the traditional scholastic mould; rhetoric (based on the classics), logic, and metaphysics dominated the curriculum. None the less, the large number of learned, cultivated, and intellectually adventurous men who emerged from this environment cannot be ignored.[6]

The chief occupation and study of the universities, however, was theology. Some distinction should be made between those undergraduates for whom the university was but one part of a general liberal education leading on to a more or less cultivated life of squirearchical responsibilities, and those for whom it was the central element in a training for holy orders. Whatever the interests of the former, the tone was set by the clerical section – intending divines and fellows of colleges. Controversial theology dominated the Cambridge of the thirties, for instance, when among the fellows were Jeremy Taylor at Caius, Crashaw and Joseph Beaumont at Peterhouse, and Cleveland at St John's. Native and foreign observers noted also the prominence of ecclesiastical controversy. The party alignment which was growing in the country was naturally earlier and sharper in the clerical university world. At Cambridge, Peterhouse under Matthew Wren and Cosin, and Pembroke under Lancelot Andrewes and his successors, led the High Church group, while the Puritan strongholds were Emmanuel, the college of so many preachers who emigrated to the New World, and Cromwell's college, Sidney Sussex. At Oxford, by tradition less Puritan, the

* A system of logic devised by the French scholar Petrus Ramus (1515-72) in opposition to the traditional Aristotelian methods: its widespread adoption formed part of the reaction against scholasticism.

division crystallized round the academic career of Laud, and religious controversy was exacerbated by personal ambitions and acrimony. By Laud's efforts as Chancellor, High Church doctrine took hold of Oxford, giving it the character it retained throughout the century.

London gained something of the character of a university town from the Inns of Court, organized in much the same way as colleges. The four Inns were the means of entry into the profitable and expanding profession of common lawyers, and their students consequently increased rapidly in this period. They were filled, however, not only by potential lawyers, but by the sons of nobility and gentry intent on at least a smattering of law in a highly legalistic age. For a future J.P. or perhaps M.P., and equally for a future landowner, some knowledge of the tortuous ways of the law was desirable. But it was not merely for their 'black-letter learning' that Ben Jonson praised the Inns as 'the noblest nurseries of humanity and liberty in the kingdom'. They were places of general education as well as of vocational training, and history, music, and dancing were among the subjects taught. Cromwell was but one who went to an Inn 'that nothing might be wanting to make him a complete gentleman and a good commonwealthsman'.[7] The core of the legal education until after the Restoration was the 'readings' and public disputations on points of law. The general education owed its quality to the society to be found at the Inns; 'the liveliest, the most intelligent, and certainly the most influential society England could furnish', it has been called.[8] Eminent lawyers, such as Bacon and Coke, remained in close touch with their Inns, while the majority of their famous contemporaries had been at one of the Inns: Selden, Strafford, and Hampden at the Inner Temple; Sir Kenelm Digby, Campian, and Suckling at Gray's Inn; Whitelocke, Hyde, and Carew at the Middle Temple; and Quarles, Benlowes, Donne, and Prynne at Lincoln's Inn. The society described in their autobiographies by Hyde and Whitelocke was obviously stimulating and absorbing. The preachers at the Inns were among the best in the country: Donne, for whose sermon in 1623 at the consecration of the new chapel of Lincoln's Inn there was such a crowd that 'two or three were … taken up dead for the time', or the Puritan Richard Sibbes at Gray's Inn, one of whose sermons, bought at the door from a pedlar, converted Baxter. The Inns delighted in dramatic entertainments combining music, poetry, and spectacle. If nothing in this period came up to *Twelfth Night*, performed in 1602 in the Middle Temple, there were masques by Chapman and Francis Beaumont to celebrate the wedding of Elizabeth of Bohemia, and the exceptionally magnificent masque, with music by William Lawes, presented to the King and Queen in 1634 by all four Inns. It is no wonder that Hyde in his student days found it difficult to tear himself away from 'study and conversation' in London.

Despite its urban aspects, English society was rooted in the land. The rhythms of society corresponded with those of agriculture, the long vacations of universities and law courts coinciding with harvest-time. In such a society the locality had a reality and attraction for its inhabitants, and the term 'my country' during the century commonly meant 'my county'. The county was the significant unit, socially and politically as well as administratively.

Although many of the nobility and gentry were acquiring town houses, the centre of life and work remained for most of them the country-house with its park and estates. Notwithstanding the economic situation, many houses (of office-holders especially) were built or extended in this period: Audley End, Hatfield, Castle Ashby, Wilton, and Bolsover are among the famous; but the mixed Jacobean and the purer Italianate styles are found in numerous country-houses, large and small. The government insisted strongly on the duties of a landowner to his neighbourhood: not only did he maintain order and provide employment, but his household was often a social and educational centre. Noblemen and frequently gentry had in their households chaplains, tutors, pensioners, 'gentlemen', and boys from neighbouring families sent to them for a training, though not everyone could make his table, like the Earl of Clare's, 'a continued *Convivium Philosophale*'. How far the absentee landlordism and the decay of 'hospitality', of which both government and moralists complained, had gone it is impossible to say. Probably it was most marked in the home counties, but in many districts the old 'hospitality' continued.

No generalization can hope to apply to all the nobility or to the 500 knights and 16,000 gentlemen (the estimate of Thomas Wilson in 1600). The incomes within a social class varied immensely; variations arose out of the different ways in which estates were utilized and land cultivated; the gentry of the home counties close to the economic and intellectual influences of London had a different environment from those of remote northern districts; those within the orbit of the Court differed from those outside it. It is a far cry from the Dorset squire, Henry Hastings, as portrayed by his famous neighbour Shaftesbury, his house littered with the apparatus of hunting, hawking, smoking, and dicing, his staple books the Bible and the *Book of Martyrs*, to the learned, cultivated Kentish gentry – the Twysdens, Sandys, Filmers, Derings, Culpepers, and Digges, who followed in the steps of the historian Lambarde. The gentry and nobility covered the whole of this range: many were denounced as boorish, many kept abreast with current learning and literature, science and philosophy, took an interest in exploration, and wrote verses in their leisure. Among the nobility, the Earl of Newcastle patronized poets and dramatists, wrote verses and treatises on horses, made chemical experiments at Bolsover, and discussed problems of optics with Hobbes. Poetry, drama, and philosophy were missing from the predominantly theological library of the fifth Earl of Bedford; interest in alchemy and American voyages was reflected in that of the ninth Earl of Northumberland. Among the gentry, 'to get learning' was common advice from father to son; libraries were becoming more common, and though the stock volumes were of theology, history, and law, literary works old and new were often there.

The normal picture is one of mixed occupations in the country; care of the estate and tenants, building, the duties of a J.P. or other commissioner of the Crown, hunting and hawking (there is a glimpse in the Knyvett letters of Thomas Knyvett, a Norfolk squire, discussing the ship-money levy with a neighbour while out hunting), entertaining, bowls and cards, music and reading. The correspondence of the Kentish Oxinden family, in the years up to the Civil War, reflects the day-to-day routine; the additions to the manor-house, the trees and hedges planted (a tree for the birth of every child), the problems of education, careers, and marriage, the hereditary service on the estate, the portrait painting by Cornelius Janssen, and the letter-writing spiced occasionally with a quotation from one of Donne's poems. This country life was still the foundation of the cultivated society to be found in London, at Court, and in the universities and Inns of Court, forming the *milieu* of most literature before the Civil War.

26

Religion before the Civil War

Religion dominated both national and personal life in the early seventeenth century; in both it was a matter of life and death. 'Whosoever bringeth in innovation in religion is a capital enemy of the Commonwealth' the House of Commons resolved in 1629; among individuals many, like Baxter, were 'serious and solicitous about my soul's everlasting state'. An intense interest in theological controversy, and to some extent in books of devotion, was common to almost all ranks of society. Probably nearly half of the books published between 1600 and 1640 were on religious topics. Their readers ranged from the nobility, through the gentry (Sir John Strode enjoined his son to read 'especially the book of God') to the yeomen, in whose inventories the books most commonly mentioned are the Bible and Foxe's *Book of Martyrs*, the citizens, and the apprentices, of whose reading and debates Lilburne and the Baptist Kiffin have left records. In such a society, virtually without newspapers, the pulpit played an outstanding part. Contemporaries were at one in seeing this; Charles I and Laud in their attempts at censorship, the Puritans in their attempts to evade this by financing 'lecturers'*, and in their attacks on preachers like Mainwaring and Sibthorpe. To all the pulpit had a political as well as a religious significance; it was a way of reaching the vast bulk of the population. Church-going was legally enforceable, but equally sermons were a genuine popular interest.

The Church of England was still an inclusive Church, numbering, except for the Roman Catholics and a few Separatists, the whole nation. Under the Elizabethan compromise it had leaned towards Calvinism in its doctrines and theology, but retained in its structure and rites traditional elements and ambiguities differentiating it from the continental Reformed Churches. These were its two points of strain at the beginning of the century. Hooker's *Ecclesiastical Polity* had already marked out the Anglican road, vindicating that Church's position in relation to both Rome and Geneva, and establishing it on the basis of history and tradition as well as of Scripture. His influence helped to make Anglicanism a favourable environment for learning

* These were clergymen, usually of Puritan leanings, who held no benefices and were appointed in market-towns and elsewhere, solely to preach. They were frequently paid by local corporations, and were virtually free from episcopal control.

and scholarship. There were, too, elements in Anglican thought making for tolerance; Anglican controversialists tended to show a lack of dogmatism, disclaiming infallibility and exclusive salvation for their Church, while the spread of Arminian views on free will softened the Calvinist conception of God. Laud himself hated this conception for its denial of mercy, and showed intellectual tolerance in some theological debates. Anglicans of the school of Lancelot Andrewes, Cosin, and Laud sought for outward beauty in churches: altars were moved to the east and railed round; stained glass, candlesticks, and organs were introduced to promote a dignity of ceremonial as 'the great witness to the world that our heart stands right'. The chapels at Peterhouse, at Little Gidding, and at Herbert's Bemerton showed also a new order and aesthetic awareness.

Much in this Anglicanism was Catholic: the stress on tradition and the return to the early Fathers; the comparative neglect of Protestant Reformers' writings; the beautifying of the churches, and the prime emphasis on the altar and the sacramental system rather than on the pulpit and the Scriptures. But intrinsically there was nothing Roman in it; although high Anglicans writing against Rome were ready (unlike their Puritan counterparts) to see in it a true if erring Church, a deep gulf lay between them and Rome. It is possible, however, to see reasons besides the sheer confusion of Catholic with Roman why their Puritan critics identified them with Popery. Laud's friend, Sir Kenelm Digby, returned to the religion of his birth; Chillingworth, Laud's godson, was a temporary convert to Rome, and numbers who moved with him in the royal circle went over. The Puritans noted that this Arminian minority among the clergy rose to power, not through weight of numbers, but through favour with a King married to a French Roman Catholic. Laud epitomized this ecclesiastical monopoly; theoretically liberal, he had, nevertheless, inflexible ideas on uniformity of worship which he enforced by means of State machinery. Busy and officious in many spheres, social and political as well as religious, he roused peculiar hatred among Puritans, and irritation among non-Puritan Anglicans like Falkland, Hyde, George Digby, and Verney. With high ideals, in practice he was unimaginative and unable to comprehend his opponents' position or even their honesty, so that his fiercest punishments were for attacks on himself and his fellow bishops.

The history of the Church in this period is dominated by Laudian Anglicanism, but throughout there was an Anglicanism which was neither Laudian nor Puritan. Under the goad of Laudian interference these Anglicans followed Puritan leadership, but the threat to the Prayer Book as distinct from the bishops in September 1641 rallied them against the Puritans. During the Civil War and Interregnum the persecution of the Laudians and the Puritan tyranny drove them increasingly towards the Laudian worship.

Undoubtedly the main swing of opinion up to the Civil War was with Puritanism. The word covers a great diversity of people, and represented rather a temper of mind within the Church of England than the nonconformity with which it is now associated. Political and economic frustration swelled the following of the Puritan leaders, and in many ways this Puritanism was based, like the early 'Protestantism' of Luther, on great negatives.

But for some, at any rate, of the Puritans there was a positive core in the teachings of Calvin and the example of Geneva. For them there was a framework for life in the Calvinist scheme of Predestination and Election deduced from the Scriptures. The convinced Puritan emerged from the despair of his doubt and remorse with a sense of salvation and of special insight into the ways of God, leading to claims to infallibility. There is undoubtedly a pattern of Puritan spiritual development revealed in many diaries, autobiographical writings, and speeches. To Puritans the rigidity of Calvinist theology and the clean break of Geneva with the hierarchy and ritual of the past seemed the only sure defence of the nation against a Rome seen as Antichrist. In the face of the European conflict of Catholic and Protestant, Laudian Anglicanism seemed a perversion of the Elizabethan Church and a betrayal of Protestant unity. Alarm and irritation grew during the thirties, a period of Habsburg victories after the death of Gustavus Adolphus and of political impotence for the domestic opposition in Church and State.

A note of fanaticism, even of hysteria, appeared among the Puritan critics of Laud at this time. If his authoritarian methods justified some of these protests, their tone often deserved his scathing references to 'the vulgar sort'. William Prynne is the typical Puritan of the textbook; between 1627 and 1640 he published nearly a score of pamphlets, among the most virulent of their kind, and spent at least six years in prison. Drinking, the drama, 'the Unloveliness of Lovelocks', and breaking of the Sabbath alike came under his indiscriminate denunciation. Plays were 'the very poison and corruption of men's minds and manners'; while in sanctioning the 'Book of Sports',* the bishops had done no more than Beelzebub, were he an archbishop, could have done 'to make it [the Sabbath] the Devil's day instead of the Lord's day'. Prynne was not alone in making such extravagant charges against the bishops: Milton's pamphlets of 1641 descend to coarse and unreasoned abuse, and significantly one of the Elizabethan Marprelate tracts was reprinted in 1642, and was followed by several imitations.

Yet to take Prynne as typical of the Puritans is to do injustice to the scope of Puritanism and the variety of Puritans. Puritanism has gained during the course of centuries a strong emotional connotation; its manifestations in New England, or in England in the nineteenth century, have drawn attention to its hostility to the arts, its intolerant morality, and its dull sabbatarianism. For many men, however, in this period, a Puritan temper was an understandable reaction to popular ignorance, indifference, and immorality; if they were serious in outlook, they often took pleasure in the arts and in sport. Cromwell's bowls, his hunting and hawking and delight in music, Milton's love of music and classical poetry, John Hutchinson's enjoyment of music, painting, and tennis suggest the need for qualifications. Nevertheless, there was the danger that the intense seriousness of the Puritan outlook would drive out what Baxter called 'the sins which go under the name of pastimes', and with them the pursuit of the arts. The attacks on traditional country celebrations like May-day games and wakes before the Civil War were followed under Puritan rule by the ban on organs in churches, the closing of the theatres, stricter control of ale-houses, and prohibition of cock-fights and bear-baiting.

The complexity of Puritanism is seen in its ambiguous relation to liberty and toleration. In its pre-Civil War form it was a protest on

---

* This royal declaration authorizing certain sports on Sundays after divine service was first issued in 1617 to settle a dispute in Lancashire, but in face of opposition not generally enforced by James. In 1633 it was reissued by Charles, who insisted that it should be read by the clergy in every church; many clergymen were penalized for disobedience.

behalf of the individual conscience against the authority of lordly bishops; John Lilburne's championship of liberty had a direct source in his Calvinist convictions. But it was not a general assertion of liberty of conscience; the Grand Remonstrance of the Commons in 1641 gave the assurance that 'it is far from our purpose or desire to let loose the golden reins of discipline and government in the Church'. Already there was among the Puritans a strong element inclining to an authoritarian uniformity, reminiscent of Laud's, which was expressed in the alliance with Scottish Presbyterianism. The more substantial Puritan contribution to liberty of thought lay with a different element, that of the Sects. Their rise to power came later, out of the confusion of the Civil War, and their very multiplication furthered a toleration which was only slowly and partially willed for its own sake.

A small tributary to the main stream of religious thought flowed from Great Tew, near Oxford. Here, separate from both Laudians and Puritans, but linked with Anglicanism of the Hooker tradition, was a small group of men, meeting regularly during the thirties at the country-house of Lord Falkland. Falkland provided for his friends a civilized background to their discussions; as his interests changed, literary men such as Jonson, Carew, and Waller were succeeded in the Great Tew circle by philosophers and theologians, several from Oxford – including John Earle, who professed to have learned more at Great Tew than ever he had at Oxford. The essential spirit of Great Tew can be gauged from Falkland's frequent quoting from Erasmus. The writings of the members of the circle, Falkland, Chillingworth, and, above all, John Hales of Eton College, show the reaction of thoughtful religious men to the bitter denominational controversy so characteristic of the age. 'Nothing troubled him more than the brawls which were grown from religion,' wrote Edward Hyde (one of the circle) of Hales. The sight of the disputes between Dutch Calvinists and Arminians at the Synod of Dort had caused him to 'bid goodnight to John Calvin'. Intolerant dogmatism and human claims to infallibility in religion seemed to Great Tew alien to the Christian spirit of charity, and a defect of the Protestant Reformers as much as of Rome. The Christian humanism of the circle led to Chillingworth's plea for religious toleration by law and Hales's for unity among all kinds of Christians on the basis of the common elements in their beliefs. Such solvents of intolerance had their echo in fashionable society; Suckling, if he lamented that Falkland was 'gone with religion', wrote, about 1637, *An Account of Religion by Reason*. Like that of Great Tew, the thought of George Herbert's brother, Lord Herbert of Cherbury, must be seen against the background of religious controversy reflected in Donne's Third Satire. Even Chillingworth, according to Hyde, in face of the rival claims to infallibility, 'contracted such a habit of doubting that by degrees he grew confident of nothing'. Lord Herbert in his search for a common denominator went outside the Christian religion. His *De Veritate*, published in 1624, was an attempt to formulate a 'natural religion' commanding universal assent. This foreshadowing of eighteenth-century deism had, as far as can be judged, little influence, but such as it was it contributed to the gradual undermining of the bases of religious intolerance in the century as a whole.

The Civil War: Disintegration and Reform Projects

The mounting opposition to the government in Church and State found vent in the Long Parliament of 1640. For its first few months the Commons were united, future Royalists and Parliamentarians joining to curb prerogative government and establish a common law monarchy. It was, however, impossible to achieve the mutual trust between King and Houses of Parliament essential for such a monarchy. The Commons started from an ingrained fear and hatred of Popery and an immovable belief in a large-scale Popish plot. The intrigues of Henrietta Maria, the Army Plot of Goring and Suckling, and, above all, the Irish massacre of November 1641, fed this conspiratorial theory. On his side Charles showed little political sense and some duplicity, although the first approach to violence, the execution of Strafford, had come from the Commons. Fear and distrust led Pym and the majority during the autumn of 1641 into novel and revolutionary claims, which alienated a substantial minority of their fellow members. This minority had appeared earlier in certain ecclesiastical debates, and now based itself not only on the Prayer Book but on the existing constitution. Gradually, and almost in spite of Charles's own unwise activities, including the attempted arrest of the five members, this minority became the King's party. Its constitutional stand was strengthened by arbitrary actions on the part of the majority, the imprisonment of the Kentish champions of the Church, among them Lovelace, antagonizing many.

The departure of the King and Queen from London in January 1642 closed a chapter: although a Court existed later at Oxford, it could not reproduce the atmosphere of the thirties, and for eighteen years Whitehall ceased to be the hub of society. Slowly, with extreme reluctance and continued negotiation, the parties aligned themselves during the summer. No single or simple explanation will account for the way men divided; political and religious issues, social distinctions played their part, but equally, personal characteristics, family traditions, and local feuds. Each county had its own variations on the theme of civil division. The broad division into Royalist north and west and Parliamentarian south and east obscures the substantial minorities in each area. Among the peers, about eighty followed Charles, some thirty supported Parliament, and another twenty took no part; the division among the M.P.s elected between 1640 and 1642, about 300 Parliamentarians and about 230 Royalists, reflected the very real division among the gentry. Tenants usually followed their lords, but freeholders might act independently, often for Parliament. The indecision and changes of side at the beginning and the splits within so many families were of the essence of the English Civil War; so were the large number of neutrals and the local neutrality agreements.[9] London was a conspicuous exception to this temper, and the determination of its trained bands prevented a speedy Royalist victory. On both sides there were a few leaders with military experience gained as volunteers on the Continent, but the trained soldiers to follow them were almost completely lacking. During the early campaigns, therefore, amateur warfare was the rule. Although volunteers were plentiful at first, both sides were reduced to impressment by 1643, and altogether no more than 60,000 or 70,000 took part in the war on each side. Soon the outcome of the war was seen to depend on which side could first organize an efficient army. Cromwell's drive gave this advantage to Parliament in the raising of the New Model Army. Regular pay, centralized control not deflected by local considerations, recruitment in strongly Puritan areas, and a single-minded concern for efficiency on the part of its commanders, gave it the decisive victory of the First Civil War at Naseby.

To estimate the effects on Caroline society of the ten years of war from 1642 to 1652 is a very difficult task, for which the materials are as yet incomplete. The fighting, if not very intensive (much of it was in skirmishes, raids, and sieges of towns, castles, and country-houses), extended to practically every county. The number of country-houses destroyed or damaged was considerable, while the pillaging and free quartering of soldiers injured whole districts. Interference by both sides with communications affected trade, and in some areas, in the south and south-west particularly, there was industrial depression. The removal of strict central control, together with the war itself, led to a breakdown of the poor law administration in many areas and the increase of distress. Even if recovery was comparatively swift in the fifties, there had been real dislocation of the economy during the forties.

The Caroline Court circle had been swiftly broken; as early as 1641 Jermyn and Suckling had fled abroad. Suckling died in 1642, 'little Sid' Godolphin was killed in 1643, and by the late forties Fanshawe, Davenant, and Denham were in exile. Great Tew also was dispersed: Falkland was killed at Newbury; Chillingworth died in 1644 after capture by the Parliamentarians at the siege of Arundel Castle; Hammond and Earle were deprived of their livings and Hales of his Fellowship, while Hyde spent his exile working for a restoration and writing his *History of the Rebellion*. In the universities, too, there was upheaval: after military vicissitudes, religious and political tests were imposed on the Fellows and many were expelled. Crashaw, ejected from Peterhouse in 1643, went abroad and became a Roman Catholic; Cowley, expelled from Trinity, became cipher-secretary to Henrietta Maria; at Cambridge a majority of the Fellows and heads of Colleges were ejected, and at Oxford a total of about 400 members of foundations. Yet if the personnel changed, the traditions of learning were upheld to a remarkable degree.

Among the aristocracy and gentry as a whole there were the casualties of war, and among the Royalists the financial oppression of taxes, fines, and confiscations. Many had already made heavy sacrifices for the King, if not on the scale of the Marquis of Worcester's £700,000. As Parliament extended its control, taxation and heavy fines forced many Royalists to sell part of their estates; some had part of their lands sequestrated, and later the Commonwealth government confiscated the lands of 700 prominent 'delinquents'. The large-scale public sales of lands – royal, episcopal, and private – benefited especially London merchants, Parliamentarian officials, and army officers, but the gentry had a substantial share. The total picture should not be made over-tragic, though it left a legacy of revenge to the Restoration period; there were many legal subterfuges whereby Royalists evaded the full penalties. Though some families were ruined by the war, many were able to weather the storm, somewhat impoverished, but by judicious sacrifice retaining the bulk of their lands. The misfortunes of the Verney family, including deaths, exile, and loss, can be curiously compared with the war-time Grand Tour of John Evelyn, who on his return bought back his father-in-law's confiscated estate, and began, literally, to cultivate his garden at Deptford.[10]

Broadly the forties saw the destruction of the traditional framework of authority in Church and State. In the Church the abolition of the High Commission removed the strongest disciplinary sanction; Laud was executed in 1645, and about a third of the parish clergy were ejected from their livings. The attempt, during the Parliamentary alliance with the Scots, to replace the Anglican order by the Presbyterian discipline had only a limited success, and Milton's 'new Presbyter' was by no means everywhere 'old Priest writ large'. In the secular sphere, if taxation ('the sinews of war') had never been so efficiently collected as in the areas under Parliamentary control, in general there was a breakdown of old controls. Without the Star Chamber central control over the localities was weakened, while for three years the traditional censorship of the Press lapsed. The symbolic climax was the execution of the King and the abolition of the House of Lords.

This unprecedented opportunity for reform and rebuilding encouraged a widespread visionary Utopianism; hopes ran high of making this 'a truly happy and wholly free nation'. Religious inspiration lay behind this reforming idealism, and an extraordinary number of men were gripped by the conviction of the imminence of Christ's kingdom. Cromwell opened the 'Parliament of Saints' in 1653 with the words, 'Why should we be afraid to say or think, that this way may be the door to usher in the things that God hath promised and prophesied of?' Such vivid consciousness of the Scriptures was common; the Puritan domination of the pulpit for the past half-century had encouraged the popular study of the Bible, and the fruits of that impulse appeared as the traditional controls and inhibitions were loosened. From 1641 complaints appeared of 'mechanick preachers': craftsmen of all kinds, apprentices, yeomen, labourers found each his own personal inspiration in the Scriptures. George Fox recorded characteristically how 'I would get into the orchard, or the fields, with my Bible by myself'. The widespread and undirected study of the Bible, added to the Puritan elevation of the individual conscience – 'conscience obliging above or against human and outward constitutions' – multiplied the sects. By 1646 a Presbyterian opponent had counted sixteen groups and over 200 'heresies' of recent growth. This vigorous, if at times eccentric, religious life could not be contained within the Presbyterian 'conscience prison'. Among the Puritans of the left the belief that God's truth was still being revealed and that they should 'stand ready to receive further light' made for liberty of conscience and toleration. The doctrine of the 'inner light' and the reaction against Predestination encouraged a shift from dogmatic religion towards a more rational theology and a more humanitarian religion.

In social terms, the religious activity of the forties meant that elements of society, hitherto silent, were becoming vocal in preaching, organizing, and writing. The spate of pamphlets was unprecedented: the bookseller George Thomason collected 20,000 published during the Civil War and Interregnum. The artificial conditions of the New Model Army and its atmosphere of religious enthusiasm encouraged the voice of the common people. 'The consciences of common men', writes Professor Woodhouse, 'were a new phenomenon in politics', and nowhere did they find clearer expression than in the debates of the Army Council in 1647-9, at which the rank and file were represented. Fundamentals of politics were discussed in the open; the debate between the conservative Ireton and the radical Rainborough moved the latter to this assertion: 'I do think that the poorest man in England is not at all bound in a strict sense to that government that he hath not had a voice to put himself under.'

The zeal for radical reform which had its roots in religion was soon applied to secular concerns, and many aspects of society came under debate. As Baxter saw, Church democracy led on easily (though not invariably) to State democracy. The Levellers, led by the first-class publicist John Lilburne, have been described as the only truly democratic party of the Civil War. In their tenets, Lilburne's Calvinist-based individualism and his vein of historicism derived from Coke mingled with William Walwyn's rational tendencies coming from classical writers and Montaigne. The Levellers demanded manhood suffrage, a fairer distribution of Parliamentary seats, and the protection of the people's rights by a fundamental law binding their representatives. Despite their name, they were not social egalitarians; the reform of the economic order as distinct from the political was the hope of the small group of Diggers. Their programme was essentially agrarian: first common lands and then private estates were to become common property, but not by violence. The earth, their leader Winstanley wrote, was to become 'a common treasury again' by all men 'acting in righteousness one to another'. Winstanley's communism seems to have sprung almost wholly from his study of the Bible, combined with a mystical temper very close to that of the Quakers. The ferment of reforming idealism found a wide variety of outlets, some curiously modern such as suggestions for woman's suffrage and free medical service for the poor. There was a strong movement for simplifying the complexities of the law and, as might be expected, education was radically debated. Earlier, the eminent Czech educationist, Comenius, had been invited over to advise on educational reform; pamphlets (including Milton's) abounded on improving education and bringing it up to date, and Parliament went so far as to make provision in Wales for State-aided education.

Towards the Restoration

An attempt at stabilization was inevitable sooner or later. With the return to something approaching normality in the mid-fifties, the pressure behind the vigorous, optimistic radicalism of the forties gradually relaxed. The end of serious fighting came at Worcester in 1651, and Cromwell, by then the key-figure, turned to the problems of peace-time organization. The Digger experiment in Surrey had been broken up in 1649, and the Leveller movement in the army had been crushed at Burford, even if Lilburne remained the irrepressible champion of a civilian remnant. Puritan Millennarianism of an undemocratic kind, rule by the elect not by the elected, found short-lived expression in the 'Parliament of Saints'. When the moderate members voted its dissolution they coincided with Cromwell's disillusion, and later, looking back, he could refer to it as a product of 'my simplicity', 'a story of my own weakness and folly'.

There had been no social revolution during the Civil War; the Diggers from a practical point of view had been insignificant, and the bulk of the Levellers strongly upheld the rights of private property. Confiscated property had been sold chiefly in large lots to comparatively wealthy purchasers including speculators. Moreover, the traditional checks on enclosure were weakened, and a new plan to safeguard copyhold tenants from exploitation failed. Under the Protectorate the country gentry and lawyers in Parliament became more influential, although the civilian groups never superseded the Army. Four years before the Restoration of the King there was a return to the older forms of government; a second chamber was restored and the Commons' privileges were guaranteed in the traditional way. Cromwell's refusal of the offer of the crown did not prevent him assuming many of its attributes, including the hereditary succession of his son. The Puritan zeal for righteousness led him still to attempt forcible moral reform, but on the whole he worked for the ideal he set before his last Parliament, to be 'the repairers of breaches, and the restorers of paths to dwell in'.

Intellectual life continued with a vigour surprising in view of the purges of Church and universities. Some of it was perforce in exile; but at home an active group, meeting first in London and then in Oxford, to discuss 'Physick, Anatomy, Geometry, Astronomy, Navigation, Staticks, Magnetics, Chymicks, Mechanicks and Natural Experiments', carried on the Baconian tradition. These men had links with Gresham College, and after the Restoration were formally instituted as the Royal Society. Many of the group were moderate Puritans, including some who had replaced Royalists in academic posts. John Wallis, who decoded intercepted Royalist despatches, became Savilian professor of geometry at Oxford: Seth Ward became professor of astronomy, and William Petty, later the originator of 'political arithmetic', professor of anatomy. The group owed most, perhaps, to John Wilkins (Cromwell's brother-in-law), who was made Warden of Wadham College in place of an ejected Royalist. As a writer on astronomy, he did much to popularize Copernican theories, and his move to Cambridge in 1659 to become Master of Trinity College brought him into contact with Benjamin Whichcote and the Cambridge Platonists. These scholars, almost all of Emmanuel College, had affinities with the Great Tew circle in their tolerance and rational leanings, but they were more concerned with the impact of science on religion, for they had to face the implications of the philosophical systems of Descartes and Hobbes. They combined a rationalism which fostered the Latitudinarianism of the later seventeenth century with a mysticism of Platonist origin. The fruitful development of both these movements continued after the Restoration.

Meanwhile, moving from one continental state to another, Prince Charles and his followers were suffering the hardships of exile. The embittering and demoralizing effects of their experiences were to play an unfortunate part in forming the temper of the new reign, together with the French and Catholic influences which took hold of Charles while abroad. All these were to combine with his subjects' experiences in England during the Interregnum to make up the complicated pattern of Restoration politics and society.

NOTES

1. The discussion on the relative economic positions of the gentry and the aristocracy continues: see, in the bibliography, the articles by Tawney, Stone, and Trevor-Roper.

2. On this important and complicated subject see E. C. Burtt: *The Metaphysical Foundations of Modern Physical Science*, B. Willey: *The Seventeenth Century Background*, H. Butterfield: *The Origins of Modern Science*, Sir W. C. Dampier: *A History of Science and its Relations with Philosophy and Religion* (revised and enlarged edition 1948), and A. R. Hall: *The Scientific Revolution 1500–1800*.

3. Between 1500 and 1630 the annual production of books rose from about 45 to about 460. By 1640 the total was approaching 600 and between 1640 and 1660 the number greatly increased. D. Bush: *English Literature in the Earlier Seventeenth Century*, p. 26.

4. Quoted from Gervase Holles: *Memorials of the Holles Family*, p. 111.

5. The nature of the 'personal rule', 1629–40, and the relation between its constitutional weaknesses and its social virtues are still controversial. See, in the bibliography, the works by Gardiner, Wedgwood, Trevor-Roper, and Unwin; also E. M. Leonard: *The Early History of English Poor Relief*, and H. E. I. Phillips: 'The Last Years of the Court of Star Chamber', *Trans. Royal Hist. Soc.*, 4th series, xxi. J. P. Cooper, 'The Fortune of Thomas Wentworth, Earl of Strafford' *Ec.H.R.*, 2nd series, xi, No. 2, has recently modified this estimate of Strafford's character.

6. On this apparent paradox see W. T. Costello: *The Curriculum at Seventeenth Century Cambridge*, which describes in detail the kind of training of the

mind given by the scholastic curriculum and exercises, and M. Curtis: *Oxford and Cambridge in Transition*, which draws attention to the wider studies outside the statutory curriculum encouraged by college tutors.

7. Although Cromwell's name does not appear on the books of Lincoln's Inn (to which, according to this biographer, he went), Firth accepts the fact as probable; the quotation shows the current valuation of the education offered by the Inns.

8. By G. M. Young in 'Shakespeare and the Termers', *Proc. Brit. Acad.*, XXXIII.

9. The nature of the division in the Civil War is discussed in the works by Trevelyan, Feiling, Firth, Brunton and Pennington cited in the bibliography, and in C. Hill's recent *Puritanism and Revolution*, chapter 1. There are numerous studies of the war in particular localities; the best is M. Coate: *Cornwall in the Great Civil War*. The Marxist interpretation of this complex subject lies behind the selective anthology from contemporary sources, *The Good Old Cause*, edited by C. Hill and E. Dell.

10. The effects of the sales of land, royal, episcopal, and private, are still under discussion. See H. E. Chesney: 'The Transference of Lands in England 1640–60', *Trans. Royal Hist. Soc.*, 4th series, XV; G. B. Tatham: 'The Sale of Episcopal Lands during the Civil Wars and Commonwealth', *English Hist. Review*, XXIII; J. Thirsk: 'The Sales of Royalist Land during the Interregnum', in *Ec.H.R.*, 2nd series, V (1952), and 'The Restoration Land Settlement', *Journal of Modern History* (1954).

PART
II

A SURVEY OF LITERATURE FROM
DONNE TO MARVELL

BY R. G. COX

Lecturer in English, University of Manchester

THE interest shown by our own age in the period from Donne to
Marvell, and especially in the poetry of Metaphysical wit, amounts
almost to a rediscovery. The experience of flux and transition in the
present century seems to have given us an understanding denied to
the eighteenth century, to the Victorians, and even to the Romantics.
To those poets of our own time who have struggled to bring poetry
back into relation with the widest possible range of experience, and
to fuse thought and feeling in one act of imaginative apprehension,
Donne and his followers have seemed to be particularly relevant.
There are dangers as well as advantages here: elements of fashion and
of genuine appreciation have been inextricably mingled. An undoubted measure of affinity between the two ages must not lead us to
distort the picture by minimizing real differences. Nevertheless, much
of the revaluation is likely to be permanent, and certainly a special
interest in so vital a stage of development from the medieval to the
modern world needs no defence or excuse.

Elizabethan and Seventeenth-Century

When Donne began to write, about 1592, much of Spenser's work
was still to come; when Marvell died, in 1678, Milton had been dead
four years, and Dryden was almost half-way through his literary
career. Given that all 'periods' of literature are to some extent
arbitrary divisions, that they inevitably overlap and are blurred at
the edges, there remains a reasonable case for considering the inter-
vening decades as a separate age. A division about the time of the
Restoration, between the period of the Renaissance and that of the
'eighteenth century', is traditional and seems natural. At the other end
a division between the Elizabethan age and the 'seventeenth century',
within the general development of Renaissance literature, is harder
to fix and calls for many exceptions and qualifications; yet the differ-

ence between the age of Spenser, Sidney, Marlowe, and Hooker and that of Herbert, Marvell, Milton, and Browne seems sufficiently marked.

It cannot be claimed, however, that homogeneity is one of the main characteristics of the period. Even more than most, it deserves to be called an age of transition; here, if anywhere, medieval touches modern in all spheres of life and thought. The age inherited views of the order and structure of the universe, of the laws governing political and economic activity, of the spiritual and physical nature of man, which had their origins far back in the Middle Ages.

In recent years scholars have been busy reconstructing for us what has come to be known as the Elizabethan 'world picture'. The universe was still conceived, according to the old Ptolemaic astronomy, as a vast system of concentric spheres with the earth at the centre. The spheres carried the moon, the sun, the planets, and the stars; the substance of these celestial bodies increased in refinement and purity in proportion to their distance from the earth, and beyond the outermost sphere lay empyrean heaven, the abode of God. The whole system was bound together in a divinely appointed order, always thought of as hierarchical. From mere matter up to God there stretched a continuous 'chain of being' in which man formed the vital central link: below him animals, vegetables, and inanimate matter, above him celestial intelligences and the orders of angels. A complicated harmony was manifest in constant correspondences between different planes of existence: the order of the cosmos was paralleled in the order of the State: the State, or 'body politic', was an organic unity analogous to man himself: and man was the 'microcosm', a little world reflecting in miniature the organization of the whole universe. As the whole universe was composed of different combinations of the four elements, fire, air, water, and earth, so human temperament was the result of varying blends of the four corresponding bodily fluids or 'humours', choler, blood, phlegm, and melancholy (black bile). In such a conception of the world and man's place in it, physics, physiology, psychology, philosophy, and religion seem to the modern mind to be hopelessly intermingled; they have not yet been recognized as completely separate studies with distinct disciplines. Yet at the beginning of our period these ideas were still receiving serious and eloquent expression by, for example, Ralegh and Shakespeare, and they were to remain for many years a commonly accepted background to thought. Knowledge was still based to a considerable extent on the authority of earlier writers, on deduction from traditional theory, or on the ingenious working out of analogies, rather than on observation and experiment. The road to learning was still the traditional one of grammar, rhetoric, and logic, and university education was still largely medieval in conception and method. Above all, Faith and Reason were not commonly set in opposition to each other, and their spheres were not sharply distinguished.

At the end of the period, very different assumptions prevail. Empirical science has emerged and is claiming the whole material universe as its field; the territory of Faith is coming to be strictly limited and fenced off so as to leave all the rest to Reason; exact measurement and scientific law are replacing the older arguments from analogy and authority. It is the age of Hobbes's deterministic psychology, and of the mathematical philosophy of Descartes. There is a conscious modernity in the air, a deliberate anti-medieval movement, so that 'scholasticism' becomes almost a term of abuse. The political upheaval of the Civil War has hastened many economic and social movements that had begun earlier. London, which has doubled its population, is rapidly developing towards the urban civilization of the Augustans. Economic individualism is becoming more a virtue than a vice; and 'political arithmetic', impersonal calculation based on statistics, is coming to seem more significant than the older organic sense of the 'body politic' and its relationships.

The transformation was of course gradual. In spite of much obvious continuity, certain signs of change appear about the beginning of the century. There are grounds, in fact, for distinguishing between the Jacobean and the Elizabethan temper, though it would be absurd to suggest that the new reign was marked by an immediate reversal of mood or outlook. Rather, certain tendencies which had been developing almost parallel with the trends towards expansiveness and idealism in the Elizabethan sensibility began to appear more prominently in the later nineties and continued to grow after 1600. Much of the Jacobean expression and discussion of melancholy may be dismissed as a passing fashion, a literary exaggeration. It remains true, nevertheless, that the Renaissance delight in new human potentialities was necessarily followed by a sharper sense of the contrast with the unchanging limitations of human existence, and that signs of this kind of disenchantment are frequent in the early seventeenth century. In political and economic life, too, there were maladjustments connected with the recent growth of capitalism and industrial enterprise, and others leading to unemployment and frustration among the more thoughtful and articulate groups – scholars, writers, aspiring courtiers, and would-be public servants – while the ending of war abroad removed one obvious outlet for unused energies. At a more philosophical level, the orthodox world-picture might also be interpreted pessimistically, laying stress on man's corruption as a result of the Fall and on the ageing and decline of a world which was thought to be drawing towards its end. Moreover, the whole grand system was undermined by Copernicus and the 'new philosophy', though the effect of this was delayed; even after Galileo's verifying experiments, the new conception of the solar system was liable to be regarded as merely one theory among others. More insidious was the effect of the amoral attitude of Machiavelli, with his naturalistic political philosophy, or Montaigne's sceptical probing of human personality and behaviour. Montaigne contributed to a new interest in psychology, which helped to give more precise expression to complex and divided states of mind.

The early years of the seventeenth century, then, show an increase in scepticism, introspection, self-consciousness, and self-criticism. The specifically literary signs are a growing emphasis on satire and realism, a deeper and more inward apprehension of tragedy, and an acuter analysis of human moods and experiences. Moreover, corresponding styles were also developed: the older rhetorical method in verse with its copiousness and formal elaboration gave way to a more concentrated manner, following more closely the diction and rhythms of speech, to what were called at the time 'strong lines' and to what became known later as 'Metaphysical' wit. In prose there was a reaction away from Ciceronian eloquence as a model towards the packed terseness of Seneca and Tacitus. The first can be seen in the tragedians and Donne, the second in Bacon's Essays. As so often, the old and the new continued for a long time side by side.

Poetry and the Tradition of Wit

The primary aim of Elizabethan poetry was not the spontaneous outpouring of emotion, whatever effects of simplicity, sensuousness, and passion may be found in its best products. It was a conscious art, rhetorical in method, concerned above all to impose form and order upon experience, working equally through the senses, the emotions, and the reason, and directed (at least in theory) at the will.[1] Wit and the play of mind, argumentation, and logical development were therefore not foreign to it: artifice and convention were accepted as natural and desirable: fluency, copiousness of language, and easy regularity of verse were positive virtues. Such an art has its notable successes where true feeling informs the idealistic conventions and the rhetorical craftsmanship, or where the stylization is related to a way of life. But it is unfitted for certain kinds of directness, economy, concentration, and realistic force, and for expressing the subtler kinds of introspection and psychological analysis. It was when the need for these came to be felt that the new style began to appear, notably, of course, in the amazing development of Shakespeare's dramatic verse from *Henry VI* to *Hamlet*, and to some extent also in the verse of his sonnets, but also in the non-dramatic poetry of Donne and others. This development started, in fact, before half the best-known examples of the older manner were in existence: when Donne began to write, such typically Elizabethan vogues as those of the sonnet sequence and the Ovidian tale of classical mythology were barely established.

Certainly many poets kept up something like the earlier style well into the reign of James I, and some even beyond. Drayton, who survived until 1631, was an Elizabethan to the end, antagonistic to the new poets and their exclusiveness. Daniel, again, who lived until 1619, owed little to new fashions. These were contemporaries of Shakespeare and almost of Spenser, but there were also younger men who may be grouped together as Spenserians. William Drummond of Hawthornden (1585-1649) cultivated the Italian and French poets, from Petrarch and the Pléiade downwards, who had been the Elizabethans' chief models. His own work, which Ben Jonson judged 'not after the fancy of the time', is bookish and elaborately ornamented, ranging from love-sonnets and madrigals to *Flowers of Sion*, with its eloquent sonnet on John the Baptist. William Browne (c.

1591–c. 1643) and George Wither (1588–1667) were pastoralists, expressing a feeling for country life in a vein of fluent prettiness. More important were the brothers Giles (c. 1588–1623) and Phineas (1582–1650) Fletcher. Phineas is chiefly known for his elaborate allegory of the human body, *The Purple Island*. Giles's *Christ's Victorie and Triumph* adapts the Spenserian style to the story of the Temptation; his verse has a warmer quality and a fondness for paradoxical wit that connect him with such Catholic poets as the Elizabethan Southwell and the Caroline Crashaw. The Fletchers form an important link between Spenser and Milton.

Much Elizabethan verse had been inseparable from music, and the association proved a conservative force for some time. Songs from masques and plays and from the numerous books of madrigals, airs, and ballets continued in the Jacobean period to be conditioned by their purpose; often the poet and composer were one, as with Thomas Campian (1567–1620). The effect of writing with music in view was to preclude complexity of mood, rapid shifts of tone, or a freedom of movement suggesting the speaking voice. Simple and obvious emotions, developed one at a time, and expressed in a lucid and formally regular style, gave the most effective opportunities to the composer. The limitations are obvious, but within them the Elizabethan lyric achieved an extraordinary freshness and grace, and in the early seventeenth century Campian was still developing new subtlety and delicacy in its treatment. Verse of this kind needs, of course, its musical setting to complete the effect.

These various survivals do not alter the fact that marked changes of style and interest were taking place during the fifteen-nineties. They are suggested in some of Ralegh's poems, with their personal melancholy and intensity of argumentation; in the energetic philosophizing of Sir John Davies's *Nosce Teipsum*; in Chapman's seriousness, intellectual temper, and explicit defence of obscurity; in some of Shakespeare's sonnets, where the movement and the imagery approach the vitality of his mature dramatic style; in the general development of verse in the theatre towards freedom and flexibility; and in the vogue for satire which produced the work of Hall and Marston. But outside the theatre the main agents of change and the dominant moulders of the new tradition were John Donne (1572–1631) and Ben Jonson (1572–1637), and Donne's originality was by far the more spectacular.

As far as we can tell, it appeared at once: if Donne's juvenilia included specimens of conventional Elizabethan verse, they have not survived. In his work of the fifteen-nineties, which included besides the satires most of the elegies and the *Songs and Sonets*, there are no sonnets in the strict sense, and the title 'songs' at once points to unusual qualities. For whether or not Donne thought that these lyrics might be set to music, he seldom allowed that possibility to control their diction, movement, or form, much less their theme, attitude, or general development. It is the directness and familiar tone of speech that at once strike us:

> Busie old foole, unruly Sunne
> Why dost thou thus,
> Through windowes, and through curtaines call on us?
> Must to thy motions lovers seasons run?
> Sawcy pedantique wretch, goe chide
> Late schoole boyes, and soure prentices,
> Goe tell Court-huntsmen, that the King will ride,
> Call countrey ants to harvest offices;
> Love, all alike, no season knowes, nor clyme,
> Nor houres, dayes, moneths, which are the rags of time.

The movement of this stanza from *The Sunne Rising* is inseparable from the tone and meaning; we cannot read it unless we recognize the lover's mood of humorous exasperation and allow its scornful emphases to play against the verse pattern – '*Busie* old foole' – '*Through windowes* and *through curtaines*' (doubling the sense of officious prying) – 'Must to *thy* motions …?' – 'houres, dayes, moneths, which are the *rags* of time'. Stress, intonation, gesture almost, are imposed on us as we read; we have the sense of a living speech, individual and intimate, not of formal or public utterance. The diction has a popular, colloquial vigour; the imagery is chosen for its effect of surprise and compression – 'countrey ants', 'the rags of time' – and sound effects such as assonance and alliteration are used to reinforce the tone and feeling rather than simply to create a pattern of verbal melody. The rhythmical effect belongs rather to the whole stanza than the single line, and it is subordinate to the expression of the meaning and the general air of dramatic realism. One aspect of Donne's originality, in fact, is that he gave to the short lyric something of the flexibility, the urgent and profound expressiveness that came to be developed in dramatic blank verse.

Donne's poetry is further remarkable for its fusion of passionate feeling and logical argument. Progression by reasoning was nothing new in Elizabethan poetry, but what distinguishes Donne from, say, Sidney in this respect is the subtlety, incisiveness, and range of his thought, together with the sense that the play of intellect tended to become for him an emotional experience, and that conversely when deeply moved his mind only worked more rapidly. Thus parting and consolation lead him to contemporary beliefs about the universe, the scale of beings, the human soul, and the nature of matter, to remote astronomical phenomena and the malleable properties of gold; but the surprising argument only heightens the feeling:

> Moving of th' earth brings harmes and feares,
>   Men reckon what it did and meant,
> But trepidation of the spheares,
>   Though greater farre, is innocent.
>
> Dull sublunary lovers love
>   (Whose soule is sense) cannot admit
> Absence, because it doth remove
>   Those things which elemented it.
>
> But we, by a love so much refin'd
>   That our selves know not what it is,
> Inter-assured of the mind,
>   Care lesse, eyes, lips and hands to misse.
>
> Our two soules, therefore, which are one,
>   Though I must goe, endure not yet
> A breach, but an expansion,
>   Like gold to ayery thinnesse beate.

Some of Donne's dialectical acuteness may have derived from his Catholic upbringing and his study of scholastic philosophy; his employment of its concepts led later to the use of the term 'Metaphysical' to define his wit and his particular type of conceit, and to its extension by Dr Johnson to describe his followers and imitators. Conceits and wit were a recognized part of the Elizabethan rhetorical apparatus for amplifying a theme, but Donne's characteristic use of them involves such an extraordinary range of ideas and experience with such startling connexions between them, the whole process seems to work at a so much higher pressure, that in comparison the general Elizabethan use appears merely superficial and ingenious.[2] When it fails, the Metaphysical conceit answers to Dr Johnson's account: 'the most heterogeneous ideas are yoked by violence together'.[3] When it succeeds one thinks rather of Coleridge's remark that imagination shows itself in 'the balance or reconciliation of opposite or discordant qualities'.

Donne's style was the natural expression of his sensibility, and its originality is reflected in his choice and treatment of subject. As he rejects the melodious fluency of Spenser's verse or the decorative use of classical mythology, so he turns from the Petrarchan conventions to analyse the experience of love in a variety of moods ranging from cynical sensuality to a profound sense of union, but always with the same realistic force and eager play of mind. When he turns to religious poetry later in life there is no change of style or method: the same variety and range of experience are drawn on, and the same dramatic power expresses his mental conflicts:

> Batter my heart, three person'd God; for, you
> As yet but knocke, breathe, shine, and seeke to mend;
> That I may rise, and stand, o'erthrow mee, 'and bend
> Your force, to breake, blowe, burn and make me new. ...
> *Holy Sonnets*, XIV

Throughout, his Metaphysical wit was a means of bringing all sides of his experience into relation with the immediate subject.

The other great formative influence in seventeenth-century poetry was Ben Jonson. It is not so much that, as some older histories of literature used to assert, there was a 'school of Donne' and a 'school of Jonson'; rather that almost any seventeenth-century poet will show signs of having learnt from both, though the proportions and the nature of the blend may differ widely. Jonson's non-dramatic verse does not show such an obvious originality or such a decisive breach with contemporary fashion as Donne's; yet his different modification of the Elizabethan manner is almost equally significant. Even his songs have a greater neatness and point; they are more economical in

method, and the best of them achieve a striking sureness of movement, a kind of controlled *élan*, which is different from the limpid
Elizabethan flow, as in the 'Hymn to Diana' from *Cynthia's Revels*:

> Queene, and *Huntresse*, chaste and faire,
>   Now the *Sunne* is laid to sleepe,
> Seated in thy silver chaire,
>   State in wonted manner keepe:
> *HESPERUS* intreats thy light,
> Goddesse, excellently bright.

Apart from lyrics, including numerous songs from his plays and
masques, Jonson wrote chiefly occasional verse-epigrams, epitaphs,
odes, and epistles. He rejected equally the Petrarchan convention, the
Spenserian fluency and 'sweetness long-drawn out', and with rare
exceptions the sonnet form. For his models, he turned from the French
and Italians to the Latin lyric poets and epigrammatists, especially
Catullus, Horace, and Martial; from these he learned a detached cool-
ness of style which can unite with genuine feeling to give it restraint,
stability, and permanence, as in the epitaph on the child actor, Solomon Pavy, who acted old men so well that the Fates mistook him
for one:

> So, by error, to his fate
>   They all consented;
> But viewing him since (alas, too late)
>   They have repented.
> And have sought (to give new bi^rth)
>   In baths to steepe him;
> But being so much too good for earth,
>   Heaven vowes to keepe him.

Jonson's classicism was in no sense an escape from the contemporary world; in reaching after an ideal civilization he did not lose
touch with the interests of the life around him and a vigorous native
idiom. He translates Catullus into Elizabethan speech and English
settings, bidding Celia, after the first thousand kisses:

> ... unto the tother
> Adde a thousand, and so more:
> Till you equall with the store,
> All the grasse that *Rumney* yeelds
> Or the sands in *Chelsey* fields

> Or the drops in silver *Thames*
> Or the starres, that guild his streames
> In the silent sommer-nights
> When youths ply their stolne delights.
> > *To Celia*

Similarly he can catch the Horatian tone of balanced moderation, the quiet acceptance of the human lot, as in *To the World*, with its characteristic close:

> Nor for my peace will I goe farre,
> As wandrers doe, that still doe rome,
> But make my strengths, such as they are,
> Here in my bosome, and at home.

Even the famous song 'Drinke to me onely with thine eyes' is made up of fragments from a late Greek prose writer; but it is Jonson's art which welds them into a whole with an effect of conversational ease and spontaneity.

When he fails, Jonson can be laboured and pedantic, but his characteristic successes achieve an urbane elegance which always suggests an underlying strength. Without attempting the obviously dramatic effect of Donne's broken rhythm, Jonson yet contrives within the smooth regularity of his verse a directness and energy of statement clearly related to speech. His detachment and his epigrammatic conciseness combine to produce an effect of wit, though it is not of the Metaphysical kind and does not employ Donne's type of conceit. In *Discoveries*, his commonplace-book of critical notes, Jonson remarked that 'metaphors far-fet hinder to be understood', and the kind of strength he sought for was not to be achieved through obscurity or metaphorical complexity. If his work has 'wit', if his lines are 'strong', it is rather through the quality of 'tough reasonableness' which Mr Eliot in his essay on Marvell has noted as underlying the lyric grace of much poetry of this time. The further description of wit in the same essay as involving 'a recognition, implicit in the expression of every experience, of other kinds of experience which are possible', indicates the grounds on which both Donne and Jonson, for all their differences, may be seen as contributing to a common tradition.

That Donne and Jonson, in spite of obvious differences, have something akin, may be seen from the fact that there exists a group of elegies of which the authorship remains undecided between the two poets. The important fact for the student of seventeenth-century poetry, however, is that it was possible for the two styles to combine and interact. Some of the ways in which this might happen are foreshadowed already in such contemporaries as Donne's friend Sir Henry Wotton (1568–1639) or Lord Herbert of Cherbury (1583–1648), whose great *Ode upon a Question* ... combines Donne's intense philosophical argument and learned conceits with Jonson's smoothness and urbanity. They are clearly to be seen in younger poets, such as Donne's executor Henry King (1592–1669), remembered especially for his moving *Exequy* on his wife, in George Herbert (1593–1633), and the religious poets, and equally in Thomas Carew (1595?–1640?) and the Caroline lyrics.

The Metaphysical Manner and Religious Poetry

In its remarkable development of religious poetry the seventeenth century forms a striking contrast with the previous age, which has little to show in this field. An exception must be made for the poetry of the Jesuit martyr Robert Southwell (c. 1561–96), which shows an odd mingling of the earlier, more naïve Elizabethan rhetoric and the Counter-Reformation ardour, sensuousness, and love of paradox. If Catholic poets tended to look to Italian models, Protestants found theirs to some extent in Joshua Sylvester's translations of the didactic and encyclopaedic works of the Huguenot poet du Bartas, which appeared during the fifteen-nineties; but there was no doctrinal exclusiveness, and the strains often mingle. In the work of Phineas Fletcher, du Bartas's didacticism is married to Spenserian allegory; in that of his brother Giles, the Spenserian quality is modified by Italian warmth and paradoxical wit in a way that anticipates Crashaw and may be described as 'baroque'. Much religious poetry of this period was affected by the vogue of books of 'emblems', sets of allegorical pictures each accompanied by verses expounding its moral. The first emblem book in English had appeared in 1586, but the most significant examples of religious verse in this form were the collections of *Emblemes* by Francis Quarles (1592–1644). The indirect influence of the emblem may, however, be seen in the imagery of more important poets, such as Herbert and Crashaw.

The religious poetry of Donne shows the same qualities as his other work: the dramatic tone, the play of speech rhythms against the verse pattern, the dialectical subtlety, the startling imagery drawn from common life or from intellectual pursuits and the psychological penetration. The effects of thus applying Metaphysical wit to religious subjects are almost as varied as in the love poetry: sometimes the ingenuity predominates, sometimes Donne's religious feelings seem to be indeed, as he described them, 'devout fits' coming and going 'like a fantastic ague'. With the *Holy Sonnets*, whatever their actual date of composition,[4] the note deepens; it is for the most part one of torment and struggle, and the style expresses this passionate conflict with dramatic vividness:

> I dare not move my dimme eyes any way,
> Despaire behind, and death before doth cast
> Such terrour ...
>
> *Holy Sonnet* I

Only in the last few hymns does Donne's religious poetry communicate the sense of assured faith:

> Since I am coming to that Holy roome,
> Where, with thy Quire of Saints for evermore
> I shall be made thy Musique; as I come
> I tune the Instrument here at the dore.
>
> *Hymne to God my God, in my sickness*

Here no less than in the poems of conflict the characteristic style and imagery continue; once more, in the astonishing geographical figures which follow these lines, we feel the main theme brought into relation with the widest possible range of interests and experience.

The use of the Metaphysical style in religious poetry by George Herbert (1593–1633) owes much to Donne, with whom he had early contacts, his mother being one of Donne's friends and patronesses. There are obvious contrasts: Herbert shows neither Donne's passionate and tortured casuistry nor his aggressive unconventionality of style. His courtly urbanity of language, his varied and musical verse forms, and a certain neatness and point, suggest the further influence of Ben Jonson. But it is from Donne that Herbert derives his wit and his conceits. Drawing upon ordinary experience and practical affairs rather than scholastic or scientific learning, Herbert's wit is often distinguished as 'homely', sometimes as 'quaint', and it does at times suggest simply the play of an ingenious fancy. In his best work, however, it has imaginative intensity and the effect of surprise:

> The growth of flesh is but a blister.
>
> *Holy Baptism*

> But we are still too young or old;
>   The Man is gone,
> Before we do our wares unfold:
>   So we freeze on,
> Untill the grave increase our cold.
>
> *Employment, II*

Often it serves to keep the religious experience close to everyday life, or it enables a sense of mental alertness to temper what might have become emotional excess, as in 'Love bade me welcome ...' where, although there are no conceits, an effect of wit is achieved through the control of tone in the dialogue. Sometimes the conceit lies in a title suggesting the emblem (*The Collar*, *The Pulley*), or it may be extended into a short allegorical narrative, foreshadowing Bunyan (*Redemption*, *The Pilgrimage*). But there is always a controlling play of mind, a firm grasp of common experience, and a vivid, dramatic sense.

Herbert can suggest the speaking voice, not only with courtly politeness, but also with direct colloquial vigour:

> Call in thy deathshead there: tie up thy fears.
>
> *The Collar*

> ... as if none knew but he.
> No man shall beat into his head,
> That thou within his curtains drawn canst see.
>
> *Miserie*

His purity of diction does not exclude proverbial and racy expressions like 'snudge in quiet', while the lyrical grace of his rhythms and stanza forms will usually be found to have an expressive relation to the meaning. In *The Collar* the movement effectively presents both the rebellious mood and the way it subsides; in *Aaron* two rhyme-sounds chiming through five stanzas suggest the bells which form one

of the poem's dominant figures; elsewhere assonance and alliteration give extra emphasis and enforce the meaning in Donne's way
(or Shakespeare's):

> ... there it [my heart] was dipt and dy'd
> And washt and wrung: the very wringing yet
> Enforceth tears.
>
> *Love Unknown*

This realistic strength underlying Herbert's grace of style is related
to the maturity of his emotional and religious life. The serenity of his
faith was not achieved without suffering and conflict; while his poems
do not show Donne's dramatic terrors and agonies, many of them
convey a profound sense of dereliction and unworthiness:

> My mirth and edge was lost: a blunted knife
> Was of more use than I.
> Thus thinne and lean without a fence or friend,
> I was blown through with ev'ry storm and winde.
>
> *Affliction*, I

Passages like this, by their intense honesty, add conviction to those
expressing the resolution of conflict in faith and acceptance. At its
most characteristic this acceptance is not mere resignation: it suggests
mature choice and an enlargement of spirit, which is communicated
most naturally in images of spring and renewal of life, as in *The
Flower*. Herbert's best work embodies the religious temper of the
seventeenth century at its finest and most humane.

Richard Crashaw (1612–49) called his 1646 volume *Steps to the
Temple*, after Herbert's *The Temple*, but the two poets have little in
common. In his use of conceits Crashaw has neither Donne's intellectual range nor Herbert's homely realism. He carries on rather from
Southwell and Giles Fletcher, combining a fondness for paradox with
sensuous warmth in the manner of the Italian poets of the Counter-
Reformation, especially Marino and the Jesuit writers of Latin epigrams. Both influences lead towards a use of the conceit as isolated
ornament rather than as an integral part of a poem's total meaning;
The Weeper, with its variations on the theme of Mary Magdalene's
tears, has been called a 'rosary of epigrams'. The characteristic warmth
and lyrical glow appear in the operatic *Hymn of the Nativity*, where,

in contrast with Milton's more majestic celebration, they are linked with a tender humour:

> Poor WORLD (said I) what wilt thou doe
> To entertain this starry STRANGER?
> Is this the best thou canst bestow?
> A cold, and not too cleanly manger?

Even before his conversion to Rome about 1645, Crashaw was writing in a vein of voluptuous mysticism which suggests Italian and Spanish baroque art. He carries to extremes the traditional use of erotic metaphor to convey the ecstasies of adoration, and his uncontrolled lyric fervour sometimes collapses into an exclamatory verbal haze. Yet there are passages of eloquent and passionate conviction:

> Faith is my force. Faith strength affords
> To keep pace with those powrfull words.
> And words more sure, more sweet, than they
> Love could not think, truth could not say.
>
> *The Hymne of Sainte Thomas*

Where there is an obvious emblematic quality, or a close relation to liturgy, or both, as in some of the later poems, the conceits and paradoxes often take on a quality of formal ritual, which lessens their general poetic force. In various ways, therefore, Crashaw's poetry moves away from the tradition of Donne and Herbert, but at times, as notably in the *Answer* to Cowley's cynical poem *Against Hope*, or the lines to the Countess of Denbigh, an approximation to Metaphysical wit adds strength and substance to his ecstatic lyricism.

Like Crashaw, Henry Vaughan (1622–95) wrote some secular verse in fashionable modes, but he is chiefly remembered for the religious poetry of *Silex Scintillans* (1655). Herbert's influence is marked in his work by many obvious echoes and borrowings. Where it is strongest, Vaughan usually suffers by the comparison; the effect is thinner and less concentrated. This is true even of comparative successes like *Regeneration*, which lacks Herbert's allegorical vividness though it shows something of Vaughan's special sensitiveness to natural beauty. The common assertion of Vaughan's greater imaginative power depends chiefly on effects of sudden illumination, like the opening of *The World*:

I saw Eternity the other night
Like a great *Ring* of pure and endless light ...

or the first stanza of 'They are all gone into the world of light'. But *The World* has this quality only at the beginning and end, and 'They are all gone ...' proves rather unequal as a whole. When Vaughan uses the conceits of a star 'confin'd into a tomb' or of 'the mists which blot and fill My perspective' (i.e. telescope) he suggests Donne, but when he makes light 'trample on my days' he is using language without the characteristic Metaphysical precision, in a manner nearer to the Romantics.

Vaughan's poetry is less social, more removed from the world of action than that of Donne or Herbert; he has neither Herbert's attachment to the Anglican Church nor Crashaw's concern with Catholic ritual and dogma. His religious intuitions belong to a wider and vaguer tradition of Neo-Platonic mysticism, of solitary contemplation which turns to images from nature – sun and stars, winds and streams, the plant and the seed – to express the soul's aspiration to eternal light or the 'deep but dazzling darkness' of God. In his best work he can still use the Metaphysical conceit effectively ('Bright shootes of everlastingness'), and this, with his fresh purity of diction, marks him of his age even when he handles Wordsworth's themes. But in single-minded concentration upon his personal vision he tends to lose that constant sense of other possible attitudes and experiences which gives the tradition of wit its peculiar strength.[5]

Most other religious poetry in the Metaphysical manner may be roughly grouped round these four poets. Quarles is a kind of inferior Herbert; Benlowes (1603?–76) has some of Crashaw's ardour with a greater extravagance; Traherne (1637?–74) carries to an extreme Vaughan's Neo-Platonic mysticism, but fails for the most part to give his vision poetic embodiment. There is a Puritan sobriety in the religious feeling of Andrew Marvell (1621–78), but it is expressed in a characteristic blend of Donnean and Jonsonian wit. The poet of *The Coronet* cannot be dismissed as lacking in seriousness, but the *Dialogue between the Resolved Soul and Created Pleasure* can employ sophisticated and urbane epigram to present a morality as ascetic as that of *Comus*. Religion, in Marvell as in Herbert and Donne, is in touch with many sides of living experience.

Caroline Poets and the Courtly Lyric

The influence of the Court upon literature during this period varies with the different reigns. At Elizabeth's Court life had been stylized in the elaborate ritual of the cult of the Virgin Queen. Under her successor nothing quite took the place of this, with all its associated poetry of idealistic love; James I's Court seems to have lost much of the earlier ceremonial dignity, though in its luxury it was even more ostentatious. The masque, with its combination of poetry, music, and spectacle, became the most popular Court entertainment. Court influence on the drama tended in the direction of sophistication, exaggerated sentiment, and artificial heroics, especially in the work of Fletcher and his collaborators. Under Charles I and Henrietta Maria there was a partial return to the Elizabethan dignity and order: Court tastes acquired more refinement and wider aesthetic interests, especially in the visual arts. Much more than in the Jacobean period, it is possible to distinguish a school of courtly poetry, mainly in the form of songs and lyrics, but differing in many ways from its Elizabethan counterpart. The lyrics are more independent of music; even when obviously songs, their evolution is not so closely controlled by the needs of the composer. Their use of language is close to cultivated speech, their imagery is more intellectual and less sensuous, their method is often dialectical, and they aim at classical neatness and point. Between these poets and the Elizabethans, in fact, there stand Donne and Ben Jonson.

The leading representative of this group was Thomas Carew (1595?–1640?). If the label 'Cavalier poet' suggests that he was an elegant trifler, it hardly gives a fair notion of his best work. His elegy on Donne is both a moving tribute and a remarkable piece of criticism, successfully handling the pentameter couplet with Donne's argumentative energy. In his love poetry the Donnean conceit is usually embodied in more polished and regular verse:

> That killing power is none of thine,
>   I gave it to thy voyce, and eyes:
> Thy sweets, thy graces, all are mine:
>   Thou art my starre, shin'st in my skies;
> Then dart not from thy borrowed sphere
> Lightning on him that fixt thee there.
>
> *Ingratefull beauty threatened*

This graceful movement and logical neatness are Jonsonian, and the merging of the two influences is characteristic. The way in which a similar blend appears in many quite minor poets may be seen in the following lines from Godolphin:

> Though poorer in desert I make
> My selfe whilst I admire,
> The fuel which from hope I take
> I give to my desire.
>
> If this flame lighted from your Eyes
> The subject doe calcine,
> A Heart may be your sacrifice
> Too weake to be your shrine.
> *'Noe more unto my thoughts appeare'*

A surprising number of minor poets were able to display these qualities in one or two poems; the names of Cartwright, Fanshawe, Habington, Hall, Kynaston, Randolph, and Stanley are a mere sample selection.

The two most often taken with Carew as Cavalier poets (though both stand well below him) are Sir John Suckling (1609–42) and Richard Lovelace (1618–53). Suckling borrows Donne's lighter themes and more cynical tone, usually embodying them in simple song metres with colloquial ease and informality. Lovelace is more unequal, but at his best a more serious poet. He has given us the most famous of all expressions of the Cavalier spirit in *To Lucasta on going to the Wars* and *To Althea from Prison*. A similar grace may be found in others of his love songs, and in such Horatian moralizings as *The Grasshopper*. The distinctive quality of the Caroline lyric comes out most clearly in a comparison with that of the Restoration; even when themes and attitudes are apparently the same, the tone of the later work has coarsened, and we miss the air of civilized grace. Even Suckling, who seems temperamentally indistinguishable from the Restoration wits, has still a slightly finer manner and a shade more purity of diction; certainly Lovelace could never be mistaken for one of the later group.

An attractive sidelight on the period is provided by a number of poems dealing with great houses and their rural neighbourhoods; they suggest that the Court was still aware of its roots in the country.

Following Ben Jonson's praise of Penshurst, Carew writes of Saxham, Fanshawe of Charles I's proclamation 'commanding the gentry
to reside upon their estates'. Similar themes appear in Randolph and
later in Marvell. The poet who shows most obvious concern with
rural culture is the conscious classicist Robert Herrick (1591-1674).
Herrick's debt to Jonson is more superficial and less significant than
that of Carew or Marvell; on the other hand, he owes little to Metaphysical wit apart from an occasional conceit (night will 'make a
seizure on the light'; the lover is 'thy Protestant'). In many ways he
is nearer to the Elizabethan lyric. Writing of fairies and country
customs, he recalls Drayton or *A Midsummer Night's Dream*; lament-
ing the transience of beauty he suggests Campian. His love songs
ring the changes on the theme 'Gather ye rosebuds while ye may'
with a fanciful charm which seldom sounds any imaginative depths.

Of course, the Caroline poets are smaller personalities than Jonson
or Donne, and the assimilation of their influence could be only partial.
But it is convincing and genuine, and the result is not merely imitative; up to a point the Cavaliers could share these modes of feeling
and relate them to their own Court world. That world had its limitations, and it may be significant that the group contains no undoubted
major poet. But it is reasonable to suppose that the finely poised
urbanity of Caroline poetry at its best had some connexion, however
indirect, with actual living. Certainly the atmosphere was favourable
to the full development of minor gifts; the dominant literary influences, combining with the last phase of true Court culture in English
history, produced some of the best lyrical and occasional poetry in
the language.

Later Developments of Wit in Poetry

The middle years of the century show Metaphysical poetry under-
going various changes. With some poets the manner declines into
eccentricity and extravagance; with others, wit takes on a different
character in response to changes in contemporary sensibility. At the
same time, the tradition shapes its last great poet in Andrew Marvell
(1621-78).

Marvell's work has a central significance, gathering together many
strands of seventeenth-century thought, feeling, and style. His special
blend of wit includes the imaginative surprise of Donne and the

civilized grace of Jonson, the gallantry of Carew and the grave delicacy of Herbert. His temperament has both Puritan sobriety and a classical sophistication more flexible than Milton's. In no poet are levity and seriousness more inextricably mingled, though something of the same quality appears in Pope. The lightest pastoral may take on the resonances of religious allegory without losing its quality of delicate artifice (*Clorinda and Damon*); a fanciful love song will contain a quiet reminder of human transience, as in *The Mower to the Glow-worms*:

> Ye Country Comets, that portend
> No War, nor Princes funeral,
> Shining unto no higher end
> Than to presage the Grasses fall ...

and a fancifully elaborated comparison of garden flowers to soldiers on parade, in *Upon Appleton House*, can lead without the slightest incongruity to serious reflections on the Civil War. The wit that permits these transitions is essentially a wide-ranging play of mind which is continually making imaginative connexions between different levels of experience. It appears not only in the learned paradoxes from which Marvell constructs his *Definition of Love*, but also in the vivid force of Fate's 'iron wedges'; not merely in the comic extravagance of the first paragraph of *To His Coy Mistress*, but also in the sudden intensity of 'Times winged Charriot' and the 'Desarts of vast Eternity', the qualified triumph over time asserted by the conclusion and the linking of these stages in connected argument.

Marvell returned to favour in the nineteenth century earlier than the other Metaphysical poets, largely on account of his feeling for natural beauty. Whenever he touches this theme his verse has certainly a remarkable quality of freshness and moving intimacy, yet this is achieved without any exclusion of his usual intellectual agility or any change from the tone of mature sophistication. The tropical paradise of *The Bermudas* is related not only to political and religious interests but to art and civilization; the spring *enamels* everything, God sends the birds on *visits* and

> ... hangs in shades the Orange bright
> Like golden Lamps in a green Night.

Similarly the meadow grass of *Upon Appleton House* 'seems as green silks but newly washed'; artificial and natural beauty are not set in opposition, but illuminate each other. A sense of the emblematic possibilities of 'Nature's mystick Book' does not preclude a direct sensuous response, nor does the pleasure of the senses impede the profounder imaginative insights of the mind in *The Garden*'s 'green shade'.

The classical quality in Marvell appears in his smooth polished verse, his precision and economy of phrase, and his balanced sense of human limitations. It is nowhere seen to better advantage than in his *Horatian Ode upon Cromwell's Return from Ireland*, which contemplates the events of the Civil War with an urbane detachment which is, nevertheless, far from cynicism or irresponsibility. Cromwell is accepted as an irresistible natural force, a minister of Destiny and the instrument of England's greatness, but the personal dignity of Charles and the pathos of his fate receive due emphasis, and the conclusion is clear-sighted:

> The same *Arts* that did gain
> A *Pow'r* must it *maintain*.

Marvell's concern with politics was to increase, and eventually to crowd poetry out of his life. After the Restoration he wrote little verse apart from political satire in rough doggerel. The change has a significance related to larger changes in the temper of the age; the culture of the Restoration was not of the kind which could feed Marvell's peculiar poetic genius.

Occasional examples of conceits running to fantastic extravagance can be found in almost all the Metaphysical poets from Donne onwards, but they tend to multiply in the forties and fifties. Crashaw's faults in this kind are well known; the wit of Marvell himself sometimes misfires, as with his salmon-fishers who, 'like *Antipodes* in Shoes, Have shod their Heads in their Canoes'. The work of Benlowes is notorious for its high proportion of extreme instances of the fantastic and obscure. But the real decadence of the style is seen when ingenuity is pursued for its own sake, with no informing imaginative pressure, as in most of the verse of John Cleveland (1613–58), and much of that of Abraham Cowley (1618–67). For Cleveland wit is a game, even in an elegy like that on Edward King (Milton's *Lycidas*), where he protests:

> I am no Poet here; my pen's the spout,
> Where the rain water of my eyes run out.

When he says of his mistress:

> ... call her the square circle; say
> She is the very rule of Algebra.
> *The Hecatomb to his Mistress*

it is clear that we are dealing with something more superficial than
Marvell's geometry in *The Definition of Love*. Dryden, distinguishing
between Donne's satire and Cleveland's, said 'the one gives us deep
thoughts in common language ... the other gives us common
thoughts in abstruse words'. It is significant that Cleveland is at his
best in political satire, a mode congenial to the next age.

Cowley, like Cleveland, had an immense contemporary reputation, which he has never regained. His work is extraordinarily representative of the changing taste of his age; it shows the wit of Donne
turning into the wit of Dryden. He has all the analytical and logical
skill of the earlier Metaphysicals, the same striking openings, the
same elaborately extended comparisons, but he lacks any profound
imaginative synthesis of experience; his intellect is employed in
decorating a number of fairly simple ideas and sentiments. Wit, for
Cowley, was a matter of rational comparison, with a common-sense
basis to its ingenuity. The poem *Against Hope* provides a fair example:

> Thou bringst us an *Estate*, yet leav'st us *Poor*,
> By clogging it with *Legacies* before!
>   The *Joys* which we *entire* should wed,
>   Come *deflowr'd Virgins* to our bed;
> Good fortunes without gain imported be,
>   Such mighty *Custom's* paid to Thee.
> For *Joy* like *Wine* kept close does better tast;
> If it take air before, its spirits wast.

He had no use for the '*Cobwebs* of the *Schoolmen's* trade' which had
furnished so many of Donne's conceits; he was interested in the new
science, and wrote odes *To Mr Hobs* and *To the Royal Society*. These
indications of Cowley's rational temper acquire an additional importance when we consider Hobbes's explicit pronouncements on current
taste and the nature of poetry. In *Leviathan* Hobbes equates Imagination and Fancy as 'decaying sense': in his *Answer* to Davenant's *Dis-*

course on his poem *Gondibert* he attacks 'the ambitious obscurity of expressing more than is perfectly conceived, or perfect conception in fewer words than it requires'. The function of Fancy in poetry is simply ornamental:

> Time and Education begets experience: Experience begets memory, Memory begets Judgement and Fancy; Judgement begets the strength and structure, and Fancy begets the ornaments of a Poem.

The new insistence is all on perspicuity and directness, on poetry as a social activity; wit is more and more limited by the claims of Good Sense, until we find Dryden in his *Apology* prefixed to *The State of Innocence* defining it as 'a propriety of thoughts and words'. All this was of course part of the general movement of thought, the swing towards mathematical demonstration and scientific logic: the aims of the new Royal Society, according to its historian, Thomas Sprat, were 'to separate the knowledge of Nature from the colours of Rhetorick, the devices of Fancy or the delightful deceit of Fables' in order to obtain for mankind 'a Dominion over *Things*'. At the same time the new society emerging from the upheaval of the Civil War was increasingly to encourage the public voice in poetry, whether as easy, direct statement or as lofty formal decorum, together with subject-matter of social and political interest. The Metaphysical balance of passion and argument, imagination and reason, settles towards the rational side, and in Cowley's poetry (and in a less representative degree that of Sir William Davenant, 1606–68) we can see the process taking place. At the same time, Edmund Waller (1606–87) and Sir John Denham (1615–69) were beginning to cater for and confirm the new tastes.

Cowley was more than a decadent Metaphysical: he established the neo-classic vogue of the 'Pindaric' ode in which lofty magniloquence is allowed a certain licence of verse form, strictly limited by convention, and in the *Davideis* he made the first attempt at an epic poem on classical principles. He is at his most effective, however, in a vein of personal feeling and simple good sense which both recalls his early admiration for Spenser and looks forward to certain elegiac strains of eighteenth-century poetry; of this the most notable example is *On the Death of Mr William Hervey*.

Milton: Humanist and Puritan

The development as a poet of John Milton (1608–74) is nothing if not individual. His early work shows, nevertheless, a variety of contemporary influences. At first he seems a Spenserian, related to Drummond, Browne, and the Fletchers, carrying on the Elizabethan manner of sensuous richness and mythological decoration, and employing, as in *On the Morning of Christ's Nativity* (1629), variations upon the Spenserian stanza form. This is a typically Renaissance poem in its mingling of classical deities and 'yellow-skirted Fayes' with the Bible story: the old tradition of Christ's birth silencing the oracles provides a plausible excuse. A more direct influence from Spenser can be seen in *Comus* (1634), and the verse paragraphs of *Lycidas* recall the marriage odes in their adaptation of the Italian *canzone*. According to Dryden, Milton himself acknowledged Spenser as 'his original'. Echoes of Ben Jonson, with something of his urbane grace and neatness, appear in *Arcades* and the *Epitaph on the Marchioness of Winchester*; but Milton's classicism was, in general, to take a different direction from Jonson's. Metaphysical wit makes an occasional appearance, used facetiously in the lines on Hobson the carrier or seriously in those on Shakespeare. A further influence comes from the Jacobean dramatists. Comus's great temptation speech:

> Wherefore did Nature powre her bounties forth
> With such a full and unwithdrawing hand ...

is Shakespearian in its varied liveliness of diction and its expressive interplay of sound, movement, and imagery, though not all of the masque has this dramatic quality.

Throughout the early poems Milton was developing his own personal voice and style. He came fairly soon to abandon both Metaphysical wit and the decorative conceits of the Elizabethan or Italian kind. After *Comus* we do not find again the Jacobean dramatic complexity, or the pure lyricism of the songs which outdo Campian in exquisite verbal melody. What continues through to *Lycidas* and beyond is a type of sonorous musical eloquence already foreshadowed as early as the *Nativity* ode, especially in its rolling alexandrines:

> And all the spangled host keep watch in squadrons bright

> The wakefull trump of doom must thunder through the deep

and carried on in the sustained exaltation of *At a Solemn Musick*. In *Lycidas*, employing the elegiac pastoral conventions, Milton is concerned 'to sing and build the lofty rhyme' with ceremonial formality, even while exploring personal problems and conflicts. The characteristic Grand Style is emerging, what Tennyson called Milton's 'organ voice', which carries on through the eloquence of the sonnets to become the epic manner of *Paradise Lost*. The great power of this style is an incantatory grandeur and nobility unrivalled for the expression of large majestic conceptions and generalized or broadly simple feelings. This power was not achieved without sacrificing certain qualities of sensuous richness, flexibility, and sensitiveness present in the earlier work. A preoccupation with sonority precludes any subtle suggestion of the speaking voice; the pattern of sound is elaborated in a much broader and less direct relation to the meaning than in Comus's temptation speech. Milton's classicism played its part in the evolution of his style, not merely in encouraging learned allusiveness and the assumption of a formal vatic manner, but in an increasing tendency to handle English in a classical spirit, adopting Latin syntactical constructions, and using classically derived words in their strict etymological sense. This again tended to increase dignity and eloquence more than inwardness or vitality.

The development of Milton's style is related to his consciousness of vocation both as man and as poet. At nineteen he already wishes to employ his native language 'in some graver subject'; at twenty-three he laments his unproductiveness and dedicates his talents to God. In *Comus* he transforms the Caroline masque into a high-minded defence of chastity and temperance; in *Lycidas* the direction of his moral fervour against corrupt clergy suggests already the combination of religious seriousness and political ardour with which he greeted the Civil War. His prose works of the early forties share a jubilantly apocalyptic mood common on the Parliamentary side at this time. Disillusion was to follow, and a progressive rejection of one sect and party after another, but through all the controversy, often acrimonious, of the next twenty years, Milton never lost the sense of being a dedicated champion of true religion and liberty. Single-minded integrity, rather than flexibility and sensitiveness, is the mark of Milton's character and thought as of his style.

For the Renaissance humanist the ultimate triumph was to do for his own country what Homer and Virgil had done for theirs, to vindicate its language and culture in a Heroic poem. For the Puritan Milton this aim coalesced naturally with the propagation of moral truth. Before the various interruptions of the Civil War he had contemplated a national epic on the Arthurian theme; a little later he was planning a drama on the story of the Fall. For reasons which may have included disillusionment over national events and a feeling encouraged by the increasing rationalism of the time that national legends were 'delightful deceits' obnoxious to reason, whereas Biblical stories had the sanction of revelation, Milton eventually planned his Heroic poem as *Paradise Lost*, and set out to

> ... assert Eternal Providence
> And justify the wayes of God to men.

Many critics of different schools have noted the difficulties involved in adapting the Biblical story to the epic form, especially the prehistoric setting, the absence of truly human characters before the Fall itself, and the direct presentation of the Christian Deity in speech and action.[6] Milton exerts the full force of his art and learning to solve these problems, particularly in the width of reference and allusion permitted by epic simile, in the sonorous sweep of his verse and the sustained elevation of his style. All man's learning and achievement is brought into relation with the central event of the Fall; Milton keeps constantly before our minds the grandeur of human history and the romantic variety of lands, races, and civilizations. He draws particularly on the world of classical legend, so potent for the humanist in its suggestions of ideal beauty:

> Not that faire field
> Of *Enna*, where Proserpin gathring flours
> Her self a fairer Floure by gloomie *Dis*
> Was gatherd, which cost Ceres all that pain
> To seek her through the world; nor that sweet Grove
> Of *Daphne* by *Orontes*, and th' inspir'd
> *Castalian* Spring might with this Paradise
> Of Eden strive.

Yet few would undertake to defend altogether his treatment of God and Heaven, and it is still matter for critical debate how far the poetic presentation of Satan in Books I and II avoids a degree of interest inconsistent with the explicit degradation of him later and with the general theme. Even more important is the question whether in spite of its obvious triumphs Milton's epic manner does not sometimes involve a certain externality and insensitiveness as the complement of its formal grandeur. Many modern readers, who would not wish to deny that Milton is a great poet, have been led by considerations of this kind to question the nineteenth-century view of him as a twin peak with Shakespeare.

In *Paradise Regained*, a poem of discussion and argument whose method recalls the Book of Job, and in the strict classical tragedy of *Samson Agonistes*, the theme of which symbolizes so much of Milton's fears and hopes for his country and the Puritan cause, we have the last stage of his style. This shows an austere concentration on bare dignity of statement, and in the dramatic choruses a formal elevation, which seem to have certain neo-classic affinities, though they are at the same time a logical culmination of Milton's whole artistic development.

Eloquence and Wit in Prose

The prose of the earlier seventeenth century is even more varied than its verse, and the lines are harder to distinguish. This is partly because of the more varied functions that prose has to serve – practical, informative, persuasive, rhetorical, artistic – functions which at this time were not clearly distinguished and some of which overlap those of verse; and partly because there was as yet no prose of everyday use as a norm from which significant variations could be made for special purposes. In some respects, nevertheless, the fifteen-nineties show developments in prose roughly parallel to the rise of Metaphysical wit.

For the Elizabethans the great model of cultivated prose style had been Cicero, and the chief aim amplification and embellishment according to the rules of the classical and Renaissance rhetoricians. The new concern is with matter rather than manner, a desire for more concentration and weight, and a preference for the epigrammatic terseness of Seneca or Tacitus. It was felt, as Sir William Cornwallis put it in his essays of 1601, that 'reason ... wrapped in a few words hath the best tang'. As in verse, there was no simple succession of one style by another: Ciceronian amplitude continued well into the middle of the seventeenth century, but it is important to note the beginning of a new mode. The *Essays* of Francis Bacon (1561–1626) provide an obvious example of the new style, especially in their first version, that of 1597. Later revisions and additions were to relax somewhat the uncompromising sententiousness of these strings of aphorisms, and to give a little more continuity in the development of the thought and allow some metaphorical expansion, but the general character remains:

> Crafty men contemne *Studies*; Simple Men Admire them; And Wise Men Use them.　　　　　　　　　　*Of Studies*

> Fortune is like the *Market*; Where many times, if you can stay a little, the Price will fall.　　　　　　*Of Delayes*

> I cannot call *Riches* better, than the Baggage of Virtue.
> 　　　　　　　　　　　　　　　　　　　　*Of Riches*

From the sententious aphorism it is an easy step to epigrammatic wit, as these examples show, and a neat and witty prose is employed in the early years of the century for a variety of purposes. It appears in such flippant exercises as Donne's *Paradoxes and Problemes*; it was naturally taken up by the dramatists, and obvious instances may be found in the comedies of Jonson or the tragedies of Webster. When a minor character in *The White Devil* is described as 'A new upstart: one that swears like a Falckner, and will lye in the Dukes eare day by day like a maker of Almanacks', Webster is using the manner of the 'character', another prose genre which encouraged and developed epigram and pointed wit. The 'character' was a brief description, often didactic or satirical, of a human type; its classical model was the series by the Greek Theophrastus, and the vogue may have owed something to the Latin translation of this in 1592. But many forms of character-sketch had come down from medieval literature, and various interests combined to make the form popular – the drama generally, the new concern with realism and satire, the doctrine of 'humours' and its development in psychological theory. The first English collection of 'Characters' in 1608 was by the satirist Joseph Hall, whose packed style earned him the title 'our English Seneca'.

The most famous of the many imitations were those of Overbury (1614, with enlarged later editions), which were really by a group of writers including Webster; and the *Microcosmography* of John Earle (1628). The former is as famous for its 'Fair and Happy Milkmaid' as for 'A Roaring Boy'; the latter ranged from the academic satire of 'A Critic' to the meditation on innocence of 'A Child', but always with a neat wit approaching the Metaphysical: 'He is nature's fresh picture newly drawn in oil, which time, and much handling, dims and defaces'. The manner continues in Fuller's *Holy and Profane State* (1642), which mingles the 'character' form with maxims, essays, and biographies.

It is an important characteristic of this period that one of the most popular forms of prose writing was the sermon. Here, too, effective use was made of the new terseness and pointed antithesis; while, as in religious poetry, Metaphysical wit proved an effective way of expressing the great paradoxes of faith. The most famous exponents of this kind of sermon oratory were Lancelot Andrewes (1555–1626) and Donne himself, though Donne's style has other qualities. Andrewes is intellectual and analytical, teasing every possible significance out of the words of his text and playing equally with meaning and sound: 'the word within a word, unable to speak a word'; 'if He had not *beene made*, we had beene marred': or employing startling metaphor from common life – 'the *Conduit pipes* of His *Grace*'. Donne combines this wit with a more expansive rhetoric, even approaching at times the looser kind of long period: the result is a greater emotional charge, a dramatic urgency and poetic power recalling his verse:

> ... though in the wayes of fortune, or understanding, or conscience, thou have been benighted until now, wintred and frozen, clouded and eclypsed, damped and benummed, smothered and stupefied till now, now God comes to thee, not as in the dawning of the day, not as in the bud of the spring, but as the Sun at noon to illustrate all shadows, as the sheaves in harvest, to fill all penuries, all occasions invite his mercies, and all times are his seasons.
>
> *Eighty Sermons*, 1640, Sermon II

The mingling of wit and eloquence in Donne's oratorical style is, like his highly individual verse, the expression of his mind and personality, in which scholastic learning, acute introspective analysis, and a restless intellect playing over the whole range of contemporary life and thought are inseparable from sensuous directness and passionate feeling.

A somewhat similar blend of epigrammatic wit with heightened eloquence may be seen in writers other than preachers. Robert Burton (1577–1640), in his encyclopaedic *Anatomy of Melancholy*, claimed to follow Seneca in respecting matter rather than words, but his habit of piling up learned references and examples, and his liking for strings of synonyms, made for long sentences which have been described as 'clause-heaps'. Sometimes these will approach the more elaborately articulated Latin sentence; more usually they seem shapeless and rambling. Burton can show at times a certain colloquial vigour, and his garrulity fits with his wide-ranging curiosity about human life and his immense reading. Sir Thomas Browne (1605–82) is chiefly famous as an exponent of sonorous eloquence and the swelling period, but in his earliest work, *Religio Medici*, there is something of colloquial familiarity and epigrammatic sententiousness, while a love of paradox and a kind of Metaphysical wit appear in all his writings. Wishing to state that he limits his desire for wealth, he says, 'I have not Peru in my desires, but a competence'; in his soul he finds among his passions 'the battail of Lepanto', and man appears to him 'that great and true *Amphibium*, whose nature is disposed to live ... in divided and distinguished worlds'. Browne's own nature was certainly so disposed; he is constantly making unexpected connexions between different fields of knowledge and experience – scholastic philosophy, classical legend and history, Christian and Biblical tradition, contemporary scientific theory, individual observation and personal musings and emotions. Similarly he plays off against each other the Latin and Teutonic elements in the language, speaking of 'the funambulatory Track and narrow Path of goodness' or 'a vanity almost out of date, and superannuated piece of folly'.

But Browne is increasingly concerned with effects of sonority, rhythm, and cadence; and in any classification of seventeenth-century prose styles his place must be with the renewed turning to expansive eloquence apparent in the pamphlets of Milton and the sermons of Jeremy Taylor (1613–67). All these writers show a deliberate and conscious rhetorical art, with a marked use of Latinized diction and syntax and a preference for the long period. Milton, indeed, is the most notable Ciceronian in English, though the anti-Ciceronian reaction had set in long before his time. His *Areopagitica*, conceived as a classical oration addressed to the Lords and Commons of England, is a sustained and glowing plea for liberty of expression; through its swelling rhythms we feel the lofty hopes of the Puritan Revolution's more idealistic phase:

> Methinks I see in my mind a noble and puissant nation rousing herself like a strong man after sleep, and shaking her invincible locks. Methinks I see her as an eagle mewing her mighty youth, and kindling her undazzled eyes at the full midday beam; purging and unscaling her long-abused sight at the fountain itself of heavenly radiance; while the whole noise of timorous and flocking birds, with those also that love the twilight, flutter about, amazed at what she means, and in their envious gabble would prognosticate a year of sects and schisms.

Such heightened eloquence could not, of course, be the staple manner of Milton's prose writings, though it maintains a generally formal and rhetorical level. The last lines of this extract suggest the vein of harshness and pedantry which sometimes appears in more heated passages of controversy; a certain inflexibility in the style makes the occasional excursions into colloquial directness seem forced and heavy. In his most memorable passages Milton handles prose as oratory or poetry. The third of these writers who preferred the long, constructed period, Jeremy Taylor, is equally a prose-poet, noted for his fluent vocabulary and copious metaphor. Like Browne he has affinities with Metaphysical wit, but even more a love of sonority and cadence together with an ornate imagery of sensuous beauty. Neither Browne nor Taylor shows Donne's urgency and intensity.

In writers like Milton and the preachers, one might expect to find a considerable influence from the Authorized Version of the Bible (1611). This is obvious in direct allusion and echoes, or in the use of the parallelism and Oriental imagery of Hebrew poetry which fitted in well with seventeenth-century exuberance. But in stately and eloquent rhythms it is not always easy to distinguish the influence of the Bible from other contemporary factors, such as the general state of the language and the study of classical rhetoric. The Authorized Version was the work of a committee of scholars, which inevitably produced an impersonal style at times somewhat conservative in its dignity and elevation; nevertheless, many of the narrative passages had a more direct simplicity which was to blend easily with homely speech in some of the Puritan pamphleteers and in Bunyan.

The pursuit of eloquence and wit, either singly or in various combinations, made possible the expression of many fascinating or impressive examples of seventeenth-century thought and sensibility. But while genius had free play, there was no check upon eccentricity; the age had no standard prose for logical argument and no normal medium for ordinary discussion and communication. It was these intellectual and practical needs which were increasingly to discipline and restrict extravagances and to lead towards the emergence of a prose of everyday use after the Restoration.

Prose as an Intellectual Instrument

As the language of learning and thought, English at the beginning of the seventeenth century had to compete with Latin, still the universal language. Bacon planned his great unfinished *Instauratio Magna* in Latin, and Hobbes used Latin for *De Cive* and *De Corpore*, translating them later. Burton would have written in Latin had not his publishers dissuaded him, and Browne used English for *Pseudodoxia Epidemica* only on second thoughts. Works were often translated into Latin to give them a European circulation; among these may be mentioned Browne's *Religio Medici* and Hooker's *Ecclesiastical Polity* (translated by John Earle, the 'character' writer).

English prose of intellectual argument as we understand it today may be said to begin with Hooker's *Laws of Ecclesiastical Polity*, but it was Bacon who fully launched it, in *The Advancement of Learning* (1605). Here in a manner more connected and flowing than that of the *Essays*, yet equally concerned for 'matter' rather than 'words', he sets out the conditions of all rational investigation of nature and human life. Claiming that 'nothing parcel of the world is denied to man's enquiry and invention', he sees as 'the root of all error' 'too untimely a departure and too remote a recess from particulars'. He advocates a radical change in intellectual habits, a transfer of interest from abstract speculation to direct observation and experiment. Bacon was the great propagandist for a kind of knowledge which should lead to practical control of the world. Though not himself a scientist, he established the basic methods of science and furthered its rapid development later in the century; by the time of the Restoration, Cowley was hailing him as the Moses who had reached the border of the scientific Promised Land. With such preoccupations it is hardly surprising that Bacon developed a prose style recognized even in his own time as aiming rather at 'Masculine, and clear, Expression, than at any Fineness, or Affectation of Phrases'.[8] Without rejecting some degree of eloquent heightening, and without losing altogether the concrete force of popular speech, he develops particularly the rational possibilities of language, using metaphors primarily as vivid intellectual illustration, and showing some distrust of imaginative writing: poetry

> doth raise and erect the mind by submitting the shews of things to the desires of the mind; whereas reason doth buckle and bow the mind unto the nature of things.
>
> *The Advancement of Learning*, Book 2

Here we have the beginnings of an attitude which was to grow more common later in the century, with important repercussions on prose style.

Prose appears as an instrument of thought about literature in the important fragments that survive of Ben Jonson's criticism. *Timber: or Discoveries* is a collection of notes from his wide reading in ancient and contemporary rhetoricians and critics, with original comments and examples. As elsewhere, Jonson makes his borrowings his own, and the considered conclusions on literature and life are expressed with a weight and authority recalling Bacon.

An approach towards a more scientific method and temper can be seen in various kinds of prose writing throughout this period. Ralegh's *History of the World* (1614) has an encyclopaedic or epic inclusiveness, beginning with the Creation and interpreting Biblical and classical events and legends according to theological and philosophical beliefs still largely medieval. In marked contrast, Bacon's *History of the Reign of Henry VII* is an attempt at a coherent and rational interpretation of a limited period. Burton, in so many ways medieval and lacking in historical sense and scientific method, yet shows a genuine observation and understanding of human psychology: it is interwoven with religious beliefs, medieval philosophy, traditional medicine, popular superstition, literary interests, humour, and satire, but one strand in the complex fabric is a true scientific curiosity. Browne, again, shows himself in part a follower of Bacon; in the *Pseudodoxia Epidemica* or *Vulgar Errors*, he takes up a project of Bacon's own, and in so far as he refers common beliefs to the test of experiment, he is a true scientist. Experiment, however, is only one of Browne's weapons: he appeals also to general reason and learned authority, and he recognizes no separation of the fields of science and religious belief. Moreover, he often shows an imaginative interest in curious notions for their own sake; even in a work whose professed aim is scientific and practical. Browne does not feel it necessary to separate rational thought from poetic imagination, and his style reflects this freedom, varying between straightforward exposition and his more characteristic vein of eloquent meditation. A more single-minded and practical development along Baconian lines may be seen in the discussions during the forties and fifties, which led to the foundation of the Royal Society in 1660.

The tendency towards disengaging the quality of clear and logical argument from the various other possible uses of prose was not confined to scientists, professional or amateur. It appears in the writings of those more Latitudinarian divines who were concerned to demonstrate the rational and philosophical basis of religious truth; among these may be mentioned John Hales (1584–1656) and William Chillingworth (1602–44). The group known as the Cambridge Platonists shared the general preoccupation with reason, but for them right reason was inseparable from true faith, the two being reconciled in an idealistic philosophy which did not hand over all truth other than that of revelation to materialistic empiricism. This philosophy was often expressed in an ornate and poetic language, especially by Henry More (1614–87) and John Smith (1615–52); but the style of others of the group, such as Benjamin Whichcote (1609–83) and Ralph Cudworth (1617–88) partakes of the growing movement towards clarity and directness.

The movement of contemporary events provided a wide field for intellectual prose, and one extensively cultivated, in the discussion of politics. Here the more extended writings include the work of Sir Robert Filmer (1588?–1653) in defence of absolute monarchy; the

Oceana of James Harrington (1611–77), a description of an ideal republic which bears upon the economic and agrarian causes of the
Civil War, and the *Leviathan* of Thomas Hobbes (1588–1679). To
these may be added the controversial pamphlets of Milton and of the
Left-Wing theorists of the Commonwealth period, especially John
Lilburne the 'Leveller' (1615–77) and Gerrard Winstanley (1609–
after 1650), the leader of the 'Diggers'. Milton, as we have seen,
expressed his political thought in mannered eloquence, and the revolutionary pamphleteers show at times a Biblical fervour, but for the
most part political discussion produced a plainer prose concentrating
on logical exposition and argument.

Many of these movements of thought and style combine in the
political and philosophical writings of Hobbes. As a philosopher, he
carries further Bacon's empiricism, applying it to human psychology
and developing a theory of knowledge as based on sense-impressions,
which are themselves ultimately reducible to the impact of bodies in
motion. From the standpoint of this thorough-going materialism
and determinism, Hobbes surveys the world in general and more
especially the constitution of society. In *Leviathan* he produces a
tightly argued philosophical theory of absolutism, bringing the whole
force of his logical and scientific mind to the task. It is only natural
that for the expression of these ideas he should have evolved a strong
and unadorned style which carried still further the concern with
matter rather than manner, rejecting as far as possible all the emotional qualities of language and concentrating on rational lucidity.
The following passage from *Leviathan* gives some idea of the geo-
metrical logic with which his argument advances, though he does
not always employ such a staccato brevity of sentence:

> To this war of every man, against every man, this also is
> consequent: that nothing can be unjust. The notions of right
> and wrong, justice and injustice, have there no place. Where
> there is no common power, there is no law: where no law
> no injustice. Force, and fraud, are in war the two cardinal
> virtues. Justice, and injustice are none of the faculties neither
> of the body, nor mind. If they were, they might be in a man
> that were alone in the world, as well as his senses, and passions.
> They are qualities, that relate to men in society, not in
> solitude ...   *Leviathan*, Part I, Ch. 13

By this stage, prose as an intellectual instrument has acquired both precision and force.

Familiar and Miscellaneous Prose

Apart from the prose of conscious art and serious intellectual discussion, this age saw a great expansion of the more miscellaneous and utilitarian types of writing: accounts of travels, biography, autobiography, diaries, letters, pamphlets, and the beginnings of journalism. Here there was a general movement away from such formal models as existed towards a simpler and more straightforward manner, and an increasing adjustment of style to the practical needs of ordinary communication. On the whole, this tendency fitted in easily with the growing intellectual concern for logic and clarity.

Among the travellers may be mentioned first the eccentric figure of Thomas Coryate (1577?–1617). The title *Coryat's Crudities Hastily gobled up in five Moneths travells* suggests the extent to which he was still a showman displaying his wit, in a manner related to the Elizabethan pamphleteers and the character-writers. Fynes Morison (1566–1630), in his *Itinerary*, wrote in a more straightforward manner of his travels in Europe. Captain John Smith (1580–1631), the historian of the founding of Virginia, was concerned primarily with communicating factual and practical information and recommending the cause of colonization. Samuel Purchas (1577–1631), no traveller himself, but devoted to the study of geography and the explorations of others, attempted to carry on the work of Hakluyt and planned a history of the world based on all existing travel literature in the vast compilation *Purchas his Pilgrims*. Generally speaking, accounts of travels tended to employ a plainer and more straightforward prose style.

The seventeenth century shows considerable development in the field of biography. In 1605 Bacon remarked that it was surprising how few lives of famous historical personages existed; by the end of the century this was no longer true, and the word 'biography' itself appeared in English soon after the Restoration. The chief starting-points for those attempting this genre were the classical model of Plutarch and the generalized 'character' depicting a social type. These influences combine in the short sketches of contemporary figures which appear in the work of historians of their own times like Arthur Wilson (1595–1652), Sir Philip Warwick (1609–83), and pre-eminently Edward Hyde, Earl of Clarendon (1609–74) in his *History of the Rebellion*. Fuller, in his *History of the Worthies of England*, mixes informal sketches and anecdotes with his biographical information in a characteristically unsystematic fashion. What may be called the first true English biographies are the *Lives* by Izaak Walton (1593–1683) of Donne, Wotton, Hooker, Herbert, and Sanderson. These were written at various times between 1640 and 1678, but even the earliest show a style which, though related to the sententious and witty manner, achieves a remarkable degree of simplicity and directness. After the Restoration, biographies multiplied; mention may be made of two whose materials were in process of collection earlier: one Puritan, the *Life of Colonel Hutchinson* by his wife Lucy (1620– after 1675); the other Royalist, the *Life of the Duke of Newcastle* by his second wife Margaret (1623?–73). Allied to biography was the report of conversation, exemplified in Drummond's notes of his talks with Ben Jonson, and in the *Table Talk* of the broad-minded lawyer and politician John Selden (1584–1654), recorded by his secretary.

Autobiography showed a similar progression towards a plainer style. Sir Kenelm Digby (1603–65) treats his *Private Memoirs* as a kind of romance, in a vein of artificial eloquence; Lord Herbert of Cherbury, on the other hand, writing his *Autobiography* in old age during the Civil War, employs a style that is informal and even negligent. Intimate accounts of the author's own tastes, opinions, and activities form part of the attraction of Walton's *Compleat Angler*, and Cowley's essay *Of Myself* shows the autobiographical interest expressed in measured conversational simplicity. Among the diaries that were to be published later, those of the Presbyterian Richard Baxter (1615–91) and the Quaker George Fox (1624–91) may be mentioned; after the Restoration come the more famous diarists Pepys and Evelyn.

Letter-writing, again, moves from rhetorical formality and elaborate wit towards a more straightforward manner. The letters of Donne show many of the qualities of his other prose, as do those of Bacon and other literary figures. Sometimes, as in the *Epistolae Ho-Elianae* of James Howell (1593?–1666), we find genuine letters mingled with an artificial use of the form to record miscellaneous reflections and observations; here the conscious art appears also in the style. But there survive from this period a large number of letters with no pretension to art, informal communications between scholars and men of affairs, practical information exchanged between soldiers and politicians of the Civil War, and the normal commerce of domestic life between relations and friends. Some of these are preserved in family collections like the Verney papers. The increase of this kind of everyday writing naturally encouraged a style nearer to ordinary speech; the letters of Dorothy Osborne (1627–95) to William Temple, whom she married in 1654, embody her belief that 'all letters ... should be as free and Easy as ones discourse'.

An important factor in the evolution of a plainer prose was the rise of journalism. Regular sheets of foreign news, called 'corantos', had begun to be published as early as 1620; at the beginning of the Civil War, in response to a natural demand, there appeared the first accounts of politics and events at home. Growth was rapid, and the Royalist *Mercurius Aulicus*, which continued from 1642 to 1645, had many imitators. Its chief political opponent was the *Mercurius Britannicus*, and later, during the fifties, the *Mercurius Politicus* had an official status under the government. At the same time a host of short-lived 'diurnals' and controversial pamphlets fed and developed the appetite for political discussion, and by their very nature encouraged a simple and forthright style, approximating ever more closely to the tone and movement of informal speech. The result may be seen in later pamphlets, like the anti-Cromwellian *Killing No Murder* by the notorious one-time Leveller Colonel Sexby (d. 1658) or the attack on Milton by Roger L'Estrange (1616–1704) called *No Blind Guides*.

The number of religious writings – sermons, controversial tracts, and spiritual autobiographies – from the various Puritan sects was no less than the political. Here the raciness and vigour of popular speech is usually modified by a strong Biblical influence. How fruitful this mingling could be is shown pre-eminently in the work of John Bunyan (1628–88), whose mind was formed under the Commonwealth, though his written works appeared after the Restoration. Bunyan represents a different side of Puritanism from Milton the scholar and humanist. His strength is to a great extent that of a popular culture close to the soil, with a language of homely vitality which had earlier formed the basis of Elizabethan pamphleteering and much dramatic dialogue. It is a culture that has its roots in the Middle Ages on both the religious and the secular side; behind the vivid allegory of *The Pilgrim's Progress* lies a long line of popular preaching, with illustrations and examples drawn from common life and appealing to practical experience and shrewd folk wisdom. To this vigour and realism of conception and style the study of the Bible added dignity and eloquence, making possible the classic expression of a religious attitude to life which went deeper than doctrinaire Calvinism or the fanaticism of a sect. It has often been noted that Bunyan anticipated the novelists of the next century. This is true not only of his narrative power and dramatic dialogue, his lively portraits of characters like Mr By-ends and Mr Worldly Wiseman and the sombre realism of parts of *Mr Badman*, but also of his record and analysis of inner conflict, especially in *Grace Abounding*, which looks forward beyond Richardson to Rousseau's *Confessions* and the psychological novel of the nineteenth century.[9]

Towards the Augustan Age

It will be apparent that by the time of the Restoration various lines of development were converging to establish a new poetry and a new prose. In both, modifications of style were symptoms of change in sensibility, intellectual habits, the general orientation of culture, and the nature of society.

In poetry the taste for 'strong lines', highly charged with meaning and employing startling figures of speech, yields gradually to a desire for perspicuity, for clear general conceptions, appealing, so to speak, to the social rather than the inner ear. Metaphysical wit changes to an epigrammatic neatness based on polite rationality and Good Sense; passionate thought gives place to urbane argument, satire, or compliment, or to a formal eloquence and magniloquence for the loftier and graver themes. The most appropriate form for the expression of the new interests was found to be the sequence of self-contained pentameter couplets, handled with a smooth regularity that owed something to the more obvious qualities of Ben Jonson's lyrics. Waller and Denham were regarded by the Restoration critics as the pioneers of the new versification – 'Mr Waller', said Dryden, 'reformed our numbers' – though in fact they had forerunners, especially among translators like Fairfax (d. 1635) and Sandys (1578–1644). The new manner and the new interests are well illustrated in Waller's *A Panegyrick to My Lord Protector* (1655):

> Your never failing Sword made War to cease,
> And now you heale us with the arts of Peace,
> Our minds with bounty, and with awe engage,
> Invite affection, and restrain our rage:
> Less pleasure take brave minds in battles won,
> Than in restoring such as are undon.

The new social style and subject-matter fitted in easily with the existing strain of conscious classicism in seventeenth-century poetry, which was reinforced through the French contacts of the royal exile; the Court returned anxious to assert its modernity and civilization according to continental standards.

In prose various causes were leading towards the emergence of a normal style of everyday use, of a kind which hardly existed at the beginning of the century. Eloquent persuasion and authoritarian assertion were giving way to a tone of polite discussion and the assumption that the reader would be a gentleman of equal status and amenable to rational argument. Similarly the lighter types of prose were moving away from the self-conscious exhibition of cleverness; wit was increasingly regulated by a sense of 'good form' and social decorum. The new scientific interests, too, helped to foster a plain prose of exposition and reasoning. Hobbes's limited view of figures of speech, and his assertion of the superiority of judgement to fancy, have already been mentioned. Sprat's much-quoted lines on the Royal Society's requirements in style should not be given an exaggerated importance, but they remain a significant pointer:

> They have exacted from all their members a close, naked, natural way of speaking, positive expressions, clear senses, a native easiness, bringing all things as near the Mathematical plainness as they can, and preferring the language of Artizans, Countrymen, and Merchants, before that of Wits and Scholars.

At the same time the practical needs of political discussion, pamphleteering, and journalism under the Commonwealth, aided by social developments in the direction of an urban culture such as the rise of the coffee-house, all helped to encourage the growth of a plain prose of ordinary use. In prose as in poetry the effects of the Court exile helped to confirm developments at home. Familiarity with French prose certainly did not dispose the minds of the returning Royalists against the new plainer style, and it may have helped to add something of polish and urbanity.

In this survey the drama has received little attention, since its later Jacobean and Caroline development is more appropriately considered in relation to the period of its triumph. But it is worth noting that the Restoration drama was not a completely new start. Marked developments towards both the comedy of manners and heroic tragedy can be seen in such writers as Fletcher, Massinger, and Shirley well before the closing of the theatres in 1642, and to a great extent the Restoration playwrights picked up the tradition from where it lapsed.

If the culture of the Restoration had its roots far back in the century, so equally a number of figures not usually thought of as 'Restoration' lived on well into the new reign – not only Bunyan, Milton, and Marvell, but also Browne, Herrick, Vaughan, Walton, and even Hobbes, who had been Bacon's secretary. It is convenient, nevertheless, to treat these as individual exceptions and to draw the general line at 1660, by which date the new spirit and the new modes of expression were reasonably well established.

NOTES

1. See the previous volume in this series: *The Age of Shakespeare*.

2. Rosemond Tuve's *Elizabethan and Metaphysical Imagery* argues that the Metaphysical 'reaction' against Elizabethan conventions has been both exaggerated and inaccurately defined. While some revision of the terms in which the contrast is stated may be desirable, it seems idle to minimize the difference. For an answer to Miss Tuve, see W. Empson's article, 'Donne and the Rhetorical Tradition,' in *The Kenyon Review* for autumn 1949. The problem is also discussed in my article 'The New Scholarship?' in *Scrutiny* XIX, no. 2 (1952–3).

3. In his *Life of Cowley*, which discusses Metaphysical poetry from an eighteenth-century point of view.

4. Miss Helen Gardner's edition of the *Divine Poems* argues for a date between 1609 and 1611 for most of these sonnets.

5. A rather higher opinion of Vaughan than is suggested here is given in M. M. Mahood's *Poetry and Humanism*, chapter 8.

6. Particularly Sir Herbert Grierson in *Cross-Currents in English Literature of the Seventeenth Century* and *Criticism and Creation*, pp. 18–22.

7. See J. Middleton Murry: *The Problem of Style*, pp. 108–21 and note; T. S. Eliot: 'A Note on the Verse of John Milton' in *E.S.M.E.A.* XXI, and 'Milton' in *Proc. Brit. Acad.* XXXIII (reprinted with some omissions in T. S. Eliot: *Selected Prose*, Penguin Books, and in *On Poetry and Poets*); F. R. Leavis: *Revaluation*, chapter 2, and 'Mr Eliot and Milton' in *The Common Pursuit*. A different point of view is represented by E. M. W. Tillyard: *Milton*, and *The Miltonic Setting*; C. S. Lewis: *A Preface to Paradise Lost*; Douglas Bush: *Paradise Lost in Our Time; Some Comments*. Attempts to sum up the argument have been made by A. J. A. Waldock: *Paradise Lost and its Critics*, and John Peter: 'Reflections on the Milton Controversy,' in *Scrutiny* XIX, no. 1 (1952).

8. By William Rawley, Bacon's chaplain, in his life of Bacon, 1657.

9. The point is made by Sir Herbert Grierson in *Cross-Currents in English Literature of the Seventeenth Century*, p. 203.

PART
III

THE EUROPEAN BACKGROUND TO
BAROQUE SENSIBILITY

BY ODETTE DE MOURGUES

Lecturer in Modern Languages, University of Cambridge

IT is always a temptation to think of England as being, metaphorically as well as geographically, an island; the more so perhaps when we consider the impressive bulk of Elizabethan and Jacobean literature. Scholars may trace the influence of Italian and French sonneteers on English Court poets; they may count up the number of translations of du Bartas and Montaigne; it hardly alters the general picture of an age when strong national characteristics were emphatically stamped on drama, prose, and poetry. But an attempt to connect English literature of the period with the Continent through the study of direct literary influences is bound to be a short-sighted process. On the other hand, a bird's-eye view of the late Renaissance in Western Europe, in a prize-giving spirit, might be misleading and unprofitable: England stands out with a baffling grandeur which reminds us of the summit of Greek literature in the fifth century B.C.; so does Spain with the splendour of its Golden Age; whereas Italian culture shows signs of decadence, and France and Germany display a confused pattern of uncertain literary values. Yet, whatever the ultimate aesthetic judgement passed on the artistic output of these countries during this period, we have come to think of the late Renaissance as a sort of 'crise de la conscience européenne'. Recent criticism on French, Spanish, and German literatures has not only been concerned with the revaluation of individual writers of the late sixteenth and early seventeenth centuries; it has been more and more attracted by this age of transition as a time when something of portentous importance was happening to the mind of Europe. We all know the rough outlines of that crisis which originated in the impact of Renaissance and Reformation on the medieval universe of Christendom: the clash between the pagan and the Christian worlds, and inside Christianity between Protestants and Catholics; political unrest and religious wars; the absence of a systematized philosophy which could have suggested some coherent answer to these new problems. We are used to thinking of the period as an era of pessimism, chaos, and violence succeeding the optimism of the Renaissance when Man, having asserted his birthright as the centre of the universe, felt the world was his, and himself and the world were one harmonious whole.

The conflicts, political, religious, or economic, assumed different forms in the different countries, but there was a certain mood which was common to all, a mood which is elusive when we come to defining it. Some would call it 'baroque' – a dangerously fashionable word in the terminology of literary criticism – but this term may be helpful if we use it in order to characterize certain manifestations of the sensibility of the late Renaissance. This sensibility reacted so violently to the problems of the age that intelligence was not always able to control it, and we may perhaps call baroque the artistic outcome of this destruction of the balance between feeling and intellect, this distortion of reality through the cravings of unruly emotions and the desperate vagaries of imagination. The word sensibility must be taken as meaning the senses as well as sentiments (and, in fact, the two connotations are more than once confused in baroque consciousness).

The conflict between the spirit and the senses was not a new one. But if we compare an Italian sacred opera published in the early seventeenth century, *Rappresentazione di anima e di corpo*,[1] with the old morality plays or even with Petrarchan ratiocination on the respective importance of the body and the soul, we realize that the intensified claim of bodily pleasures now made any kind of balance a very precarious one. Renaissance humanism had proposed the *mens sana in corpore sano*, but that was too obviously an enticing pagan tag. The solution of the Jesuits and of devout humanism was to enlist the senses in the service of God. This was one of the most impressive attempts towards preserving at least part of the unity of a threatened universe. It gave birth to the stern *Spiritual Exercises* of Ignatius Loyola, the art of the Counter-Reformation, the Emblem-books of the Jesuits, and an enormous bulk of religious poetry (poetry like that of Crashaw). In its excesses this appeal to the senses *ad majorem Dei gloriam* leads to a distorted vision of life in which religious themes, such as the repentant Magdalene, the ecstatic Teresa, the Sacred

Heart, the crucified Saviour, the Holy Innocents, are translated into undulating marble raptures in sculpture or pictorial symbolic metaphors in poetry. They compose a decorative pageant based on an emotion which is of doubtful quality: a strange mixture of crude pathos and sensuous pleasure. It leaves us with the impression that senses and imagination have been indulged out of all proportion to the needs of religion. This carnal mysticism leads us to suspect that something has gone wrong in this interpenetration of spirituality and materiality, and that one thing has been substituted for another: the roses, pearls, flaming hearts, and doves for some kind of escapism into fairy-land; the voluptuous tears of sinners for the bitter-sweet delights of masochism, and the raptures and swoons of saints for erotic experiences. Baroque sensibility has subtle, contorted by-paths and oblique vistas. If we leave aside the questionable expressions of sacred love, we find even in novels, epics, or pastorals dealing with profane love a perverted preference for ambiguous situations: Honoré d'Urfé's shepherds disguised as girls spend days and nights with chaste heroines; Tasso's amazons fight in lascivious tussles with warriors, under the tantalizing protection of golden armour.

But sometimes the balance between the body and the spirit was destroyed in favour of the spirit. Spanish mysticism was still soaring on those supreme heights which St John of the Cross had reached, where, all material life annihilated, the soul rejoices in a luminous void. In France the early seventeenth century is marked by a conflict between abstract mysticism and the last champions of devout humanism; before coming down to the rational and psychological standpoint of Bossuet, French spirituality struggles towards a direct union with pure Divine Essence.

These contrasts and contradictions show that Renaissance man had lost his self-confidence. The hero of Jacobean drama is often torn between a horror of life and a terror of death. So is perhaps the Picaro, the hero of the Spanish novel at the end of the sixteenth century. Renaissance humanism had relied on Nature and Reason to make Man a harmonious whole. But the age of geographical discoveries had become an age of more upsetting explorations: explorations of the mind by itself. St Teresa's autobiographies and Montaigne's essays had found disturbing recesses in human personality; they had passed the frontier which separates the conscious from the subconscious mind. Montaigne especially had shown our psychic life as a threateningly elusive, ever-moving, ever-changing flow, and baroque sensibility vacillated at times over dark rivers. Montaigne was eminently sane, but doubt and uncertainty were not for his contemporaries or followers the 'mol oreiller' they were for him: they had bad dreams. Uncertainty became distrust: the dry, stiff distrust of the politician and the courtier, which stands out in Bacon's essays or in the works of the Spaniard Gracian. Bad dreams invaded day-life, and in the heated brains of some men recurrent nightmares started to draw odd and terrifying pictures. Melancholy was to be anatomized by Burton. It had indeed many shapes and many faces during the late Renaissance. These faces became more clearly outlined as they dropped the fragile mask of Stoicism so carefully put on by the sixteenth century, and one of the faces was the flat face of Death. A second Dance of Death passed over Europe. A taste for the macabre permeated French drama of the period as well as the Jacobean drama. The skeleton became a decorative element of Italian mortuary monuments and the grim companion of the poet's love. Yorick's skull, Donne's shroud, Tourneur's horrors are paralleled on the Continent. In French lyrical poetry, Agrippa d'Aubigné decorated his bedroom with bones, and we owe to dark meditations on physical decay the superb sonnets on death by Jean de Sponde.[2] From the Dance of Death we pass to the dance of worms and the dance of evil spirits. The natural disintegration of the human body is not enough to satisfy an imagination which is doggedly determined to go on to the bitter end. In contrast with the rosy paradises of mystical writers like Crashaw or Fletcher, we find the harrowing obsession with Hell. The epic, solemnly terrifying hell into which d'Aubigné's enemies are hurled in a blast of heavenly vengeance; the phantasmagoric, grotesque, crude Visions of the Spanish writer Quevedo; the picturesque, Bosch-like description of Davies of Hereford's *House of Time* with frozen hearts floating on sulphured streams and a 'goblin, grisly grim, fishing for a Soule'. The horrifying supernatural element crept into the life of the living, taking the form of magic and witchcraft. It is hardly surprising that some of the writings of the time reveal a divided personality in the writer or even a disjunction in his vision of reality which may go as far as the absurd. In Italy, the poet-philosopher Bruno (put to death in 1600) expressed in sibylline incoherence the boldest theories, and the visionary Campanella dabbled in occultism and wrote violent and dark poetry, involved and abrupt. In France a puzzling ode by Théophile de Viau presents us with a mad universe where everything is upside down.

Reality is thus viewed in distorted and grinning mirrors. For the Renaissance the solid wholeness was implicitly given by the complementary union of the Macrocosmos, the totality of things, with the Microcosmos, the 'little world', Man. The Renaissance poets, like Ronsard, had with patience and love tried to build up the cosmos into a harmonious whole, where Nature's eternal laws ruled in magnificent hierarchy the rose, Man, and the stars. But now the sense of proportion vanished. The giddy imagination is attracted by the colossal, the limitless: continental poets, like d'Aubigné, wander like roaring giants in interplanetary spaces, hurling down stars and suns. The sense of disaster pervading the period had to take apocalyptic proportions, and one of the favourite themes of late Renaissance poetry is that of the Last Judgement:

> At the round earth's imagin'd corners, blow
> Your trumpets, angels. ...

Donne is concerned with his own relationship with God and for him the theme is just a starting-point, but many continental poets seem to take an almost malignant delight in describing this colossal disorder in Nature. Fragments of the cosmos, magnified by anxiety and made more terrifying by their isolation, haunted the poets of the late Renaissance and provided them with a rich store of poetic images. Such are the moons and suns which Shakespeare placed on the face of Antony.

But on the other hand baroque sensibility delights in the diminutive. Devout humanism spent endless hours contemplating a dewdrop on the petal of a carnation; the French Libertin poets, Théophile and St Amant, reduced seascapes to the dimensions of a gold-fish bowl and landscapes to that of a Chinese garden. In Italy, Marini was conspicuous for his myopic vision of the universe.

Not only were the proportions of the world so strangely altered, but, as if under the effect of some invisible crack, reality split apart and fell into separate pieces. The trumpets of Doom were not even necessary. The poets mentioned above, Théophile and St Amant, offer us pictures which are disconnected as well as diminutive. They pass from one object to another without supplying any logical link. Their technique is a kind of *pointillisme*, which reminds us of impressionist pictures. The disorderly enumeration of various objects which appeal to their fancy is furthermore stressed by the jerkiness of the rhythm. Perhaps, as Professor Forster remarks in his study *The Temper of Seventeenth Century German Literature*,[3] the fragmentation of subject is linked with the fragmentation of time: 'Time is felt to be split up into a series of moments, of *occasiones*. . . . The poet sees one thing at a time, in its momentary, changing aspect, and the change is an abrupt one.'

This juxtaposition of images or moments which fail to fuse into unity may well recall to our mind Coleridge's well-known distinction between Imagination and Fancy, in which Fancy is 'a mode of Memory emancipated from the order of Time and Space' receiving 'all its material ready-made from the law of association'. In fact, the word *fantaisie* is a key-word when judging the works of some baroque writers; the Libertin poets mentioned it all the time and asserted their right to follow the capricious meanderings of their *rêverie*, and the English Metaphysical poets have been grouped in a recent anthology under the title of the Fantasticks.[4] Coleridge's definition would perhaps account for the impression of extreme artificiality and, at times, extreme monotony we have when reading some of the late Renaissance poets. Crashaw, Théophile, St Amant, Gongora, Marini replaced the living universe by a world of correspondences. A network of recurrent motifs is constantly being interposed between reality and ourselves: tears, wounds, flaming hearts, the turtle-dove. and the phoenix, the grave and the nest in the mystical baroque poets; tritons, shells, water-fowl and rushes, grottoes, the Naiad, and the poppy in the French Libertin poets. The shimmering quality of this network is made even more artificial by a riot of colours and a profusion of jewels. In Crashaw's poetry blood-drops are like rubies and tears like pearls. In the universe of Marini and the Libertin poets, the sea is green enamel and cut jasper with diamonds at the crest of the waves'. In the extremely elaborate texture of Gongora's *Solitudes*, Nature is in the same way made tame and ornate, infinitely artificial, sparkling with gold and silver, an object of supreme luxury. In spite of the endless flow of metaphors and metamorphoses, this baroque poetic universe retains a hard, glittering solidity even though things appear as if they were melting away – this was no romantic escapism into a kind of Shelleyan ecstasy. But it is difficult to assess whether such poets were satisfied with gliding over the surface of things with dazzling brilliance or whether they wanted to convey a particular experience of the world. Some of Gongora's most common adjectives – *confuso, incierto, inconstante, inquieto*[b] – are disquieting, as if imagination was desperately trying to seize some ultimate reality beyond clouds of uncertainty.

Thus life appeared as a series of *fantasques tableaux*, to use St Amant's own words. Life as a picture, life as a stage, life as a dream. We come to the fundamental uneasiness which underlay this deliberate artificiality, these shifting visions, this playing up to a sort of super-reality. The senses and the spirit are usurping each other's vested interests; time has split into unconnected moments; the cosmos, magnified into prodigious infinity or reduced to derisive minuteness, has dissolved into fragments; the irregular beats of the human heart swing from Paradise to Hell; what is reality? Baroque sensibility was bound to question the intrinsic value of its wild flights of fancy. Hence this theme of the confusion of reality and illusion, which is one of the most important themes of the first half of the seventeenth century. In Germany the themes of the 'Theatre of the World', of 'Life as a Dream', the interplay of *Sein* and *Schein*, are characteristic of the literature of the period. They are also to be found in Shakespeare, in the French dramatist Rotrou, and in the famous play of Calderon, *La vida es sueño*. The puzzling qualities of Corneille's comedies *L'Illusion comique* or *Le Menteur* may be partly due to the impact of illusion on reality. Misunderstandings, lies, or magic are not merely dramatic devices – they illustrate and stress the repeated assertion that human beings are not what they seem to be, that night is very dark and love uncertain. The fashionable Pastoral, French, Italian, or English, and later the Opera, open the gates of a paradise of fallacies and disguises, an earthly compensation for frustration and failure. And of illusion and reality, which is the more valuable? On the threshold of the baroque era, Cervantes's *Don Quixote* seems to stand like a warning that man loses his life when he loses his illusions.

This simplified study has emphasized the most violent reactions of European sensibility to the spiritual crisis of the late Renaissance. It has been more concerned with what men of that age felt than with what they thought. I have mentioned what they feared or were attracted by rather than what they were endeavouring to do in order to solve their contradictions. The tortured, restless, tense sensibility which led writers to a distorted vision of the universe – mystical or macabre, morbid or absurd, colossal or diminutive – could be and was checked, transcended, or otherwise made harmless. We know that the English Metaphysical poets, controlling their imagination and sensibility, achieved a perfect balance in a blend of passion and intellectual subtlety. Men like Herbert certainly escaped the dark vistas of the baroque. In most continental countries the seventeenth century is marked by a quest for certainty and absolute values, for order and safety. Wild passions were curbed by Court life and drawing-room standards. It is interesting to see how the most disturbing baroque themes, the end of the world and churchyards, were turned into the frivolous hyperboles of gallant poetry. Dangerous moods were tidily classified by Court poets and *précieuses*; the Libertin poets' landscape neatly trimmed into landscape gardening. It is significant also that the formidable baroque sun which, either black or dripping with blood, had presided over many an apocalyptic catastrophe, was reassuringly transformed into a mere adjunct to human glory and, carved in homely timber, became with Louis XIV the symbol of solid royalty whose task it was to provide order and hierarchy. Men of the seventeenth century were responsible for the rise of the absolute power of kings. In France and in Germany, this absolute power with which the readers of the English seventeenth-century theorist Hobbes are familiar, was strongly built on a well-ruled, tidily stratified, courtly world.

French classicism was the first and the most spectacular reward of that quest for order within the boundaries of Reason and Nature. But even before the time when the sobered humanist, overcoming the metaphysical crisis of the late Renaissance, had become the 'moralist' for whom 'The proper study of mankind is man', we see the early-seventeenth-century man opposing the threatening nightmares and the deceptive appearances of a confused reality with forces from within. A haughty *culte du moi* developed during the first half of the seventeenth century, based on will-power. Man challenged the world and stiffened into an uncompromising code of honour, himself sought to be superior to his own nature. 'I can rise higher than my-self', says a character in one of Calderon's plays, and is echoed by Corneille: '*Je suis maître de moi comme de l'univers.*' Quietly but confidently Descartes states that even if everything is a deceitful dream, '*Cogito, ergo sum*'.

We may now come back to our starting-point: England as an island. Keeping in mind the European traits of this crisis of sensibility and the baroque themes which swept over England as well as over Spain, Italy, France, or Germany, we may realize better the essential Englishness of a Donne, a Thomas Browne, a Milton. This rapid survey may also help us to understand better some of the reasons for that 'dissociation of sensibility' which, according to T. S. Eliot, is a characteristic feature of the latter part of the seventeenth century.

NOTES

1. Emilio de' Cavalieri's *Rappresentazione di anima e di corpo*, produced in 1600 at San Filippo Neri's Oratory in Rome.

2. Sponde: an early-seventeenth-century French poet whose works have recently been discovered and edited by Professor A. Boase.

3. Inaugural Lecture delivered at University College, London (published London, 1951).

4. *The Fantasticks*, by W. S. Scott (London, 1945).

5. See *The Literature of the Spanish People*, by Gerald Brenan (London, 1951).

THE POEMS OF JOHN DONNE

BY R. G. COX

JOHN DONNE, we sometimes forget, was an Elizabethan. Scholars do well to warn us against over-simplifying the pattern of literary change into a simple succession of movements and 'reactions', and to remind us that in periods of heightened vitality developments in different directions often exist side by side.[1] By no means all of what we now consider typically Elizabethan poetry was in existence when Donne began to write. It remains true, nevertheless, that Donne chose to do something different from his predecessors and from those of his contemporaries who were still exploiting and developing the existing modes; and younger followers like Carew looked back on this choice as revolt or reform:

> The Muses garden with Pedantique weedes
> O'rspred, was purg'd by thee; The lazie seeds
> Of servile imitation throwne away
> And fresh invention planted. . . .
>> *An Elegie upon the death of the Deane o,*
>> *Pauls, Dr John Donne*

Modern students of rhetoric have argued that Donne's innovations did not run counter to contemporary rules,[2] but even if he is to be regarded as implementing existing theoretical possibilities, his practice remains the kind of new departure which marks a decisive alteration in the course of literary history.

In considering the nature of Donne's poetic originality, it is common to begin with his development of the metaphysical conceit. Yet there is a great deal to say on the subject of his verse style before broaching the topic of imagery at all. The first point likely to strike the reader who comes to Donne from the smooth fluency of the average Elizabethan lyric or sonnet is the surprising directness of the speaking voice conveyed by his rhythms and diction:

> For Godsake hold your tongue, and let me love,
>> Or chide my palsie, or my gout,
> My five gray haires, or ruin'd fortune flout,

> With wealth your state, your minde with Arts improve,
>   Take you a course, get you a place,
>   Observe his honour, or his grace,
> Or the King's reall, or his stamped face
>   Contemplate, what you will, approve,
>   So you will let me love.

> *The Canonization*

Here the occasional inversions of normal speech-order and the fact that line 4 by itself might come from an eighteenth-century couplet hardly affect our general impression that technique and conception are essentially dramatic; the colloquial outburst of line 1, the heavy stresses on 'palsie' and 'gout', the contemptuous alliteration of line 3, above all the play of an exasperated splutter of short phrases across the intricate stanza form, all impose on the reader the desired emphasis, tone, and mood. Plainly the aim here is not sweetness, grace, or verbal melody, either for its own sake or to accommodate any possible musician who, as Donne complains in *The Triple Foole*,

> his art and voice to show
> Doth Set and sing my paine.

It is rather a realistic expressiveness of the kind developed in the 1590s by the dramatists, above all by Shakespeare, and nothing quite like it had previously appeared in lyric poetry,[3] in spite of certain foreshadowings in Wyatt. As in dramatic verse, the aim of realism is, of course, not absolute; whatever metrical licences are taken, the pattern of line and stanza remains, to reinforce, modify, or generally play against the rhythms of speech with the effects of heightened intensity and concentration proper to poetry. When we speak of realistic expressiveness we use a shorthand term for the maximum of realistic expressiveness compatible with a sense of artistic form. Donne's lyrics have a music of their own, though the immediate effect is of vivid speech rather than song:

> Deare love, for nothing lesse than thee
> Would I have broke this happy dreame,
>   It was a theame
> For reason, much too strong for phantasie,
> Therefore thou wakd'st me wisely; yet

My Dreame thou brok'st not, but continued'st it,
Thou art so truth, that thoughts of thee suffice,
To make dreams truths; and fables histories;
Enter these armes, for since thou thoughtst it best,
Not to dreame all my dreame, let's act the rest.

The Dreame

That Donne could write with a simple lyrical sweetness when he
chose is shown by one or two songs to existing airs, especially
'Sweetest love, I do not goe, For wearinesse of thee',[4] though even
here his originality comes out in the careful subtlety of the poem's
argument. He was a conscious artist, and his avoidance of conventional fluency of movement and courtliness of diction must be
assumed to be deliberate.

As with the lyric stanza, so in his satires and elegies with the couplet
Donne makes use of licences similar to those of dramatic blank verse.
Always the formal devices of poetry – metre, rhyme, alliteration, and
other effects of sound – are made to serve an expressive purpose; a
constant control of pause, stress, and tempo works to the same end.
It is interesting to compare the formal dignity of Spenser's last two
stanzas on mutability at the end of *The Faerie Queene* with Donne's
tone of passionate argument on the same theme in *The Second
Anniversarie*:

And what essentiall joy can'st thou expect
Here upon earth ? What permanent effect
Of transitory causes ? Dost thou love
Beauty ? (And beauty worthy'st is to move)
Poore cousened cousenor, *that* she, and *that* thou,
Which did begin to love, are neither now;
You are both fluid, chang'd since yesterday;
Next day repaires, (but ill) last dayes decay.
Nor are, (although the river keepe the name)
Yesterdaies waters, and todaies the same.

Here the play of the sense across the couplet pattern produces what is
essentially a dramatic emphasis, setting 'permanent effect' against
'transitory causes' with a feeling of scornful *reductio ad absurdum*,
contrasting 'yesterdaies waters' and 'todaies' in a strong argumentative climax, and making colloquial concessions and qualifications in

the rapid parentheses. There is a characteristic use of the slight pause at the end of a line in the question

> Dost thou love
> Beauty?

to produce the conversational effect of an implied 'for example' or 'shall we say?' before coming down with special stress on the important word. Examples may be multiplied; in the much-quoted passage on truth in *Satyre III*:

> On a huge hill,
> Cragged, and steep, Truth stands, and hee that will
> Reach her, about must, and about must goe;
> And what the hills suddennes resists, winne so;

critics have noted that the verse-movement imposes on the reader incipient muscular movements which seem to enact the meaning, and that this way of using language is remarkably close to Shakespeare's in directness and concreteness of suggestion.[5] It is for reasons of this kind that we are not so ready as earlier readers to blame Donne for harshness and ruggedness or a 'defective ear'.

Another aspect of this dramatic quality of Donne's rhythms and diction is his controlled variety of tone. If it is a speaking voice that strikes us in the *Songs and Sonets*, it is a voice with many inflexions and intonations, from the assertive forthrightness of *The Broken Heart*:

> He is starke mad, who ever sayes,
> That he hath beene in love an houre,

to the meditative musing of *Loves growth*:

> Me thinkes I lyed all winter, when I swore
> My love was infinite, if spring make it more.

From the coarse cynicism of *Loves Alchymie*:

> Hope not for minde in women; at their best
> Sweetnesse and wit, they are but Mummy, possest.

to the enigmatic irony of *The Funerall*:

Who ever comes to shroud me, do not harme
   Nor question much
That subtile wreath of hair, which crowns my arme;
The mystery, the signe you must not touch,
   For 'tis my outward Soule....

Even more remarkable are the transitions of tone in a few lines of
the same poem: *Lovers infinitenesse*, for example, begins on a note of
simple tenderness, passes through a bewildering series of doubts and
suspicions, worked out in riddling casuistry, and returns at the end to
more wholehearted expressions of love. *Aire and Angels*, in its second
stanza, moves from conventional hyperbolic adoration of beauty to
insolent disparagement of women's capacity for feeling.[6] The effect
is always that of hearing a particular tone of voice rather than of
merely following words on a page.

Donne's imagery has always impressed readers by its range and
variety and its avoidance of the conventionally ornamental. *The
Good-morrow* refers to the familiar processes of suckling and weaning,
snoring, dreaming, and waking, but also to voyages, maps, and
hemispheres, scholastic theories of the nature of pure substance and
general philosophical speculations about our experience of space.
The Extasie draws on theories of the nature of souls and the way
heavenly influence may work on man, on physiological notions of
animal spirits, on medieval cosmology, on alchemy and chemistry,
but also on negotiations between armies during a truce, imprisoned
princes, sepulchral monuments, the transplanting of flowers, and
threading beads on a string. Some of Donne's most powerful images
are learned and scientific, as when in *A Valediction: forbidding
mourning* the idea that the higher nature of the lovers' relationship
will lead them to avoid outward demonstrations of grief is enforced
through an analogous contrast between the dangers of earthquakes
and the harmlessness of the more important irregularities of movement among the heavenly bodies:

   Moving of th' earth brings harmes and feares,
      Men reckon what it did and meant,
   But trepidation of the spheares,
      Though greater farre, is innocent.

'Trepidation', or trembling, of the spheres was the explanation in
medieval astronomy of phenomena actually caused by the slight

wobble of the earth on its axis. A poem which particularly depends upon learned references is *A Nocturnall upon S. Lucies day, Being the shortest day*. It begins with a solemn setting of the scene – midnight, the shortest day, the winter solstice, tempered by the wit of St Lucy's 'unmasking' for only seven hours and the ironical comparison of the sun to a flask of spent gunpowder. The short line

> The world's whole sap is sunke

states with particular emphasis the deadness of the season, which is further driven home in the medical metaphor ascribing the fall of the sap to the earth's dropsy and in the assertion that life has shrunk back to earth 'as to the beds feet'. The conceit that the lover is the 'epitaph' of the dead world warns us of the refinements upon the concepts of nothingness and death which are to follow. The second stanza depends on the reader's knowledge of the meaning, in alchemy, of 'quintessence' – the fifth, and therefore extremely pure, distillation: Love has 'pressed out'

> A quintessence even from nothingnesse,
> From dull privations, and leane emptinesse:

'privation' being used in its strict philosophical sense of 'absence' of a quality. In a further hyperbole the lover is said to have been 're-begotten' by all 'things which are not' – absence, darkness, death. In the third stanza the alchemical metaphor continues as the lover says that he has been transformed in Love's 'Limbecke' (or chemical retort) into a grave comprehending everything negative, whereas other people can take from all things the positive principles which constitute their nature and being. Then follows a series of references to the previous occasions in the relationship of the lovers when grief, distractions, or absence have reduced them to states comparable to world destruction, or the primitive chaos before the Creation, or death. But by the death of his mistress the lover has sunk much further in nothingness, becoming (again in alchemical terms) the 'Elixer' (or quintessence) of original chaos; he no longer has the self-consciousness which is the mark of man, nor the more elementary powers of response that belong to the animal, the vegetable, or even the mineral kingdoms. He has less existence than is implied by such an 'ordinary nothing' as a shadow; he lacks the solidity of a body, and the light of his sun is withdrawn. An adroit twist of the figure brings him back to the 'lesser sun' (that is, inferior, and at the same time of a wintry weakness), which at this season is in the zodiacal sign of the Goat (Capricorn); it will return in spring bringing for other lovers 'new lust' (the goat's proverbial quality), but he must prepare to join his dead mistress, who now is identified with, or replaces, St Lucy as patron of this time of midnight and midwinter, and so the poem returns to the statement of the opening line:

> Since shee enjoyes her long nights festivall,
> Let mee prepare towards her, and let mee call
> This houre her Vigill, and her Eve, since this
> Both the yeares, and the dayes deep midnight is.

These hints are intended to bring out the primary sense; it is not suggested that they exhaust the poem's full meaning. It is essentially the work of a mind trained in the handling of abstractions and the multiplying of subtle distinctions; it draws upon current beliefs in metaphysics, cosmology, natural science, medicine, and alchemy – yet the learning and the argument are controlled to generate a profound and intense emotion. In the total effect of the poem a great part is played by the grave and sombre movement of the verse with its weighty stresses on key-words, and by the stanza form with its emphatic short line at the centre and its effect of accumulation in the three consecutive rhymes of lines 5–7.

Even in the *Nocturnall* there are 'squibs' and 'beds-feet' besides quintessences and investing properties, and many of Donne's images derive their force from everyday and commonplace experience. For the lover in *The Sunne Rising* 'houres, dayes, moneths' are 'the rags of time'; death, in *The Second Anniversarie*, becomes

> ... a Groome,
> Which brings a Taper to the outward roome,
> Whence thou spiest first a little glimmering light ...

and every now and then, as in the letter *To Mr T. W.*, we have a vivid glimpse of the contemporary scene:

> As in our streets sly beggers narrowly
> Watch motions of the givers hand and eye,
> And evermore conceive some hope thereby.

In the past the learned element in Donne's imagery has perhaps received more stress than the familiar, and particularly his use of medieval theology and contemporary science.[7] Drummond seems to have had Donne in mind when in 1630[8] he objected to the modern attempt to 'abstract poetry to metaphysical ideas and scholastic quiddities', and Dryden later complained that 'Donne affects the metaphysics not only in his satires but in his amorous verses', and 'perplexes the minds of the fair sex with nice speculations of philosophy'.[9] Dr Johnson spoke of Donne and his followers as 'the metaphysical poets',[10] referring particularly to their exhibition of their learning, and 'metaphysical poets' they have remained ever since. The term may be regarded simply as a label, of no precise significance, and it is often convenient to leave it at that. On the other hand, it may be justified in a general sense; the best known and most satisfactory attempt of this kind is Sir Herbert Grierson's.[11] The word does not apply to Donne, he admits, as to Dante or Lucretius, poets inspired by a whole philosophical conception of the universe. Yet it lays stress, he says, on the right things: the reaccentuation in the work of the seventeenth-century poets of the metaphysical strain in medieval Italian poetry, 'the more intellectual, less verbal character of their wit compared with the conceits of the Elizabethans; the finer psychology of which their conceits are often the expression; their learned imagery; the argumentative, subtle evolution of their lyrics; above all, the peculiar blend of passion and thought, feeling and ratiocination, which is their greatest achievement'. A more precise justification may be found in Professor James Smith's essay 'On Metaphysical Poetry'.[12] This isolates an element in the poetry of Donne and his followers where the poets seem to come up against fundamental problems and oppositions of a strictly metaphysical nature and to express them by a special kind of paradoxical metaphor, of which Marvell's 'green thought in a green shade' and Donne's

> ... her pure and eloquent blood
> Spoke in her cheekes, and so distinctly wrought,
> That one might almost say, her body thought

are typical examples. This definition of the term 'Metaphysical' involves, of course, a careful restriction of its use, which is not yet generally accepted.

The points made by Sir Herbert Grierson have been taken up in various forms by many other critics. He recognizes that conceits and wit were common in Elizabethan poetry, but stresses the learning and the greater play of mind brought in by Donne. To the range of subject-matter drawn upon we must add the remarkable power of perceiving relations between different levels of experience, the sense of a mind always aware of various points of view, the continual effects of surprise and intensity. Mr T. S. Eliot has remarked[13] that these sometimes depend upon the extreme elaboration of a comparison, as with the famous compasses of *A Valediction: forbidding mourning*, sometimes on a development by rapid association calling for great agility of mind in the reader, as in the second stanza of *A Valediction: of weeping*, sometimes on sudden contrasts of associations concentrated in brief phrases.

When, in *The Will*, we come upon the lines

> And all your graces no more use shall have
> Then a Sun dyall in a grave ...

the effect depends on the shock of passing at once from associations of summer and sunlight to those of darkness and death: when *Loves Exchange* begins

> Love, any devill else but you,
> Would for a given Soule give something too

we are startled into attention by the unexpected term 'devill' as applied to Love. Even more arresting are the complex juxtapositions of *Twicknam Garden*:

> The spider love, which transubstantiates all
> And can convert Manna to gall. ...

Here, long before we have recovered from the surprise of considering love as a spider, with its various possibilities of irony, we come to all the metaphysical and scriptural reverberations of 'transubstantiate', 'Manna', and 'gall'. This is again a device associated with the dramatists, though Shakespeare uses it already in the *Sonnets* with his 'Lilies that fester'.

Dr Johnson's objection to Metaphysical wit was that, as he said, 'the most heterogeneous ideas are yoked by violence together'. Most modern critics would admit the heterogeneity, but deny that 'yoked by violence' was a fair description of the general effect. At its best the Metaphysical conceit communicates a unified experience; what matters is the sense of imaginative pressure and intensity; it is only where this is absent that the ingenuity seems obtrusive and we feel impelled to speak of 'frigidity' and 'fantastic hyperbole'. The extreme cases are easy enough to pick out; against the successes already quoted we may set the extravagance represented by the following:

> Pregnant again with th' old twins Hope and Feare ...
> > *To Mr T. W.*

> Or as sometimes in a beheaded man,
> Though at those two Red seas, which freely ranne,
> One from the Trunke, another from the Head,
> His soule be sail'd, to her eternall bed ...
> > *The Second Anniversarie*

but there must necessarily be an indeterminate region where the degree of success is a matter of opinion. The chief advantage of the conceit as Donne uses it is the quality of inclusiveness it makes possible. It is a way of bringing effectively into poetry all his interests, activities, and speculations. No part of his experience is regarded as intrinsically unpoetical; all is equally available to him in the act of composition. Here again the parallel is with the dramatists, especially the mature Shakespeare, Ben Jonson, and the Jacobean tragedians.

It was with both the dramatists and the Metaphysical poets in mind that Mr Eliot made his famous remark about 'a mechanism of sensibility which could devour any kind of experience', and suggested that in the later seventeenth century 'a dissociation of sensibility set in, from which we have never recovered'. These phrases have been taken from their context and made to bear more weight than they were designed for; they have been treated as philosophical definitions rather than suggestive hints, and are at present the victims of a strong reaction of scholarly disapproval. Yet they remain useful pointers to qualities in the poetry of this period, and of Donne in particular, that all critics must find some way of describing, however careful they may be to avoid the loose and facile use of phrases like 'felt thought' or 'unified sensibility'. Sensation, emotion, and thought are interfused in the best work of Donne and his followers in a way and to an extent that they never are in the poetry of the eighteenth and nineteenth centuries. Sir Herbert Grierson, as we have seen, speaks of the blend of passion and ratiocination as their greatest achievement. It is certainly characteristic of Donne that profound emotion generally stimulates his powers of intellectual analysis and argument, and that for him the process of logical reasoning can be in itself an emotional experience. As he brings to the lyric poem a new realism and urgency and a new penetration of psychological analysis, so he carries further than any previous poet the use of dialectic for a poem's whole structure and development. And as reasoning and analysis are not incompatible with feeling and sensuous immediacy, so there is no antithesis between wit and seriousness; seriousness, for Donne, never becomes simple solemnity.

There are, of course, in Donne as in all other poets, passages where the vitality lapses – where the rhythmical irregularities seem a tiresome mannerism, the conceits mere displays of ingenuity, and the argumentation tedious casuistry. But these are not nearly so numerous or characteristic as the general opinion assumed up to about 1920, and it seems unlikely that any readjustment of critical values will lead to a return to all the old objections of harshness, perverse obscurity, frigid intellectualism, and the rest. The criticism that Donne shows little feeling for beauty, and particularly for natural beauty, deserves a somewhat closer examination. It is not always easy to know how serious a charge is intended: if it is meant that certain attractions in the poetry of Spenser, Keats (before the revised *Hyperion*), or Tennyson are not to be found in Donne, it may be argued that his verse offers other, and equally (if not more), important qualities: if the comparison is with Dante or Shakespeare his inferiority may be readily conceded; if with Marvell, then it must be admitted that Marvell shows the possibility of combining many of the merits of Donne's style with others not characteristic of him. But it is as well to remind ourselves that just as there are exceptions which show that Donne could write smooth lyrics if he chose, so there are passages which suggest that the comparative rarity of natural beauty as a theme in his poetry was not due to complete insensibility; there is the fine passage on the sun, the elements, and the seasons in *Elegy XII*, the unexpected simile in *Elegy XIX*:

> Your gown going off, such beautious state reveals,
> As when from flowry meads th' hills shadow steales;

the stanza on the birds in the Palatine Epithalamion, and, perhaps more significantly, the feeling for natural growth in one or two of the *Songs and Sonets*:[14]

> Gentle love deeds, as blossomes on a bough,
> From loves awakened root do bud out now.
>
> *Loves Growth*

Any attempt to trace Donne's poetic development or to relate his work to the events of his life is made extremely difficult by the uncertain dating of the poems, very few of which were published before his death. Broadly speaking, his adult career falls into three main periods: from his arrival in London to his marriage, from his marriage to his ordination, and from his ordination to his death. Born in 1571 or 1572, he was educated as a Catholic and remained one until about 1598. In 1592 he entered Lincoln's Inn, and before this he may already have travelled abroad. During the nineties he appears as a student and man of fashion about London, and as an adventurer in Essex's expeditions to Cadiz (1596) and the Azores (1597). To this period belong most of the *Satyres* and *Elegies* and probably a good many of the *Songs and Sonets*. In 1598 Donne became private secretary to Lord Keeper Egerton, but in 1601 his hasty marriage to Anne More, the niece of Egerton's second wife, led to his dismissal and ruined a promising career. For the next ten years or so he lived in poverty and melancholy, dependent on the charity of friends and with no constant occupation. The poems of this time include many verse-letters and occasional poems of compliment and condolence, as well as the rest of the *Elegies* and *Songs and Sonets* and the first of the religious poems. In 1611 and 1612 there appeared the two *Anniversaries: An Anatomie of the World* and *Of the Progresse of the Soule* (not to be confused with the earlier fragment of satire) commemorating Sir Robert Drury's daughter, whom Donne had never seen. In the same period he wrote certain prose works of controversy and meditation, including *Biathanatos*, a discussion of suicide. In 1615, after years of persuasion and postponement, Donne was finally ordained, becoming Reader in Divinity at Lincoln's Inn the following year, and Dean of St Paul's in 1621. His wife died in 1617. To this last period may belong the *Holy Sonnets*[15] and the rest of the *Divine Poems*, as well as the sermons and other religious writings.

The first collection of his verse was published in 1633, two years after his death.

Donne's poems, then, may be considered in three main groups: the love poetry, the miscellaneous and occasional poems and verse-letters, and the religious poems – corresponding roughly, but not exactly, to the early, middle, and late periods of his career. The first contains the work by which he is probably best known. It is remarkable for realism, psychological penetration, and above all for the range and variety of mood, corresponding to the variety of tone and style already discussed. This extends from ecstatic and passionate poems, like *The Sunne Rising*, *The Dreame*, or *The Good-morrow*:

> And now good morrow to our waking soules,
> Which watch not one another out of feare;
> For love, all love of other sights controules,
> And makes one little roome, an every where.

to the deliberately cynical flippancy of *The Indifferent* or *The Flea*; from poems of fulfilment and happiness in love like *The Anniversarie* to *A Nocturnall upon S. Lucies day* with its intensity of privation and desolation; from the convincing affirmation of constancy in absence in *A Valediction: forbidding mourning*, or in a different way in *Elegy V*, to the savage bitterness of *The Apparition*. The poet who writes 'Goe, and catch a falling starre', or *Communitie*:

> Chang'd loves are but chang'd sorts of meat.
> And when hee hath the kernell eate,
>   Who doth not fling away the shell?

also gives us the profound sense of spiritual union in love in *The Extasie*:

> A single violet transplant,
>   The strength, the colour, and the size,
> (All which before was poore, and scant,)
>   Redoubles still, and multiplies,
> When love with one another so
>   Interinanimates two soules,
> That abler soule, which thence doth flow
>   Defects of lonelinesse controules.

In between these contrasting extremes are many poems difficult to classify, of mixed mood and shifting tone, or qualified by subtle ambiguities. In poems like *Aire and Angels* the total attitude can be defined only through a complete analysis of the whole poem. Even so apparently simple an expression of feeling as *A Valediction: of weeping* may be shown to carry overtones of a number of other possible responses to the situation, even if these are not perhaps so many or so complex as Mr Empson's analysis in *Seven Types of Ambiguity* would suggest. Further, there remains a group of poems in which Donne returns for special purposes to a modified and highly personal use of the Petrarchan convention to express platonic love and friendship to such great patronesses as Lucy, Countess of Bedford, and Mrs Herbert. In these poems genuine personal feeling, the playing of a conventional game, irony, and a certain imaginative fire in elaborating a dramatic situation, all contribute something to the total effect; there is no simple way of summing up *The Funerall*, *The Relique*, or *Twicknam Garden*.

Classification of this kind must always remain very tentative: many poems cannot be made to fit simply into any scheme. There is a natural temptation to try to find biographical explanations; but this opens the door to conjecture of all kinds, and except in the most general and provisional form it is not likely to further disinterested appreciation. The only safe procedure is to treat each poem on its merits, and analyse carefully what it communicates, remembering that the relation between art and the raw material of experience may vary almost infinitely. In answering the criticisms of Professors C. S. Lewis and J. E. V. Crofts on Donne's love poetry, Mr Leishman and Mrs Bennett are right to insist on the need for a sensitive discrimination of tone. But they are both inclined to move a little too easily to deductions about Donne's personal experience; in this connexion 'sincere' and even 'serious' are slippery terms to handle, and considerable vigilance is needed to see when the interest shifts from the literary to the biographical side. What is always constant throughout the changing moods of Donne's love poetry is the habit of introspection and analysis, the heart 'which love[s] to be Subtile to plague [it]selfe',[16] the turn for realistic and dramatic presentation and for making connexions between the given situation and many other aspects of experience.

The miscellaneous poems form perhaps the least successful group of the three, though there are interesting exceptions. For the most part the *Satyres* are the adaptations to contemporary life of stock Latin themes. The third stands out for its penetrating and serious discussion of the problem of choosing between rival religious beliefs, the alternative possibilities being embodied in short satirical portraits. The vogue for satire declined somewhat after the ban of 1599, and the satirical spirit found an outlet elsewhere, but Donne's fragment of 1601, *The Progress of the Soule*, which was to have attacked the Queen, belongs, with its bitter and sceptical quality, to this division of his work. Of the *Elegies*, some go with the love poems and invite similar comments; others are linked to the *Satyres* in their use of classical models and their witty and dramatic tone. No. IX, *The Autumnall*, seems connected with the poems of platonic love and the complimentary epistles to great ladies. These form one section of the group of verse-letters; it includes also the brilliant descriptions *The Storme* and *The Calme*, which won Ben Jonson's praise, and such urbane intercourse with friends as the letters to Sir Henry Goodyere and to Sir Henry Wotton 'at his going Ambassador to Venice'. The *Epigrams* are mere displays of ingenuity; the *Epicedes and Obsequies*, with their involved and elaborate hyperbole, are very little to modern taste. It is easy to believe Jonson's story that the elegy on Prince Henry was written 'to match Sir Ed. Herbert in obscurenesse'. The *Epithalamions*, on the other hand, have their rewarding moments: they show Donne for once celebrating courtly pleasures – 'warmth and light and good desire'. Two are dated 1613 and one much earlier, but all three show some approach to the melodious strophes of Spenser with a recurring refrain-line – further proof, as Mr Leishman has said,[17] that Donne wrote as he usually did from choice and not incapacity.

The religious poems form the second in general interest of the three main groups. The earliest, which include the *La Corona* sonnets and several meditations in couplets, hardly show Donne's characteristic power, though *The Litanie* is notable for the balanced psychological insight of some of its petitions asking for deliverance

> From being anxious, or secure,
> Dead clods of sadnesse, or light squibs of mirth,
> From thinking that great courts immure
> All, or no happinesse, or that this earth
> Is only for our prison fram'd,

and

> From needing danger, to bee good.

The *Anniversaries* belong to this group in that they are in essence less about Elizabeth Drury than life and death in general, meditations on the corruptions of this world and the glories of the next. They show Donne at his most extravagantly fantastic, and also at his most powerfully imaginative. Within twelve lines of the notorious invocation to the 'immortall maid' to be a father to his muse, he can rise to the sublimity of

> These Hymnes thy issue, may encrease so long
> As till God's great *Venite* change the song.

The two poems are in accord with many aspects of contemporary thought and sensibility, besides constituting a remarkable expression of Donne's own speculation, scepticism, and melancholy. But Donne's chief power as a religious poet is shown in the *Holy Sonnets* and the last hymns. Only in the *Hymne to God the Father* do we find an assured faith; elsewhere there is always an element of conflict and doubt or fear. The best of the *Holy Sonnets* express these struggles with unparalleled force. There is no essential change of style: Donne can stop to remember that the round world's corners are 'imagin'd' without destroying the power of his vision of Judgement Day; he treats God as a conqueror or a ravisher, or employs the kind of wooing used to his 'profane mistresses'. As in the love poetry, too, there is a considerable variety of tone and method, ranging from mere casuistry and debating tricks to a profound urgency and conviction, and sometimes both may be found in the same poem. The best show the characteristic wit reinforcing the emotional intensity:

> Onely thou art above, and when towards thee
> By thy leave I can looke, I rise againe;
> But our old subtle foe so tempteth me,
> That not one houre my selfe I can sustaine;
> Thy Grace may wing me to prevent his art,
> And thou like Adamant draw mine iron heart.

Donne's poetic fame remained high up to the Restoration, but sank to a low level in the eighteenth century. Nineteenth-century taste was hardly more favourable to him, in spite of some discriminating praise from Coleridge and the enthusiasm of Browning.

During the early years of this century critical opinion turned in his favour to an extent that raised him by the twenties to unprecedented heights. This was of course closely connected with a general reaction against the decadent remains of the Romantic tradition and the rise of a new poetry which found a special stimulus in the work of the seventeenth-century poets and the Jacobean dramatists, and it is not surprising that Mr T. S. Eliot should have contributed considerably to the change of opinion. Donne's vogue in the twenties, however, was to some extent a matter of fashion, as Mr Eliot himself suggested in an essay of 1931,[18] prophesying a reaction in the future. This has been perhaps slower in coming than he anticipated, but there are signs of it here and there, and it is worth while considering how far the rehabilitation of Donne may be a temporary phenomenon. There are those who would like to suggest that it was merely a typical aberration of the post-1918 period, and that it implied an irresponsible reaction against mature values and mastered experience, a preference for sharply realized fragments over achieved wholes. This seems an extreme view, going much further than Mr Eliot's 1931 essay, which nevertheless contains sentences that appear to give it some partial countenance. But it is difficult to discuss the question without precise reference to examples. Donne is certainly not Shakespeare or Dante, but it seems pertinent to ask whether his best poems are not achieved wholes, whether some kind of mastery of experience is not present in *The Good-morrow*, *The Extasie*, *The Valediction: forbidding mourning*, and the *Nocturnall*, to go no further. Mr Eliot's considered conclusion, however, that Donne would never sink back to his earlier obscurity, and that he would always remain as 'a great reformer of the English language, of English verse', will be recognized by those familiar with his critical ideas and terminology as by no means faint praise. After twenty years it still seems a safe minimum claim.

NOTES

1. The point has been made by Esther Cloudman Dunn in *The Literature of Shakespeare's England*, and by J. B. Leishman in *The Monarch of Wit*, among others.

2. See particularly Rosemond Tuve: *Elizabethan and Metaphysical Imagery*, and the answer by W. Empson: 'Donne and the Rhetorical Tradition' in *The Kenyon Review* for autumn 1949.

3. The point is made by T. S. Eliot in his essay on 'Donne in Our Time' in *A Garland for John Donne*, ed. Theodore Spencer.

4. Certain MSS. carry the note that this and one or two other poems were 'made to certain ayres which were made before'. See Grierson's edition of the *Poems*, Vol. I, note to p. 18.

5. See especially F. R. Leavis in an essay 'Imagery and Movement' in *Scrutiny* XIII (1945).

6. See F. R. Leavis: *Revaluation*, Chapter I.

7. The special significance that certain images seem to have possessed for Donne is discussed interestingly in M. M. Mahood: *Poetry and Humanism*, Chapter IV.

8. In a letter quoted by Hebel and Hudson: *Poetry of the English Renaissance*, p. 906.

9. In the *Discourse concerning the Original and Progress of Satire*, essays, ed. W. P. Ker, Vol. II, p. 19.

10. In his *Life of Cowley*.

11. See the introduction to *Metaphysical Poems and Lyrics of the Seventeenth Century*.

12. In *Determinations*, ed. F. R. Leavis.

13. See his essay on 'The Metaphysical Poets' in *Selected Essays*.

14. Professor L. C. Knights has some illuminating discussion of this point in his essay 'The Social Background of Metaphysical Poetry' in *Scrutiny* XIII, p. 37.

15. Miss Helen Gardner, in her recent edition of the *Divine Poems*, has argued for a date between 1609 and 1611.

16. See Donne's *The Blossome*.

17. See *The Monarch of Wit*, p. 116.

18. The essay 'Donne in Our Time' in *A Garland for John Donne*, ed. Theodore Spencer.

THE PROSE OF DONNE AND BROWNE

BY GILBERT PHELPS

THE word 'Metaphysical' as used by literary historians usually refers to the group of seventeenth-century poets who explored their experience by way of the intellectual excitements and preoccupations of their day. The label can, however, be equally well applied to many of the prose writers of the period, and in this restricted sense it is possible to compare the work of John Donne (1572–1631) and Sir Thomas Browne (1605–82).

But even if we start at a level where the superficial resemblances are most likely to appear, important differences at once emerge. Take, for example, the way in which each writer, according to the Metaphysical fashion, 'played' with an idea. *The Garden of Cyrus* (1658), by Sir Thomas Browne, is a fanciful dissertation on quincunxes (that is, the arrangement of objects in sets of five – like the five spots on a die), which leads him into an elaborate investigation of the possibilities and implications of the theme, artistic, historical, botanical, magical, and so on. He observes, for example, that:

> In the Laureat draughts of sculpture and picture, the leaves and foliate works are commonly thus contrived, which is but an imitation of the *Pulvinaria*,* and ancient pillow-work, observable in *Ionick* peeces, about columns, temples, and altars. To omit many other analogies, in Architectonicall draughts, which art itself is founded upon fives, as having its subject, and most graceful peeces divided by this number.

Donne could fasten upon a fanciful idea just as doggedly. In *Paradoxes and Problemes*, his earliest prose writings, which are contemporary in date with his early poems (and in many respects similar in mood and temper), he will take some conventional theme and then conduct elaborate, and paradoxical, five-finger exercises upon it. In the first of these, for example, he begins:

* Couches used for the images of gods in Roman antiquity.

That Women are *Inconstant*, I with any man confess, but
that *Inconstancy* is a bad quality, I against any man will
maintain: For every thing as it is one better than another, so
it is fuller of change; The *Heavens* themselves continually
turn, the *Stars* move, the *Moon* changeth; *Fire* whirleth, *Aire*
flyeth, *Water* ebbs and flowes, the face of the *Earth* altereth
her looks, *time* staies not; the Colour that is most light, will
take most dyes: so in Men, they that have most reason are the
most alterable in their designes, and the darkest and most
ignorant, do seldomest change; therefore Women changing
more than Men, have also more *Reason*. They cannot be im-
mutable like stocks, like stones, like the earth's dull Center;
Gold that lyeth still, rusteth; Water, corrupteth; Aire that
moveth not, poysoneth; then why should that which is the
perfection of other things, be imputed to Women as greatest
imperfection? ...

A Defence of Women's Inconstancy

Obviously there are great differences here in the texture of the
prose, and in the attitudes of the two writers towards their medium.
In the extract from *The Garden of Cyrus* the balance of the words and
clauses, the leisurely spacing and punctuation, induce a slow, relaxed
rhythm. The effect is to make the reader curious as to what might
follow – but not excited. There is no pressure or urgency: the connexion between the separate ideas is tenuous, and it is possible to
break off at the end of almost any sentence without loss of continuity.

In the Donne passage, on the other hand, it is very difficult to cut
across the constant jet of the thought: clause springs from clause and
sentence from sentence (in spite of a strong Euphuistic element) as it
takes fresh impetus; there is a complex criss-cross and overlay of ideas,
a continual reference back and catching up with the sense. The punctuation itself is part of this progression: there are few real rests, for the
thought hardly ever comes to a definite stop, and the punctuation-
marks for the most part serve as a momentary slowing down, pre-
paratory to a fresh spurt.

This is really another way of saying that Donne is more immediately
engaged with his material – that even in his flippancy he is the more
serious writer. Some readers may find this suggestion surprising, because the anthologies have familiarized us with examples of Browne's
prose which are reckoned among the most famous in English litera-

ture – whereas Donne's is as a rule only sparsely represented. The fact that a writer lends himself to this selective process, however – that there are such immediately recognizable 'fine passages' in his work that can be lifted out bodily – may be symptomatic of weaknesses as well as of merits.

One of the most famous of these passages is from *Hydriotaphia, Urne Buriall; Or, a Discourse of the Sepulchrall Urnes lately found in Norfolk* (1658), in which Browne, inspired by the funeral-urns and the human bones that they contain, launches out into his favourite meditation:

> But the iniquity of oblivion blindely scattereth her poppy, and deals with the memory of men without distinction to merit of perpetuity. Who can but pity the founder of the Pyramids? *Herostratus* lives that burnt the Temple of *Diana*, he is almost lost that built it; Time hath spared the Epitaph of *Adrian's* horse, confounded that of himself. In vain we compute our felicities by the advantage of our good names, since bad have equall durations; and *Thersites* is like to live as long as *Agamemnon*.* Who knows whether the best of men be known? or whether there be not more remarkable persons forgot, then any that stand remembered in the known account of time? Without the favour of the everlasting register, the first man had been as unknown as the last, and *Methuselahs* long life had been his only Chronicle.
>
> Oblivion is not to be hired: The greater part must be content to be as though they had not been, to be found in the Register of God, not in the record of man. Twenty-seven Names make up the first story before the flood, and the recorded names ever since contain not one living Century. The number of the dead long exceedeth all that shall live. The night of time far surpasseth the day, and who knows when was the Aequinox?† Every hour adds unto that current Arithmetique which scarce stands one moment. And since

---

* In the *Iliad* Thersites is the contemptible and foul-mouthed man of low birth who rails at Agamemnon, King of Argos and leader of the Greek host before Troy.

† This refers to the current seventeenth-century belief that the Creation was in process of 'running down'. It affected the imagery of many contemporary writers (e.g. Donne in his poems *A Nocturnall upon S. Lucies Day* and *The Second Anniversarie*).

death must be the *Lucina** of life, and even Pagans could
doubt, whether thus to live, were to dye. Since our longest
sunne sets at right descensions, and makes but winter arches,
and therefore it cannot be long before we lie down in dark-
nesse, and have our light in ashes. Since the brother of death
daily haunts us with dying *memento's*, and time that grows
old in it self, bids us hope no long duration: Diuturnity is a
dream and folly of expectation.

It is interesting to set against this undoubtedly fine and impressive
piece of prose, a passage from Donne on a similar theme. It is taken
from one of his best-known sermons, preached 'at the Earl of Bridge-
water's house in London at the marriage of his daughter, Nov. 19th,
1627':

There are so many evidences of the immortality of the
soule, even to a naturall man's *reason*, that it required not an
article of the Creed, to fix this notion of the Immortality of
the soule. But the Resurrection of the *Body* is discernible by
no other light, but that of *Faith*, nor could be fixed by any
lesse assurance than an *Article* of the *Creed*. Where be all the
splinters of that Bone, which a shot hath shivered and scattered in the Ayre? Where be all the Atoms of that flesh,
which a *Corrasive* hath breath'd, and exhal'd away from our
arms, and other Limbs? In what wrinkle, in what furrow,
in what bowel of the earth, ly all the graines of the ashes of a
body burnt a thousand years since? In what corner, in what
ventricle of the sea, lies all the jelly of a Body drowned in the
generall flood? What cohaerence, what sympathy, what dependence maintaines any relation, any correspondence,
between that arm that was lost in Europe, and that legge that
was lost in Afrique or Asia, scores of yeers between? One
humour of our dead body produces worms, and those worms
suck and exhaust all other humour, and then all dies, and all
dries, and molders into dust, and that dust is blowen into the
River, and that puddled water tumbled into the sea, and that
ebbs and flows in infinite revolutions, and still, still God knows
in what *Cabinet* every *seed-Pearle* lies, in what part of the
world every graine of every mans dust lies; and *sibilat
populum suum*, (as his Prophet speaks in another case) he
whispers, he hisses, he beckons for the bodies of his Saints,

* An ancient Italian deity presiding over childbirth.

and in the twinckling of an eye, that body that was scattered over all the elements, is sate down at the right hand of God, in a glorious resurrection. A Dropsie hath extended me to an enormous corpulency, and unwieldinesse; a Consumption hath attenuated me to a feeble macilency* and leanesse, and God raises me a body, such as it should have been, if these infirmities had not interven'd and deformed it.

Fifty Sermons, 1649: Sermon I

In the Browne extract there is the same tempo as in the passage we have already quoted from *The Garden of Cyrus* – though now the tread is stately rather than leisurely. The 'spreading out' is again achieved by the firm punctuation, by the rhythmical balance of the clauses, and their slow unfolding ('... and deals with the memory of men without distinction to merit of perpetuity'); and it is heightened by the careful incidence of the latinisms ('... and time that grows old in it self, bids us hope no long duration: Diuturnity is a dream and folly of expectation'). By these means Browne creates a deliberate, architectonic effect, as of a lofty vault filled with reverberating echoes. But this very deliberation produces a distancing of the emotion; the funeral urns have somehow been too much in the nature of 'an occasion', and the impact on the reader is in consequence less palpable. We are invited to solemn admiration rather than to emotional participation.

In the Donne extract there is the passionate re-creation of an experience. As in *Paradoxes and Problems*, clauses and sentences take fire from each other, and there is continual heat and motion. It is interesting, too, to notice that as a quotation it again seems incomplete; we feel that we want to know what goes before and after. And indeed any quotation from Donne must seem torn from its context, producing an effect of broken tissue and ligaments, for each of his prose works is an organic whole, and the total effect cannot be satisfactorily judged apart from that whole.

He does not merely examine his theme academically and from a safe distance, articulating its various parts at leisure. He *experiences* it, in the mind and 'on the pulses', in all its exact sensuous connotations. Ideas, theories, doctrines, quotations, allusions, imagery are all devoted to this end, they are inherent, all caught up in the intensity of

* Thinness (i.e. emaciation).

the emotion. The repetition and alliteration, the internal assonance and the rhythms, all drive inwards to its core. For example, the actual *sensation* conveyed by the verbs that follow 'corrasive' – 'breath'd, and exhal'd away' – is heightened by the subsequent concrete reference to 'consumption' and the active preposition 'away from' itself adds preciseness to this sensation of the stripping away of flesh. In the same way the repetitive questions – 'In what wrinkle, in what furrow, in what bowel of the earth' and 'In what corner, in what ventricle of the sea', and the unexpected rhyme of 'and then all dies, and all dries', all these communicate a sense of physical exploration. Even the so-called 'morbidity'[1] is symptomatic of the same intensity of contact.

Some critics have deplored Donne's morbidity as a lapse into bad taste. We must distinguish, however, between the morbidity of decadence, in which the symbols of death and decay are arranged from outside, either in a haphazard fashion (as in the later Jacobean dramatists; contrast the way in which they introduce the skull, for example – in order purely to heighten the horror – with its precise implications in Tourneur's *Revenger's Tragedy*) or with deliberate effect in the service of a romantic self-pity or self-advertisement (as in Shelley's *The Cenci*, or in writers of the Romantic decadence, such as Thomas Lovell Beddoes) – and the morbidity that is a concrete manifestation of a profound inner awareness of mortality. It is in this serious and fundamentally moral sense that Dr Johnson and Swift are morbid. This, too, is the morbidity of the medieval *danse macabre* (or of Hamlet's preoccupation with death and decay – working from inside the agonizing discovery that 'this majestical roof fretted with golden fire' is at the same time 'a foul and pestilent congregation of vapours'), and it is a kind of morbidity that springs not from weakness but from a mature acceptance of life in death. In the extract from Donne we have just quoted, the 'humour of our dead body' that 'produces worms', the worms that 'suck and exhaust all other humour', the 'Dropsie that hath extended me to an enormous corpulency', and the Consumption that 'hath attenuated me to a feeble macilency and leanesse', convey in tangible terms the determination to probe with the mind and the senses along the nerves and into the very marrow of the experience, and is in no way a 'morbid' surrender to it.

This distinction between a prose which translates experience directly and palpably and a prose of the literary occasion is inherent in any examination of Browne and Donne, and is apparent in every aspect of their work. Take, for example, the use that each makes of his learning. In the one case a curious and roving mind delights in illustrating an argument with all kinds of unexpected references, examples, and allusions – and in embellishing the theme with numerous quotations. But it *is* properly speaking 'embellishment' – that is, an extraneous arrangement of objects related to the theme, but not urgent or intrinsic to it. And the attention Browne invites is also of a roving and curious kind: he speaks as an amateur and a spectator, rather than as a participant, and much of our pleasure is thus of a detached and bookish nature. When he rises to his great perorations on death and decay he is, of course, more universal – but at the back of them we are still conscious of the museum and the study. In Donne, however, there is none of this whimsical rolling of the pellets of learning on the tongue. The impulse is altogether different. He is completely caught up in the excitement of the moment – whether spiritual, intellectual, or sensual, and the quotations and allusions are functional, entirely related to that excitement and subjugated to it.

There are in addition considerable differences in the actual nature of their learning, or at any rate in the emphasis they laid on different parts of it. Browne's mind is stored with an extraordinary medley of classical and medieval learning, of folk-lore, magic, archaeology, and pseudo-science. In *Religio Medici* (published 1642, written probably 1635) he adopts a rational and liberal attitude, typical of the seventeenth-century reaction against authority. In *Pseudodoxia Epidemica* (1646) he reveals, among a mass of medieval superstition, an occasional approximation to the Baconian 'spirit of enquiry'.

There is little of this in Donne. In spite of his vivid interest in contemporary currents of thought, the energy and originality of his mind, and his metaphysical imagery, he is closer to the medieval traditions of thought than Browne.[2] He is not even a true humanist – for he seems to have studied Greek only in Latin translations, and he always quotes the New Testament in the Vulgate. He shows, however, a minute knowledge of the works of the Fathers, the Schoolmen, the medieval jurists, and the Roman and Protestant controversialists. His method of argument, too, was medieval, founded on syllogistic reasoning, and with frequent appeals to authority, while his philosophy was a continuation of the ideas of Augustine and Aquinas. And this firm grounding in medieval culture gives his work discipline and coherence (in spite of the passionate, frequently helter-skelter nature of his thought and language), while Browne's amateur playing with the 'new ideas' increases the fragmentary and desultory nature of his writing, to which his dilettante temperament in any case inclined him.

But Donne is also steeped in the language of the medieval and Tudor preachers, and of the translators of the Prayer Book and the Bible. Browne's grandiloquent style has often been compared to that of the Bible, but a glance at the two passages we have quoted will show how much closer is Donne's language, in spirit and texture, to this tradition than is Browne's. Donne, while never letting go of his theological argument, in all its complexity, uses as his staple style the muscular, sensuous language and imagery of common speech. Thus the dust of our dissolution becomes 'puddled water tumbled into the sea'; as for the Prophet – 'he whispers, he hisses, he beckons' and 'in the twinckling of an eye, that body that was scattered over all the elements, is sate down at the right hand of God'. Time after time in the sermons the most subtle of scholastic arguments are brought to a climax and driven home, in the manner of the parables or the *exempla* of the medieval and Tudor preacher, by some homely idiom or image, which extracts from the mass of theory and doctrine the human and universal truth it was designed to communicate.

In Sermon LXVI (*Eighty Sermons*, 1640), for example, he concludes an argument on Divine Grace:

> ... yet if God with-draw not his spirituall blessings, his Grace, his Patience, If I can call my suffering his Doing, my passion his Action, All this that is temporall, is but a caterpillar got into one corner of my garden, but a mill-dew fallen upon one acre of my Corne; The body of all, the substance of all is safe, as long as the soule is safe.

And in Sermon IX (*Eighty Sermons*) he urges his congregation:

> Pay this debt to thy selfe of looking into thy debts, of sur-veying, of severing, of serving thy selfe with that which is truly thine, at thy noone, in the best of thy fortune, and in the

strength of thine understanding; that when thou comest to pay thy other, thy last debt to thy self, which is, to open a doore out of this world, by the dissolution of body and soule, thou have not all thy money to tell over when the Sun is ready to set, all the account to make of every bag of money, and of every quillet of land, whose it is, and whether it be his that looks for it from thee, or his from whom it was taken by thee; whether it belong to thine heire, that weepes joyfull teares behinde the curtain, or belong to him that weeps true, and bloody teares, in the hole in a prison.

Even in the most characteristic of his metaphysical images the preoccupation is serious and entirely human:

Upon this earth, a man cannot possibly make one step in a straight, and a direct line. The earth it selfe being round, every step wee make upon it, must necessarily bee a segment, an arch of a circle. But yet though no piece of a circle be a straight line, yet if we take any piece, nay if wee take the whole circle, there is no corner, no angle in any piece, in any intire circle. A perfect rectitude we cannot have in any wayes in this world; In every Calling there are some inevitable tentations. But, though wee cannot make up our circle of a straight line, (that is impossible to human frailty) yet wee may passe on, without angles, and corners, that is, without disguises in our Religion, and without the love of craft, and falsehood, and circumvention in our civill actions.

Eighty Sermons: Sermon LXVII

By comparison with the variety and richness of Donne's language and imagery – subtle, witty, intellectually tough, at the same time that it is vivid, sensuous, and dramatic – Browne's stylistic resources often seem threadbare and his effects limited and contrived. The range of feeling and human observation in Donne's language is symptomatic of a mind in touch with experience at every point, while even the finest of Browne's 'fine passages' are by comparison academic and second-hand (the sentiments expressed in them are, after all, the commonplaces of Elizabethan and Jacobean literature). They have charm and even grandeur, but they are fundamentally 'safe'.

There is certainly nothing safe about Donne's prose. It forces the reader, not to the solemn ruminations of the detached observer, but to a struggle, intellectual, sensuous, and spiritual. There is nothing fixed or static in his prose. In the sermons he may adopt a medieval structure – analysing in minute detail the several parts of his text, illustrating each step in the analysis with arguments drawn from the Fathers and the Schoolmen, and then reconstructing it from these elements (this process can perhaps be seen at its most typical in the moving sermon on the text 'Remember now thy Creator, in the days of thy Youth' – *Twenty-six Sermons*, 1660: Sermon XIX).[3] But the combination of formal structure and molten fluidity of style serves to heighten the intellectual and emotional tension which is the product of a profound sensibility of mind and senses in direct contact with the issues of human destiny. With Donne it really *is* a matter of life and death.

The personality that emerges, in consequence, is itself fluid and restless – always changing, expanding, struggling, developing – exploring new channels, sometimes tortuous, always original, into which to pour its restless energy. It is impossible, therefore, ever to say that we have isolated Donne's personality – not, of course, because he is not present in his work, but because the term has no real meaning apart from the organization of words into which it has been absorbed. He is too deeply committed to his experience: as an artist he remains in control – but as a man he surrenders to it. Indeed, to speak of the personality of a writer as if it were a separate element in his work is, as a general rule, beside the point. It is not irrelevant here because in reading Sir Thomas Browne we *do* come away with a definite picture of character. He means that we should – for to him personality is an important part of his stock-in-trade.[4] He is one of the first English prose writers to set out deliberately to cultivate 'the gentle reader'. He takes him into his confidence, inviting admiration for his learning, indulgence for his foibles and eccentricities, and awe in the face of his perorations. In addition, he has no hesitation in commenting in *Religio Medici* upon his own courage, charity, pity, tolerance – and freedom from pride. But it is not only in these obvious ways that Browne parades his individuality – the whole of his writings are devoted to the careful distillation of a distinctive personal aroma.

Now this deliberate exploitation of personality, with the self-conscious attitude towards literature that it involved, was one of the symptoms of the changes that were taking place in English culture in the seventeenth century. The reasons for these changes are examined elsewhere in this volume; briefly they relate to the gradual break-up of the Elizabethan 'world picture' and of the medieval tradition of learning and belief that lay beyond it, and to the consequent irruption of new and revolutionary ideas and theories. In a period when everything was in a state of flux, many writers turned in a more deliberate way than they had hitherto to the exploration of the quirks and oddities of personality. There was, for example, the vogue of eccentricity, practised with varying degrees of self-consciousness, by such writers as Thomas Coryat (1577?-1617), Robert Burton (1577-1640) and Sir Thomas Urquhart (1611-60) – the pedantic nature of Urquhart's eccentricity is apparent even in his titles: *The Trissotetras, Pantochronocanon, Ekekubalauron, Logopandelteision* (though of course there was more to it than that, and the tendency stood him in good stead in his translation of Rabelais). This cultivation of eccentricity might perhaps be considered as a form of escape from the perplexities of a period of instability, a kind of frantic thrusting upwards of the personality at a time when the roots were in danger of becoming parched through lack of nourishment.

The 'eccentrics' were an extreme case, but this shift of perspective in the attitude towards the writer's self reveals itself in other contemporary developments – in the growth of autobiography and memoirs (for example, Lord Herbert of Cherbury, 1583-1648, and Kenelm Digby, 1603-65); in the appearance of intimate 'table talk' (notably, of course, John Selden, 1584-1654); and in the gossip and self-revelation of the famous diarists Samuel Pepys (1633-1703) and John Evelyn (1620-1706). In the essay, too, moral analysis as practised by Francis Bacon (1561-1626) and Abraham Cowley (1618-67) was accompanied by a degree of personal analysis, which was to become gradually more pronounced – growing worldly and urbane in Lord Halifax (1633-95), Sir William Temple (1628-99) and Lord Shaftesbury (1671-1713), but nevertheless pointing forward to the more intimate confessions of the essayists of the Romantic Revival. A similar heightening of the personal element can be seen, too, in such writers as Izaak Walton (1593-1683), Thomas Fuller (1608-61), and John Aubrey (1626-97) in whom charm, whimsicality, quaintness, and temperament are dispensed with a certain air of self-conscious artifice which was comparatively rare among the earlier writers.

This increase in the awareness of the writer's personality as part of his stock-in-trade was attended by a more detached approach in the observation of the elements of character, and a tendency to isolate them for curious examination, notably, of course, in the Character-writers Sir Thomas Overbury (1581–1613) and John Earle (1601–65). A similar shift in the point of view, with an emphasis on the external traits of colourful personality in place of the old unity of character and background, might be detected in seventeenth-century drama. There are, for example, the rapid thumbnail sketches thrown off by Flamineo in Webster's *The White Devil* and by Bosola in *The Duchess of Malfi* (with their obvious affinities to the Character-writers), which, though they are woven into the fabric of the plays, slow down the tempo and detract from the unity of the effect. At the same time in the actual 'persons of the play' there is, in much later Jacobean drama, a sense of wavering perspective, of incompleteness and scrappiness that reflect the increasing uncertainty about themes and values. They are closer to 'characters' in the actor's sense – prolific of grimaces, gestures, witticisms, and 'dark sayings', but with little organic rela-tionship one with another or with the common background of Nature. The Elizabethan and early Jacobean dramatists, on the other hand, dealt with the great human themes *through* the characters, who remained real 'selves' (where, that is, that kind of differentiation was relevant – in many cases, of course, the characters were purely personi-fications), but without any distortion of their natural function in the play as a whole.

Now these tendencies must be set side by side with the emergence of a new kind of prose, which was designed to further scientific speculation and investigation, and which was to a large extent the work of Francis Bacon. It was not that his writings exhibited any particular technical innovations. In many respects he was a typical Elizabethan prose writer. It was his *attitude* towards his medium that was revolutionary. Whereas the gradual exhaustion of the Elizabethan inspiration left many of his contemporaries uncertain and aimless – driving some of them, as we have seen, into eccentricity and whim-sicality – Bacon was in no doubt whatever as to his purpose. It was to adapt prose to the great task of achieving mastery over the material world, and he did, in fact, succeed in creating an instrument that was admirably suited to its purpose, and without which scientific advance might have been impossible. But in achieving his utilitarian purpose he inevitably narrowed the resources of English prose. His imagery, for example, was subordinated to a purely intellectual purpose; he deployed his various figures of speech, as we can see in *The Advancement of Learning*, not in order to express the whole range of his feelings about the case he is arguing, but in order primarily to gain a dialectical victory.

In Tudor prose, however, the imagery was used primarily to increase the emotional effect and to heighten the muscular sensation rather than to enforce a strictly logical meaning, because it was exactly here – in expressing the whole texture of an idea or a situation – that the writer's chief interest lay, and not so much in the desire to analyse, argue, and prove.

There had, in fact, been little specialization or differentiation of function in Tudor prose – because there had been no overriding necessity for it. It had been at the same time the prose of narrative, description, theology, controversy, and the senses. It appealed, as Professor L. C. Knights has said, not only to the eye that measures and calculates, but also to the hand that feels and weighs. The muscular content was part of the meaning. The relationship between word and sensation, word and action, was more intimate than it is today – and the thought (as in Donne) was itself 'felt'. This was true not only of writers such as Greene and Nashe, who were particularly close to contemporary idiom, but in a sense also of the theologians such as Hooker and even of the Euphuists. Lyly and Sidney, for example, were more elaborate than Sir Thomas Browne in their stylistic devices, but these sprang more directly from their emotional commitment and were not picked up and laid down like objects in a collection. Their use of literary convention, moreover, was bound up with a powerfully nostalgic feeling for the past, and in addition there was the energy and excitement of experimentation in a comparatively new medium. In reading Hooker's great perorations on Order and the Light of Reason, too, one has the sense of absorption in the material in a passionate, unequivocal way, so that the eloquence rises naturally out of an amalgam of the theology, the thought, and the feeling.

This account of Tudor prose and of the changes that followed in the seventeenth century is, of course, much simplified and compressed. It does not give sufficient weight to the survivors of the Elizabethan tradition, and notably Milton, or to the vitality and resilience of the Tudor tradition in prose, and its resurgence in Bunyan, the religious controversialists, and the Puritan pamphleteers. It does not examine the ways in which the new self-consciousness on the one hand and the new Baconian objectivity on the other enriched our culture, for example, in the development of the novel. Above all, it leaves out of account the creation of another kind of cultural unity and 'world picture' (narrower, perhaps, but with its own toughness and energy – and with its roots, moreover, in the past) in the Restoration and Augustan periods. Nevertheless, its main contention is, I think, a valid one: that in the seventeenth century a split in the functions of English prose begins to make itself felt, between, at the two extremes, the Baconian prose of inductive reasoning and the whimsical over-literary prose of Sir Thomas Browne (and in this connexion it is interesting to note Browne's popularity with the most whimsical of the essayists of the Romantic Revival) – and that this carried the possible implication that the prose of the new instauration of learning was the really serious vehicle for contemporary thought and endeavour, while that of literature might, in consequence, be regarded as fanciful and remote.

The fissure between these two kinds of language had not gone very far in the seventeenth century, but the prose of Sir Thomas Browne is already symptomatic of it. As we have seen, he is not unequivocally absorbed in his experience: he is not so passionately caught up in it that it speaks powerfully through his medium in spite of himself; on the contrary, he can stand back and calculate his effects. His great passages in consequence do not grow inevitably out of his material – they are externalized and their connexion with it is not organic. At the same time there is a new element of self-consciousness in his relation to his audience. He has no passionate concern to communicate with his fellow men from the deepest level of his being – to share his experience and *live* it side by side with them – as Donne does; he is concerned rather in showing off his learning, skill, charm, and whimsicality in front of a select audience composed of people of similar tastes and interests. His attitude towards literature, in other words, is already that of the dilettante or the belle-lettrist – who treats literature as something separate from the main-stream of contemporary life.

Hitherto prose had been a medium for the whole range of human experience; Browne demonstrates how its pitch can be screwed up or down, not according to the emotional demands of the situation, but at the whim of the curious and experimental manipulator. Donne's prose, on the other hand, shows no sign of self-consciousness or literary artifice: he still belongs to a tradition in which the 'whole man' is used up in writing, and when he rises to the heights of eloquence, he is driven to them by the cumulative force and energy of his intellectual, sensuous, and spiritual explorations.

Thus the comparison between Browne and Donne is particularly fruitful because it throws into relief the changes that were taking place in English sensibility in the seventeenth century, and is therefore valuable for an understanding of the period; and because in doing so it emphasizes the distinction between literature and belles-lettres. Donne emerges from the comparison as the greater writer because as a man and an artist he was in complete organic relationship with his material. When the whole man is thus engaged, the language is both sensuous *and* functional, and the 'fine passages', if indeed they can be isolated from the total effect, grow out of the greatness of the theme and the degree of passion and sincerity with which it is envisaged.

NOTES

1. For an examination of Donne's philosophical views as to the relationship between body and soul, see *A Study of the Prose Works of John Donne*, by E. M. Simpson.

2. For an examination of Donne's debts to the medieval tradition of teaching, see 1 above.

3. This can be read in full in *Poetry and Prose of John Donne*, selected by W. S. Scott. Another sermon, the famous 'Death's Duel', can be read in full in *Complete Poetry and Selected Prose*, edited by John Hayward. See also *Sermons*, edited by George R. Potter and E. M. Simpson (10 vols.).

4. See *Hours in a Library*, 2nd series, by Leslie Stephen.

BEN JONSON'S POETRY

BY F. W. BRADBROOK

Lecturer in English, University College of North Wales, Bangor

THE revival of interest in Ben Jonson as a dramatist in recent years has perhaps led to an undue neglect of his non-dramatic poetry. There has also been a fashionable interest in John Donne and the Meta-physical poets, which has not always recognized that Ben Jonson was closely associated with John Donne both in actual life and as a literary influence. That Ben Jonson was the leader of a group of poets known as 'the tribe of Ben' is generally known. But his influence extends beyond them into the eighteenth century, and among modern poets W. B. Yeats, T. S. Eliot, and W. H. Auden are indebted to him.

In many ways Jonson occupies an unusual position in English litera-ture. This is partly owing to the length of time that he was a dominant force in drama and poetry. 'Like Bacon, Jonson mediates between the age of Shakespeare and the age of Milton.'[1] By 1598 Francis Meres, who wrote a survey of English literature from Chaucer to his own day called *Palladis Tamia*, had come to the opinion that Jonson was one of 'our best for tragedy'. In 1616 the poet received official recog-nition in the form of a pension from James I, and this was continued and enlarged by Charles I. Jonson collected his poems, plays, and masques for publication in a folio volume in the same year that he received this royal favour. Until his death in 1637 he held a command-ing influence over his fellow poets, and after his death his memory was celebrated with affectionate esteem by his admirers in a volume of elegies entitled *Jonsonus Virbius*. A further collection of his poems was published in 1640.

Jonson's poetry is notable for its range and variety, and this is re-flected in the breadth of his social contacts. From the beginning of the century Jonson had presided at the famous meetings of writers held at the Mermaid Tavern,[2] and it was here that Shakespeare en-gaged in the famous wit combats with him described later by the chronicler Fuller. Jonson was 'like a Spanish great galleon ... built far higher in learning, solid but slow in his performances'; while

Shakespeare, like 'an English man-of-war, lesser in bulk but lighter in sailing, could turn with all tides, tack about, and take advantage of all winds, by the quickness of his wit and invention'.[3] Perhaps this account has rather prejudiced later views of Ben Jonson. He was certainly a much more learned poet than Shakespeare, but the general view of his contemporaries, as suggested, for example, in the poem addressed to him about 1606 by Francis Beaumont, is that there was nothing clumsy or heavy about the conversations at the Mermaid. On the contrary, it is the wit, the nimbleness, and subtlety that are stressed, and Ben Jonson himself is praised as one who makes smooth and plain the way of knowledge for others. Jonson, however, did not rely solely on the Mermaid for his company. With John Donne (whom he considered 'the first poet in the world in some things'), Drayton, and several other poets, he shared the inspiring friendship of Lucy Harington, Countess of Bedford. Others who entertained the poet informally at their houses were Sidney's daughter, the Countess of Rutland, and his niece, wife of Sir Robert Wroth, themselves both poets. Sir Robert Sidney and the Earl of Pembroke, son of Sir Philip's sister, were also friends, and from the latter Jonson received £20 every New Year's day to buy new books.[4] Jonson describes in one of his poems the lavish hospitality he enjoyed at the ancestral home at Penshurst.

The theatre, the tavern, and the country-house each played their part in shaping Ben Jonson's genius, and it is hardly surprising that his poetry ranges from some of the crudest to some of the most refined and urbane in the English language. In literature the most important influence, apart from Donne, was exerted by the classical poets on whom Jonson deliberately modelled himself, but the vitality that characterizes all his writing and gives the most derivative of poems its special timbre is his own.

Like Sidney, Jonson was a critic as well as a poet. His views on poetry are given in the notes which Drummond of Hawthornden took in 1619 when the poet visited Scotland, and in Ben Jonson's own commonplace-book called *Discoveries*. From these two sources, knowledge of both Jonson's theories and practice in poetry can be gained. In *Conversations with William Drummond* there are brief remarks on many of Jonson's predecessors and contemporaries, and even those whom he admired are commented on with typical pungency. Never reluctant to talk about himself, he reveals his own method of writing poetry: 'That he wrote all his first in prose, for so his master Camden had learned him'; while the robust assertiveness of his views about his position in English literature is characteristic: 'He was better versed and knew more in Greek and Latin, than all the poets in England.'

Timber, or Discoveries made upon men and matter, as they flowed out of his daily readings is not, in any sense, an original work. In his critical ideas, as in his poetry, Jonson drew heavily on classical models.[5] 'I know nothing can conduce more to letters than to examine the writings of the ancients', he says. But he adds a recommendation 'not to rest in their sole authority, or take all upon trust from them ... for to all the observations of the ancients we have our own experience, which if we will use and apply, we have better means to pronounce'. The ancients are, for Jonson, guides not commanders. 'Spenser, in affecting the ancients, writ no language.' To write well, a man must read the best authors, observe the best speakers, and exercise his own style. Jonson himself cultivates style deliberately: 'No matter how slow the style be at first, so it be laboured and accurate.' He is no enemy of inspiration, provided it is genuine, but he is an enemy of facility. Care and industry are needed in the writer as in any other craftsman; it is his duty to revise and polish his work. The best writers 'did nothing rashly; they obtained first to write well, and then custom made it easy and a habit'. Jonson's ideal in style is a modest one: 'Pure and neat language I love, yet plain and customary.' His abomination is a barbarous phrase.

Jonson is both independent and a believer in tradition which he calls 'custom' ('that I call custom of speech which is the consent of the learned'). But he is opposed to any dictatorship of ancient models ('as the schools have done Aristotle'), and he will not confine a poet's liberty 'within the narrow limits of laws which either the grammarians or philosophers prescribe'. At the same time Aristotle 'understood the causes of things; and what other men did by chance or custom he doth by reason; and not only found out the way not to err, but the short way that we should take not to err. ...'

This combination of respect for tradition and a sturdy independence is what gives Ben Jonson's poetry its variety and flexibility. He can range from the most formal classical style to the racy idiomatic utterance befitting a popular dramatist and the leading spirit of the meetings at the Mermaid. It is, in fact, not at all easy to separate these two sides of his genius. His most classical poems have a racy idiomatic quality, while his most colloquial poems frequently follow classical models. Jonson made no attempt to impose the idiom and syntax of the classical writers on the English language. The spirit in which he uses the classics is very different from that of Milton.

A typical example of the Jonsonian lyric is his *Song to Celia* modelled on the familiar theme of Catullus (*'Vivamus, mea Lesbia, atque amemus'*).

> Come my CELIA, let us prove,
> While wee may, the sports of love;
> Time will not be ours for ever:
> He, at length, our good will sever.
> Spend not then his gifts in vaine.
> Sunnes that set, may rise againe:
> But, if once wee lose this light,
> 'Tis, with us, perpetuall night.
> Why should we deferre our joyes?
> Fame, and rumor are but toyes.
> Cannot we delude the eyes
> Of a few poore household spyes?
> Or his easier eares beguile,
> So removed by our wile?
> 'Tis no sinne, loves fruit to steale,
> But the sweet theft to reveale:
> To bee taken, to be seene,
> These have crimes accounted beene.

This has been described as 'mediocre' by his Oxford editors, 'merely smooth and insignificant', and is compared unfavourably with 'the superb Elizabethan romanticism'[6] of the poet Campian's treatment of the same theme. Others have referred to the poem in very different terms. 'Jonson's effort was to feel Catullus, and the others he cultivated, as contemporary with himself; or rather, to achieve an English mode that should express a sense of contemporaneity with them. ... This mode ... may be described as consciously urbane, mature, and civilized.'[7] Obviously a poet who is able to arouse such difference of opinion among those qualified to judge is still very much alive. Perhaps the point that should be stressed is that Jonson was not alone in this use of the classics, though despite earlier examples, such as the poem of Campian, it was he who was largely responsible for transposing the spirit of the classical *lyric* into English. Jonson's combination of a classical sense of form and restraint with a native English vigour gave the seventeenth-century lyric its distinctive quality. Andrew Marvell, in such a poem as *To His Coy Mistress*, as in many of his other poems, is writing in the tradition initiated by Ben Jonson, modified by the more colloquial manner and the imagery typical of the lyrics of Donne.

Jonson's *Song to Celia* is, in a special sense, dramatic. It is sung by Volpone in the third Act of the play. To be fully appreciated it must be read in its dramatic context. However closely related they are, there is an ironic contrast between Catullus's poem in praise of Lesbia and the song of Volpone the Fox, who is attempting to seduce Celia, the wife of the merchant Corvino. Volpone immediately follows up the song with the offer to his lady of diamonds and jewels:

> . . . a carbuncle,
> May put out both the eyes of our St Mark.

A typical satirical flavour is added to the apparently simple lyric. The idea, expressed at the end of the poem, that it is no sin to steal but only to be found out, was a belief held by the Spartans that Jonson may have absorbed directly or indirectly from the classics. But it comes with superb irony from the mouth of Volpone the Magnifico, who has just been described by the misguided husband (who had willingly prostituted his wife) as 'an old decrepit wretch, That has no sense, no sinew'. Such a satirical undertone is quite lacking in Campian's charming lyric.

There is a similar treatment of Catullus in Jonson's other poem to Celia ('Kiss me sweet'), which perfectly catches the tone and accent of its original in the opening lines. Then, in the enumeration of the kisses, the lyric deviates ironically, and contrasts Catullus with the Cockney background of the contemporary lover:

> Adde a thousand, and so more;
> Till you equall with the store,
> All the grasse that *Rumney* yeelds,
> Or the sands in *Chelsey* fields,

Or the drops in silver *Thames,*
Or the starres, that guild his streames,
In the silent sommer-nights,
When youths ply their stolne delights.

In the last four lines of the lyric Jonson returns to the urbane and poised accent of the opening. Such flexible and controlled transitions from an ideal classical world to the actualities of seventeenth-century London, with the accompanying sense of ironical contrast, distinguish Jonson from a poet such as Campian, and are a proof of his greatness. Because of the restraint imposed by Jonson's sense of form, these transitions are always easy and graceful. There is none of that deliberate shock of contrast such as T. S. Eliot exploits in his early poetry. But for the general method, the ironical opposition of the actual and the classical which is one of the characteristic effects in *The Waste Land*, Mr Eliot could find numerous models and examples in Jonson's poetry.

The edition of Jonson's poems printed in 1616 contains his epigrams and a collection called *The Forest*. In some of the epigrams there would appear to be some justification for adverse comment. When Jonson is not at his best, his poems are too elaborate, lacking in spontaneity and flexibility, clumsy and harsh. Yet there are also to be found in this collection some of the most sensitive and delicate of his lyrics. In poems such as *On My First Daughter, On His First Sonne*, together with the epitaphs on Solomon Pavy and Elizabeth L. H., Jonson writes in a style of limpid clarity that conveys by its simplicity and restraint the deepest of human feelings. *The Epigrams* also include the fine tribute, written in an unusual tone of humility, to Jonson's master William Camden, and poems to his friends John Donne, Francis Beaumont, Lucy, Countess of Bedford, and Mary, Lady Wroth. Such poems are the natural product of that intellectual, courtly, and refined society where intimacy and friendship naturally express themselves in formal written compliment. 'Rare poems aske rare friends,' as Jonson writes to the Countess of Bedford when sending her Donne's satires. In such a world only the best is good enough: the standard set implies selection. Jonson and his circle were consciously writing for the few. Moreover, there was for Jonson a complete harmony between this actual world and the ideal one of classical literature. In the witty and learned lines *Inviting a Friend to Supper*,

Jonson describes at length the food and wine to be offered to his friend. He also dwells on the talk that is to follow, about Virgil, Horace, and Anacreon. This natural association of the ideal with ordinary everyday things looks forward to the eighteenth-century poets, particularly to Pope. Penshurst itself is the home of the Dryads, Pan, Bacchus, the Muses, and Satyrs, but it is also a very real place:

> The lower land, that to the river bends,
> Thy sheepe, thy bullocks, kine, and calves doe feed:
> The middle grounds thy mares, and horses breed.
> Each banke doth yeeld thee coneyes. ...[8]

The attitude to the great house and its surroundings, the feeling for nature, together with the style of formal, dignified compliment, are echoed in Pope's lines at the end of Epistle IV (*Of the use of Riches, to Richard Boyle, Earl of Burlington*):

> Whose cheerful Tenants bless their yearly toil,
> Yet to their Lord owe more than to the soil;
> Whose ample lawns are not ashamed to feed
> The milky heifer and deserving steed.

Later, in describing 'thy orchard fruit', 'thy garden flowers', 'the blushing apricot and woolly peach', there is a direct sensuous appreciation of nature that brings to mind *The Garden* and *Bermudas* of Andrew Marvell. The same combination of interests is to be found in the poem *To Sir Robert Wroth*.

Some of Jonson's finest lyrics appear in the masques that he wrote for the Court. The plays also contain numerous songs, some of which were set to music by Jonson's friend, Alfonso Ferrabosco. Generally, under the influence of Jonson and Donne the lyric extended its range, expressing more profound thought and deeper feeling. But in the masques and plays the tradition of the Elizabethan song was continued, and a number of Jonson's finest lyrics are in the earlier, simpler manner. 'Queen and huntress, chaste and fair', 'Still to be neat, still to be dressed', 'Slow, slow, fresh fount', and 'If I freely may discover' are perhaps the best-known examples. Here Jonson casts his learning aside and writes with ease and grace some of the most sensitive and delicate of English songs. If one compares them with a song of Donne's such as 'Sweetest love, I do not goe', it will be seen how much more ingrained in Donne's poetry is the intellectual conceit. The rhythm of Donne's songs is much nearer to colloquial speech, and even the simplest ones would not appear to lend themselves very easily to musical accompaniment.[9]

The series of poems addressed *To Charis* are Jonson's main contribution to the love lyric. They are playful in tone rather than passionate, with the exception of the finest of the pieces, *Her Triumph*. Here, and particularly in the final stanza, 'Have you seene but a bright Lillie grow?', there is a strong direct expression of feeling rare in Ben Jonson's love poetry, though there is another passage in the seventh poem of the series with an echo of the scene with Helen in Marlowe's play *Dr Faustus* and a reminiscence of Donne's *Extasie*:

> Joyne lip to lip, and try:
> Each suck the others breath.
> And whilst our tongues perplexed lie,
> Let who will thinke us dead, or wish our death.

Such passages are unusual. Generally speaking, emotion is suggested and implied rather than directly presented. The neatness of form is what appeals to the reader, and this involves restraint and control. The concern with form and style hardly allows for the intensity that Donne gains in such a poem as *The Canonization*:

> For Godsake hold your tongue and let me love. . . .

Typical of the Jonsonian lyric is the courtly expression of platonic love beginning:

> Faire Friend, 'tis true, your beauties move
>   My heart to a respect:
> Too little to bee paid with love,
>   Too great for your neglect.

The poem has been attributed to Sidney Godolphin, one of Jonson's admirers, and resembles the Cavalier poets in manner and style though it has a weight and dignity characteristically Jonsonian. Jonson too combines depth of feeling with a graceful lightness of touch. Though emotion does not directly appear in the poem, the very moderation and modesty of his claims emphasizes the sincerity. The poet is calmly and impersonally recognizing both the reality and the limitations of his love:

'T is not a passions first accesse
   Readie to multiply,
But like Loves calmest State it is
   Possest with victorie.

It is like Love to Truth reduc'd,
   All the false values gone,
Which were created, and induc'd
   By fond imagination.

'Access' includes the sense of 'attack' (reflected in the image of the victorious man-of-war at the end of the stanza), 'approach', 'advance', and an 'outburst' of feeling. In 'multiply' there is a similar pun on the sexual and mathematical implications, carrying on the suggestions implied in the 'first access'. The verse flows evenly until there is a sudden stress on the word 'possessed'. The poet indicates at one and the same time that he has gained a victory over his passions and that he has all the pleasure of 'possession' in the obvious sexual sense. Like the beauty of Keats's *Grecian Urn*, love has been disciplined until it is 'reduced' to truth. Though this love does not involve physical separation like that described in Andrew Marvell's *The Definition of Love*, it is still primarily 'a conjunction of the mind'. The style, the sophisticated recognition of physical desire at the same time that it is transcended, and the tone and accent combine to make this a particularly 'modern' poem. It is from Donne and Jonson that a poet such as W. H. Auden gains his appearance of 'tough reasonableness', even when the appearance is obviously a façade and he is at his least mature:

Soul and body have no bounds:
To lovers as they lie upon
Her tolerant enchanted slope
In their ordinary swoon,
Grave the vision Venus sends
Of supernatural sympathy
Universal love and hope.

The two powerful odes *To Himself* are written in Jonson's more robust and assertive style. When scorn, contempt, or satire are required, Jonson is at his most vigorous best, and here he bitterly attacks the theatre-going public that he fundamentally despised, and the playwrights, including Shakespeare, who pleased them. In the ode beginning:

> Where do'st thou carelesse lie,
> Buried in ease and sloth?

there is again a use of imagery and the intellectual conceit reminiscent of Donne. The taste of the public is contrasted with and 'placed' by Jonson's own classical tastes. The final lines:

> But sing high and aloofe,
> Safe from the wolves black jaw, and the dull Asses hoofe

were remembered by W. B. Yeats in the closing rhyme at the end of *Responsibilities*. Yeats with his concern for 'ancient ceremony' and seeking

> ... under that ancient roof
> A sterner conscience and a friendlier home

is perhaps of all modern poets the nearest in spirit to Jonson. In the second ode ('Come leave the lothed Stage'), written in a superb mood of contemptuous indignation, Jonson again turns to the classics as a relief from the crudities of the groundlings. That in the final stanza he should associate Alcaeus, Horace, Anacreon, and Pindar with King Charles and 'the acts of his sweet raigne' is one of the finest testimonies to the civilization of that age given by a poet who was no servile flatterer. The form and style of the poem recall Marvell's *Horatian Ode*.[10]

Jonson's religious lyrics show the same virtues of surface simplicity, clarity, intellectual discipline, and depth of feeling that are revealed in the best of his other lyrics. The attitude of the poet in *To the World* is stoical rather than Christian, but elsewhere, as in *To Heaven*, he writes in a passionate mood of self-examination and self-reproach. The resemblance here is to Herbert rather than to Donne. Such a poem as Jonson's *A Hymne to God the Father* is closer technically and in every other way to Herbert's *Discipline* ('Throw away thy rod') than to Donne's *A Hymne to God the Father*. The mingling of the doctrinal and the personal in *The Sinners Sacrifice: To the Holy Trinitie* again recalls Herbert. *A Hymne on the Nativitie of my Saviour* contrasts with Milton's longer hymn, though there are certain resemblances in detail. In the religious lyric, as in his other poetry, it is to the line of wit that Jonson belongs. He provided with Donne the foundation on which later poets were to build.

Jonson himself summarizes his character and achievement, and gives a characteristically long negative list of the people and things that he disliked in *An Epistle answering to one that asked to be Sealed of the Tribe of Ben*. His final claim for himself is the classical virtue of self-knowledge:

> First give me faith, who know
> My selfe a little; I will take you so,
> As you have writ your selfe. Now stand, and then,
> Sir, you are Sealed of the Tribe of *Ben*.

NOTES

1. *Ben Jonson*, ed. C. H. Hereford and Percy Simpson, Vol. I, p. 127.
2. But see L. A. Shapiro, *Modern Languages Review* XLV (1950), pp. 6–17, and XLVI (1951), pp. 59–63.
3. Fuller's *Worthies* (1662), 'Warwickshire', p. 126.
4. For details, see C. H. Herford and Percy Simpson, Vol. I.
5. For Jonson's indebtedness in his criticism, see the edition of *Discoveries*, by M. Castelain. Hardin Craig has some sensible remarks on 'imitation' and borrowing in *The Enchanted Glass*, pp. 254–5.
6. *Ben Jonson*, ed. C. H. Herford and Percy Simpson, Vol. II, pp. 386–7.
7. F. R. Leavis: *Revaluation*, p. 19.
8. See Maurice Castelain: *Ben Jonson: L'Homme et l'œuvre, 1572–1637*. Paris, 1907; *Ben Jonson*, ed. C. H. Herford Percy and Evelyn Simpson, Vol. VIII, p. 94.
9. But see p. 100 and note 4, p. 115.
10. This is pointed out by F. R. Leavis in *Revaluation*, p. 21.

GEORGE HERBERT AND THE
DEVOTIONAL POETS

BY D. J. ENRIGHT

Professor of English, University of Singapore

THERE is no longer any immediate need to defend George Herbert
(1593–1633) against the charges of 'quaintness' brought against him
during the eighteenth and nineteenth centuries; his 'realism' in metaphor and what Coleridge described as his 'neutral style' accord well
with contemporary preferences.

'Neutral' though Herbert's style may be, he has one of the strongest
poetic personalities in English. Devotional though his poetry is – and
he certainly considered devotion the better part of poetry – it has
nothing to do with the tepid, characterless verse which we call, by
way of apology, 'devotional'. The Herbertian note is pervasive, but
it is not easy to define. First of all there is the quietness of tone, so far
removed from ecstatic exaltation, which yet allows him so incisive
and exalted a climax as 'You taught the Book of Life my name'.
Elsewhere he describes man as the 'Secretary of (God's) praise'; a
secretary has little to do with ecstasy, his concern is to be exact,
methodical, and modest.

Yet Herbert will argue with God, and the peculiar effect of rebellion and reconciliation, of complaint and resolution, is often achieved
by the alternation of long sweeping lines with short pointed ones.
The latter frequently owe their pointedness to their proverbial form
and to Herbert's Metaphysical wit, which is generally less brilliant
than Donne's and more homely and more immediately apprehended:

> Love is that liquor sweete and most divine,
> Which my God feels as blood; but I, as wine.

That is superb; there is not the slightest 'oddity'. But elsewhere –
and we can afford to admit it – the 'conceits' are sometimes a little
self-conscious and laboured; in *Prayer* (I)[1] – where among other comparisons prayer is described as 'reversed thunder' – we are aware of a
tour de force rather than of a forcefully created experience.

In imagery, Herbert is especially fond of church furniture, flowers, trees, herbs, stars, music, and the law (particularly regarding debt, for man's great debt to Christ). In this connexion, the rough obvious difference between Donne and Herbert is that while the former arrives by strange means at an unorthodox end –

> Kill, and dissect me, Love; for this
> Torture against thine own end is,
> Rack'd carcases make ill Anatomies

– the latter arrives by simple means, put to unorthodox uses, at orthodox ends; the one explores, the other reveals. Thus Herbert's *The Bag* centres on an identification of Christ's wounded side with the diplomatic bag:

> If ye have any thing to send or write,
> (I have no bag, but here is room)
> Unto my fathers hands and sight
> (Beleeve me) it shall safely come,
> That I shall minde what you impart;
> Look, you may put it very neare my heart.

Arguing with himself, or with God, Herbert makes effective use of the rhetorical question followed by the telling answer or second thought; of the 'King of grief' he demands, 'how shall I grieve for thee?':

> Shall I weep blood? Why, thou hast wept such store
> That all thy bodie was one doore. ...

Paradox, too, is one of his Metaphysical habits, and *Repentance* ends with the aphoristic line, 'Fractures well cur'd make us more strong'. But a more interesting and personal characteristic is the poet's use of personification. This often occurs so quietly that we are not conscious of it as such –

> I scarce believed,
> Till grief did tell me roundly, that I lived

– and it is found, of course, in the 'play-poem' so common in Herbert, or the dramatic parable, of which *Love* (III) is one of the most perfect examples: a volume of theological commentary lies behind each short phrase:

Love bade me welcome: yet my soul drew back,
      Guiltie of dust and sinne.
But quick-ey'd Love, observing me grow slack
      From my first entrance in,
Drew nearer to me, sweetly questioning,
      If I lack'd any thing.

A guest, I answer'd, worthy to be here:
      Love said, you shall be he.
I the unkinde, ungratefull? Ah my deare,
      I cannot look on thee.
Love took my hand, and smiling did reply,
      Who made the eyes but I?

Truth Lord, but I have marr'd them: let my shame
      Go where it doth deserve.
And know you not, sayes Love, who bore the blame?
      My deare, then I will serve.
You must sit down, sayes Love, and taste my meat:
      So I did sit and eat.

Thus *Humility* (with the Virtues and the Animals) is a mixture of masque and beast-fable, while *The World*, *Redemption*, and *The Quip* bear a certain resemblance to the morality play. *The Pilgrimage* and *Love Unknown* look forward as well as backward – to Bunyan's *The Pilgrim's Progress* – and remind us that Herbert combines in his work both courtly and popular elements:

I travell'd on, seeing the hill, where lay
      My expectation.
A long it was and weary way.
      The gloomy cave of Desperation
I left on th' one, and on the other side
      The rock of Pride.

And so I came to Fancy's meadow strow'd
      With many a flower:
Fain would I here have made abode,
      But I was quicken'd by my houre.
So to Care's copse I came, and there got through
      With much ado. ...
           The Pilgrimage

Yet we have not defined that sense of drama which is everywhere in this poetry, and is independent of personification or dialogue-form; it is identical with the freshness and vividness of his best passages, the feeling that we are now seeing, for the first time, something we had always heard about from others. The note is struck by the gentle intimacy of an opening like 'Deare Friend, sit down ...' or in the Elizabethan accent of:

> Ladies, look here; this is the thankfull glasse,
> That mends the lookers eyes: this is the well
> That washes what it shows. ...
>> *The Holy Scriptures*

It sounds more humorously in this description of an astronomer observing the stars:

> He views their stations, walks from doore to doore,
> Surveys, as if he had design'd
> To make a purchase there ...

and, with a most 'un-devotional' force, in 'My friend may spit upon my curious floor', though still in a most devout context.

That he sometimes betrays a weakness in his use of dramatic imagery must be allowed, and it may be felt that too much strain is placed on the favourite image of the box in the second section of *Good Friday*, where the heart is likened to a writing-case containing at the same time ink and sin. The breakdown in the relation between thought and metaphor is more serious in the final lines of *The Dawning*:

> Christ left his grave-clothes, that we might, when grief
> Draws tears, or bloud, not want an handkerchief.

It is a tribute to the persistence of Herbert's artistic taste that, in a poet so consciously concerned with the teaching of central Christian truths, such lapses should not occur more commonly.

Herbert's main themes are what one would expect of an Anglican minister, and foremost among them are the Incarnation, the Passion, and the Redemption. Against this debt is placed man's behaviour, both the unseemliness of his disobedience and the inadequacy of his obedience. In a similar spirit he looks quite simply (not in the manner of Marvell's *A Dialogue between the Soul and the Body*) at the dichotomy of body and soul: 'The growth of flesh is but a blister'; and considers at more length the balance between man's greatness and his lowliness. *Man* relates the former –

> Man is one world, and hath
> Another to attend him

– while *Misery* describes the reverse of the medal:

> Man is a foolish thing, a foolish thing,
> Folly and Sinne play all his game.

And, at his most cheerful, Herbert sums up in *The Church-floore*:

> Blest be the *Architect*, whose art
> Could build so strong in a weak heart.

This brings us to what is, I think, the most serious criticism Herbert's work is open to: the rather clumsy way in which the scales are occasionally weighed against earthly pleasures as opposed to heavenly bliss. There is much more of the Renaissance in Donne, even in his most fervent religious poetry, than in Herbert. 'There is no pleasure here', Herbert announces in *The Rose*, and attempts to enforce his judgement by a feeble verbal trick:

> Or if such deceits there be,
> Such delights I meant to say. ...

Humane as is his austerity in his best work – where we are not tempted to compare it with Donne's wider emotional range – 'the world, the flesh, the devil' is elsewhere set up too easily and knocked down too easily. The couplet:

> Then silly soul take heed; for earthly joye
> Is but a bubble, and makes thee a boy

betrays, by its inept rhyme, the lack of personal feeling – a formula is being repeated; and parts of *Home* impress us as mechanical, pietistic repudiation of a 'weary world' with which (the verse would here suggest) he never profoundly battled. There is an unintelligent heaviness about such outbursts; Herbert's 'sighes and groans' sometimes fall too copiously to move us. And this is not simply a question of the reader's personal preference, for we cannot but admire those poems which turn on a tactfully contrived collapse of the human before the divine, in which we experience that collapse and are not merely referred to some generalization concerning 'this world of sugared lies' which we accept or reject according to our tastes. *The Thanks-giving* is a witty poem that reaches its climax in a final relinquishment of wit, an evaporation of wit, in front of the Passion:

> Then for thy passion – I will do for that –
> Alas, my God, I know not what,

and we cannot but be convinced by the *volte-face* which concludes *The Collar* (a poem in which the typical Herbertian pattern is shown to perfection):

> But as I rav'd and grew more fierce and wilde
> At every word,
> Me thoughts I heard one calling, *Childe*:
> And I reply'd, *My Lord*.

Herbert came of a noble family, apt in the arts of war, the Court, and the mind, and Izaak Walton remarks that, while at Cambridge, 'his clothes seemed to prove that he put too great a value on his parts and parentage'. His 'parts' as a scholar were impressive, and he became University Orator, an accepted stepping-stone to high civil office. 'My birth and spirit rather took The way that takes the town', he says in a poem, but he was ordained deacon in 1625–6 and priest in 1630. It has been held that Herbert's vacillation between Court and Church was resolved by the death, around 1625, of King James and of other patrons of his, but Dr Hutchinson points out that for a man of his qualities all hopes of preferment would hardly have ended for this reason. Certainly too much has been made of the struggle between his worldly ambitions and his impulse towards a life of religious duties. In a letter to his mother written in his sixteenth year, he stated that 'my poor abilities in Poetry shall be all, and ever consecrated to God's glory'. We are not to imagine in Herbert any such division as between Jack Donne the gallant and John Donne the Dean of St Paul's, 'Apollo's first, at last, the true God's Priest'. We are told that Nicholas Ferrar (Herbert's friend and literary executor, and the founder of the religious community at Little Gidding) suffered the early temptation of 'whether there was a God, and how to be served'; Herbert's problem was the second, and never the first. Professor Knights speaks of Herbert's 'feeling of uselessness and self-distrust' and suggests that 'behind the more obvious temptation of "success" was one more deeply rooted – a dejection of spirit that tended to make him regard his own life, the life he was actually leading, as worthless and unprofitable'.

And it is true that the theme of worldly ambition and the imagery of rebellion that run through his work are linked with his sense of inadequacy as an active Christian: he chastises his feebleness by reference to the 'glory and gay weeds' of the courtier, and the implication is that so weak a servant of God might have done better as a servant of the King. In *Affliction* (I) he writes:

> I took thy sweeten'd pill, till I came neare;
> I could not go away, nor persevere.

And we must allow due weight to the words, 'nor persevere': this is the shame of inefficiency in one's profession, not of nostalgia for a different one. Barnabas Oley, writing in the mid seventeenth century, quotes Herbert as saying, 'God has broken into my study, and taken off my chariot wheels, I have nothing worthy of God'. And this discontent – hardly a selfish discontent – is silenced in the end, for 'there is no articling with thee'. His complaints of inadequacy –

> All things are busie; only I
> Neither bring honey with the bees ...

or

> I read, and sighe, and wish I were a tree;
> > For sure then I should grow
> To fruit or shade: at least some bird would trust
> Her household to me, and I should be just

– remind us of passages in the poetry of Gerard Manley Hopkins, a Jesuit priest and teacher who also suffered from ill health:

> ... birds build – but not I build; no, but strain,
> Time's eunuch, and not breed one work that wakes.

But the ultimate reconciliation is there, too; Hopkins wrote, in a letter, 'Nothing comes: I am a eunuch – but it is for the kingdom of heaven's sake'. It remains to add that Herbert's dissatisfaction is not merely personal, although it is personally felt; the final recognition is that man is by nature unable to requite his debt – even though the heart is pure, Herbert says:

> Yet one pure heart is nothing to bestow:
> In Christ two natures met to be thy cure.

Those who are sensitive enough to feel this as a personal deficiency are not always best equipped to ward off a persistent if limited melancholy which, in poetry, is merely melancholy.

But perhaps a more illuminating link between his life and his poetry may be perceived in his aspect as a parish vicar, a practical clergyman. His first task on taking orders was to rebuild the church of Leighton Bromswold and, on his induction into Fulston with Bemerton four years later, he undertook extensive repairs to both churches and to his rectory. His concern was at once with public worship – 'Down with thy knees, up with thy voice' – rather than private adoration. Further experience of practical Christianity came to him through his contact with Little Gidding, while his short country ministry reinforced both the teacher in him and, by implication, the popular elements in his style. Respecting the former, we can adduce the little book which he wrote at Bemerton, *A Priest to the Temple, or The Country Parson*, a practical guide for the practising country parson, founded on the definition that 'A Pastor is the Deputy of Christ for the reducing of Man to the Obedience of God', and purposing, through a detailed treatment of every aspect of the parson's vocation, 'to keep the middle way between superstition and slovenliness'. For his rather conscious attitude, in these last years, to the popular in his writing, we can cite a passage in which Walton says that the first sermon Herbert delivered to his parishioners was of a 'florid manner ... with great learning and eloquence', but that Herbert then told them that 'that should not be his constant way of Preaching, for, since Almighty God does not intend to lead men to heaven by hard Questions ... his language and his expressions should be more plain and practical in his future Sermons'.

It has already been suggested that for Herbert the justification of his poetic work was that

> A verse may find him, who a sermon flies,
> And turn delight into a sacrifice.

But didacticism, implying the urge towards clarity and immediate impact, is a less dangerous preoccupation, in a poet of his nature, than it usually is. It is part and parcel of his straightforwardness and of his rejection of conventional poetic devices: *Jordan* (I) is his manifesto here, 'I envy no man's nightingale or spring'; while his concern above all to be understood and useful probably served as a safeguard against eccentricity – for

> The fineness which a hymn or psalm affords,
> Is, when the soul unto the lines accords.

There is no need to suppose that this concern did not exist before he became a country rector, and we see how it agrees with the homely imagery, the recurrent box, for instance, in which either sweets or sins are kept. His attitude towards flowers is eminently practical and down-to-earth:

> Farewell, dear flowers, sweetly your time ye spent,
> Fit, while ye liv'd, for smell or ornament,
>   And after death for cures.

Despite the naïvety that has sometimes been ascribed to Herbert, his collection of poems, *The Temple*, – with its individual titles, *The Church-porch*, *The Altar*, *Church-monuments*, *Church-music*, *The Windows*, and so on – partakes of that orderly, deliberate, and business-like nature which rebuilt churches, and which, together with what Walton calls 'an almost incredible story, of the great sanctity of the short remainder of his holy life', caused his ministry of three years soon to become a classic example for the English Church. We take leave of him with a short extract from *Providence*, full of his characteristic tenderness and finely uniting his practicality with his courtesy, the country gardener with the true gentleman of the university and the town:

> Rain, do not hurt my flowers; but gently spend
> Your hony drops: presse not to smell them here:
> When they are ripe, their odour will ascend,
> And at your lodging with their thanks appeare.

* * *

Unlike Herbert, Henry Vaughan (1621–95) began by writing secular verse, either discursive or amatory. His first volume, *Poems*, contains such titles as *Les Amours* and *To Amoret: The Sigh*, and phrases like 'a woman's easy faith' and 'That face hath many servants slain'. Donne was his master here; *An Elegy* has the striking opening we associate with him – ''Tis true, I am undone' – but the poem has none of Donne's preciseness and bite, and we are more aware of a playful fancy than of the peculiar seventeenth-century imagination. *To Amoret, of the difference 'twixt him, and other Lovers* ('Just so base, sublunary lovers' hearts ...') is modelled on Donne's *A Valediction: forbidding mourning* ('Dull sublunary lovers' love ...'), but where the latter is compact, the former is dispersed and repetitive.

Perhaps another influence is to be detected: that of Herbert – the line in *To Amoret Weeping*, 'I envy no man's purse, or mines', echoes Herbert's customary forthrightness and 'I envy no man's nightingale or spring'. But despite its derivativeness, the collection hints at the kind of poetry Vaughan was later to write. *Upon the Priory Grove, his usual Retirement* anticipates that individual effect of calm and stillness which he achieves in his most famous lines, while his gift for the macrocosmic evocation is seen, if dimly, in a passage where he compares Amoret's eyes with the sun and speaks of

> ... the vast Ring
> Amidst these golden glories,
> And fiery stories. ...

The religious conversion which Vaughan experienced about the year 1648 has been attributed to the national unrest (he was a Royalist), to prolonged illness, to the death of his youngest brother. Vaughan himself, in the preface to the second edition of *Silex Scintillans* (1655), seems to ascribe it to Herbert: 'The first, that with any effectual success attempted a diversion of this foul and overflowing stream [i.e. of 'witty' amatory verse], was the blessed man, Mr George Herbert, whose holy life and verse gained many pious Converts (of whom I am the least) and gave the first check to a most flourishing wit of his time.'

From *Silex Scintillans*, the volume that contains his essential contribution to English poetry, we should quickly deduce that, in poetry at least, he was a 'convert' of George Herbert. The borrowings are abundant and unashamed. Thus,

> I have deserv'd a thick, Egyptian damp,
> > Dark as my deeds,
> Should *mist* within me, and put out that lamp
> > Thy spirit feeds
>
> > *The Relapse*

obviously derives from this passage in *The Temple*:

> I have deserv'd that an Egyptian night
> Should thicken all my powers; because my lust,
> Hath still sow'd fig-leaves to exclude thy light
>
> > *Sighs and Groans*

and even the volume's subtitle is taken from Herbert's title-page. Correspondences of this kind, both to *The Temple* and to Owen Felltham's prose *Resolves* (first edition c. 1620), are listed in the notes to Mr L. C. Martin's edition of Vaughan, and Dr Hutchinson remarks that 'there is no example in English literature of one poet borrowing so extensively from another'.

An examination of several passages in which Vaughan is clearly remembering something of Herbert's is useful in bringing out both the former's weaknesses and his originality. Our general impression is that Vaughan's advantage over Herbert lies in his longer breath, his greater fluency, and in what at first seems a more positive vitality. On the other hand, Vaughan is sadly lacking in Herbert's sense of climax – his poems generally go on a little too long – and his imagery (on the whole more intellectual and 'elevated' than the elder poet's: the recurrent image is no longer 'box' but 'star') lacks the dramatic liveliness whereby Herbert's justifies itself. *Regeneration*, the opening poem of *Silex Scintillans*, is Vaughan's equivalent of Herbert's *The Pilgrimage*; it has the same parable-form and the same theme – the necessity of struggling on in spite of hardship and disappointment. We see that Herbert is more 'primitive', nearer to the morality (to Bunyan, too), simple and dramatic. Vaughan is noticeably less simple and less dramatic, in a sense more 'personal' because less traditional. He gives the impression of going farther, perhaps because he shows us fewer landmarks. And it may be felt that parable-form is not altogether suitable for this more personal, more esoteric utterance; we are not always sure of how to interpret something that calls for interpretation:

> I wonder'd much, but tir'd
> At last with thought. ...

Vaughan is more suggestive, mysterious, than Herbert, and the poem contains some striking natural description; but he leaves us 'wondering' where Herbert leaves us *knowing*.

Didacticism enters into Vaughan's work – notably in *Rules and Lessons*, which reminds us of *The Church-porch*, though its instructions are less directly practical and down-to-earth – but it is much less pervasive than in *The Temple*. Vaughan has not the same compulsion to be understood. Here, as elsewhere, we find him, in comparison with Herbert, moving towards nineteenth-century romanticism, where the individual is the great theme rather than the social or religious community.

Vaughan, too, is concerned with the dichotomy of body and soul – especially in relation to the Resurrection – and, more important, with the Incarnation and the Passion, though he displays a less personal anguish than Herbert at man's ingratitude and lack of merit. In his inconstancy, man is contrasted with the natural creation – with birds, bees, and flowers:

> I would (said I) my God would give
> The staidness of these things to man!

And the 'fair, order'd lights' of *The Constellation* make him think of the 'Obedience, Order, Light' which man has not achieved. The injunction, 'Observe God in his works', suggests an aspect of Vaughan's originality: parts of 'And do they so?' call Wordsworth to mind:

> Go go; Seal up thy looks,
> And burn thy books –

though the lesson which Nature will teach is rather more precise. The similarities between Wordsworth's *Intimations of Immortality* and the attitude towards childhood of Vaughan and of his contemporary, Thomas Traherne, are too well known to need much comment here. Vaughan associates childhood with 'whiteness', the symbol of purity;

'dear, harmless age', it is also 'an age of mysteries'. Thus *The Retreat* runs parallel with *Intimations of Immortality* for a part of the way:

> When yet I had not walkt above
> A mile, or two, from my first love,
> And looking back (at that short space)
> Could see a glimpse of his bright-face. ...
>
> *The Retreat*

> ... the growing Boy
> ... beholds the light, and whence it flows. ...
> The Youth, who daily farther from the east
> Must travel, still is Nature's Priest,
> And by the vision splendid
> Is on his way attended. ...
>
> *Intimations of Immortality*

But their paths soon divide: Wordsworth declares himself an early-nineteenth-century thinker, while Vaughan emerges as a seventeenth-century religious 'metaphysical' – for *The Retreat*, one of his finest poems, one of the few that are exactly the right length, is not far from Donne in its 'wit', its compactness, and the physical reality of phrases like (the borrowed) 'bright shoots of everlastingness'.

Before leaving this point it should be remarked that there is a relation between the state of childhood and that of man in those other 'early days', after the expulsion from Eden. In *Corruption* he writes:

> Man in those early days
> Was not all stone, and Earth. ...
> He saw Heaven o'er his head, and knew from whence
> He came (condemned), hither ...
> still *Paradise* lay
> In some green shade, or fountain.

Both poets lament the loss of 'a white, Celestial thought' or 'celestial light' (in Traherne, 'my pure primitive virgin light'), but Vaughan, whose desiderations are more precise than Wordsworth's – the God whose nearness he describes in these nostalgic poems is more 'present' than the later poet's – finds less consolation here and now. Wordsworth was readier, in Herbert's words, to 'rest in Nature, not the God of Nature'.

Vaughan, then, is more interested in natural creation, in the nature of the country, than Herbert; it conducts him to the creator – 'rural shades are the sweet fence Of piety and innocence' – but he delights in it on the way. Yet *The Search* indicates how he is, by comparison, 'unworldly'. This poem has the final turnabout which we met in *The Temple*, the short answer to a lengthy question. 'Me thought I heard one singing thus' – and it is perhaps significant of Vaughan's greater elaborateness that the voice should be 'singing' instead of 'calling' (see Herbert's *The Collar*):

> Search well another world; who studies this
> Travels in Clouds, seeks *Manna*, where none is.

Herbert at least found manna through the imagery of this world; his 'convert' is more abstract in his language, more declamatory, and more leisurely.

This being so, it says much for the strength of the Metaphysical wit tradition that it should so often save his work from shapelessness. We may instance the poem which begins 'Joy of my life!'; it moves freely from stars to the saints, who are 'shining lights', 'candles', 'our Pillar-fires', or indeed the 'shining spires' of the City 'we travel to'. The poem seems about to disintegrate, but the final image, evoking the flaming sword in Eden, succeeds in pulling it together:

> A swordlike gleame
> Kept man for sin
> First *Out*; This beame
> Will guide him *In*.

On Herbert's ground, Vaughan is no match for him. But there is a handful of poems in which Vaughan appears as a distinctive figure both in the seventeenth century and in English poetry. These poems – and notable among them are *The Retreat*, *Peace*, *Ascension Hymn*, *Quickness*, *Regeneration* (in parts), and *The World* – turn on images of peace, majesty, security, and controlled power, 'an illuminated vision', in Dr Hutchinson's words, 'of the universe, newly apprehended':

> I saw Eternity the other night
> Like a great *Ring* of pure and endless light,
>   All calm, as it was bright,
> And round beneath it, Time in hours, days, years
>   Driv'n by the spheres
> Like a vast shadow mov'd, In which the world
>   And all her train were hurl'd. ...

They might seem to have been written, in T. S. Eliot's phrase, 'at the still point of the turning world'; but perhaps their peculiar quality is hinted at by Vaughan himself:

> But life is, what none can express,
> *A quickness, which my God hath kissed.*

* * *

Richard Crashaw (1612/13–49) is a very different kind of poet. His relation to Herbert is much slighter than might be supposed from the title of his first volume of English verse, *Steps to the Temple*, for his temple is Catholic, baroque, and Italian. The son of a Puritan rector for whom the Pope was Antichrist, Crashaw came under the Laudian High Church influence at Cambridge – he was a frequent visitor at Little Gidding – and turned to Roman Catholicism, probably in 1645, when it seemed that the 'middle way' of Anglicanism could not survive. (For the religious background to this essay, readers are referred to Part I of the present volume.) At his death Crashaw held a minor position at the Cathedral of the Holy House at Loreto. He is pre-eminently the English poet of the Counter-Reformation.

If Herbert can be related to the popular sermon and the morality play, then Crashaw must be related to Catholic ritual and the masque. Thus *Epiphany*, 'A Hymn, sung as by the Three Kings', with three solo parts and chorus, is quite operatic in form, while *The Mother of Sorrows* opens in the Handelian manner:

> In shade of death's sad TREE
> Stood Doleful SHE.
> Ah SHE! now by none other
> Name to be known, alas, but SORROW'S MOTHER.

The Sorrows are rendered remote and impersonal by their rhetorical, repetitive, and ornate presentation. We understand why the reader should not be invited to identify himself with the 'Sancta Maria Dolorum': there are to be no unseemly grovellings in the aisles; on the other hand, there is the danger that he will experience nothing – or, at any rate, nothing that could not have been prompted by some accepted aid to devotion.

Examining *The Weeper*, a series of variations on the theme of the Magdalene's tears, we realize that, though Crashaw's poems are often longer than Herbert's or Vaughan's, his poetic breath is really shorter, for his poetry is continually stopping and restarting. Some of the variations betray a lack of humour – a 'brisk cherub' sips the tears 'And his song/Tastes of this Breakfast all day long' – but others have the true dignity of the seventh stanza*. Crashaw's first publication was a collection of 'sacred epigrams', and it is the epigrammatic aspect of his work that most nearly approaches the Metaphysical school; it emerges here in

> O wit of love! that thus could place
> Fountain and Garden in one face,

and it endows the poem with an occasional and welcome neatness and intellectual force:

> Others by moments, months, and years
> Measure their ages; thou, by TEARS,

and, indeed, in its last lines *The Weeper* achieves a climax rare in Crashaw: the tears themselves take over the burden:

> We got to meet
> A worthy object, our lord's FEET.

Notorious in Crashaw's work is his sensuousness, and in particular his use, in picturing sacred love, of the metaphors – indeed, the atmosphere – of human love, both of mother for child and of man for woman. This sensuousness is rather ambiguously present in his handling of spiritual and physical torture: 'blood' and 'milk' are his characteristic references:

> To see both blended in one flood,
> The Mothers' Milk, the Children's blood,
> Makes me doubt if Heaven will gather,
> *Roses* hence, or *Lilies* rather.
> > *Upon the Infant Martyrs*

The reader may feel faintly repelled, but not shocked, for the verse has no immediacy; the experience reaches us at second hand, as if the poet is describing the picture of something and not the thing itself.[2]

The ornate, decorative image – the 'baroque conceit'[3] – is the very

---

* Numbering of the version published in 1648 and 1652.

basis of Crashaw's poetry; it is lovingly handled, but sometimes too lovingly fondled. An English taste is unlikely to find any poem entirely successful, for the locks between one level of imagery and another do not always function smoothly; but Crashaw's finest poem, as an *English* poet, is the *Hymn to Saint Teresa*. One welcomes the direct and firm opening – 'Love, thou art Absolute sole lord/OF LIFE & DEATH' – and the passage which follows:

> Those thy old Souldiers, Great and tall,
> Ripe Men of Martyrdom, that could reach down
> With strong armes, their triumphant crown;
> Such as could with lusty breath
> Speak loud into the face of death
> Their Great LORD's glorious name ...

is dramatic and unusually masculine for Crashaw. Teresa's childhood is related with that sweet tenderness, quite distinct from Herbert's or Vaughan's, for which this poet must be prized:

> She'll to the Moores; And trade with them,
> For this unvalued Diadem.
> She'll offer them her dearest Breath,
> With CHRIST's Name in't, in change for death.

And though the hymn is weakened by a cloud of abstractions ('WORKS ... SUFFERINGS ... TEARES ... WRONGS ...'), from time to time 'large draughts of intellectual day' shine out in phrases like

> 'Tis LOVE, not YEARES or LIMBS that can
> Make the Martyr, or the man.

In the previous paragraph I stressed the word *English* by way of suggesting that, though Crashaw's work is in a tradition, that tradition is not English. It is an Italian school, the 'conceited' school of Marino, to which he properly belongs, and what one misses in him is the Saxon contribution to our tradition, the forthright, masculine, and earthy elements of our literature. It is not an adequate defence of his use of English to describe him as 'primarily a European'. And one does not, finally, complain of over-excitement, 'ecstaticness', but rather the opposite; the individual beads are highly coloured, yet the fingers that thread them are cold and even mechanical. The prevailing mood, as Professor Willey has remarked, is 'at once inflamed and relaxed'. The artist who creates is, here, too separate from the martyr who suffers, and often the ecstasy is left outside, outside the language and outside our response; a formal, public act of worship which tastes simultaneously of the cathedral, the stage, and the study.

* * *

In moving from Herbert through Vaughan to Crashaw, we have noticed an increasing 'romanticism' in their work – it is not merely because of similarities in belief that Vaughan has been likened to Wordsworth and Crashaw to Francis Thompson. While this implies a certain liberation, an increased lyricism, a greater evocativeness, it also means a certain loss in intellectual impact. A comparative evaluation of 'romantic' and 'metaphysical' lies, happily, outside the scope of this essay, but it may be remarked in concluding that what we value in seventeenth-century Metaphysical poetry is, in its simplest terms, the union of hard thinking with deep feeling.

NOTES

1. Reference is to *The Works of George Herbert*, ed. F. E. Hutchinson, where numbering is adopted if two or more poems have the same title.

2. Reference may be made to *English Emblem Books* (1948), by Rosemary Freeman. Miss Freeman tends to overstress emblematic qualities in Herbert, but what she says is certainly relevant to Crashaw. Whereas Crashaw describes the emblem, Herbert makes it unnecessary.

3. See the essay 'On Metaphysical Poetry', by James Smith, in *Determinations* (1934), ed. F. R. Leavis.

THE CAVALIER POETS

BY GEOFFREY WALTON

Professor of English, Makerere College, the University College of East Africa

To appreciate the poetry associated in varying degrees of intimacy with the Court of Charles I requires, I believe, certain important mental and emotional readjustments. One is not dealing with major poetry – though there are several major poems – and therefore it is necessary to feel an especially close sympathy with the social and cultural attitudes and interests of a particular group of men and women in particular surroundings. This poetry embodies more of the life and culture of upper-class pre-Commonwealth England than do any of the other arts. It is learned and theologically minded. It is at once eminently English and strongly influenced by the classical and cosmopolitan interests – and affectations – of its writers and public. The Court was, needless to say, not puritanical, but the tone of most of the lyric poetry suggests that it was addressed to social equals, though we do not now know their names.

Cavalier poetry presents a surprising mixture of elegance and sophistication with naïvety and schoolboy obscenity, but it is rarely vulgar or sneering. One senses these qualities in reading. Further knowledge of the way of life that produced it helps to explain the paradoxical qualities. One comes to realize that in submitting oneself, with the efforts involved, to the effect of the poetry, one is submitting oneself to the influence of a phase of English civilization.[1] Our relationship with these knights and squires is a fairly close one. Their way and manner of speaking comes out directly in

> I tell thee, fellow, who'er thou be,
> That made this fine sing-song of me,
>   Thou art a rhyming sot.
>
> (Suckling)

> Now you have freely given me leave to love
>   What will you doe?
>
> (Carew)

or again in:

> Hearke, reader! wilt be learn'd i' th' wars?
>
> (Lovelace)

The idiom is the conversation of the Court circles in all its variety, cultivated and colloquial, with that tendency to the racy and the slipshod which has been characteristic of English aristocratic speech ever since the speech of the educated became formalized, and which has produced so remarkable a succession of literary achievements from this time to Byron's.[2]

The body of Cavalier poetry is remarkably homogeneous, as perhaps the foregoing generalities have suggested. The four or five principal talents have certain individually distinctive qualities, but the lesser figures can be more easily classified as being better or worse poets or as being nearer to, or farther from, their masters than by personal characteristics. As the poetic masters of these poets, Donne and Jonson formed an almost ideal partnership, at once stimulating and disciplining, arousing exuberant feeling and ingenious elaboration of the fancy and exerting a dignified restraint and a sensitive literary tact.[3] The influence of Donne is the most obvious. One has cases of the direct imitation of his conceits, such as Carew's *Upon a Ribband*:

> This silken wreath, which circles in mine arme,
> Is but an Emblem of that mystique charme,
> Wherewith the magique of your beauties binds
> My captive soul ...

which is clearly based on *The Funerall*. One also finds the wider influence of themes and attitudes. Donne's *The Extasie* and *A Valediction, forbidding Mourning* are behind a long series of poems, including Lord Herbert's *Ode upon a Question moved, Whether Love should continue for ever?*, Lovelace's *To Lucasta, going beyond the Seas*, and Suckling's *To Mistress Cicely Crofts*, which characteristically reverses the theme:

> There rests but this, that whilst we sorrow here,
>   Our bodies may draw near;
> And when no more their joys they can extend,
> Then let our Souls begin where they did end.

Beyond this again is, of course, the spirit of Metaphysical wit, that
source of imaginative strength which enabled more or less irresponsible young men about Court to analyse their feelings and build up
sustained poetic arguments, and to bring into their poetry their miscellaneous dabblings in theology, philosophy, natural science, and
whatever else caught their interest. The Cavalier elegies on Donne
make their debts to him explicit and, if one allows for the customary
obituary hyperbole, show in at least one case remarkable critical insight and power of definition; while their couplets clearly derive
from his *Satyres* and the *Anniversaries*. From the work of Lord Herbert,
Falkland, Carew, Mayne, Cartwright, Godolphin, and Porter – the
last almost neo-classically elegant – one must select Carew's (1595 ?–
1640?) for examination. He presents a very full account of Donne as
a 'reformer and preserver of the English tongue' in poetry, e.g.:

> The Muses garden with Pedantique weedes
> O'rspred, was purg'd by thee; The lazie seeds
> Of servile imitation throwne away,
> And fresh invention planted, Thou didst pay
> The debts of our penurious bankrupt age;
> Licentious thefts, that make poetique rage
> A Mimique fury, when our soules must bee
> Possest, or with Anacreons Extasie,
> Or Pindars, not their owne; The subtle cheat
> Of slie Exchanges, and the jugling feat
> Of two-edg'd words, or whatsoever wrong
> By ours was done the Greeke, or Latine tongue,
> Thou hast redeem'd, and open'd Us a Mine
> Of Rich and pregnant phansie, drawne a line
> Of masculine expression. ...

One only wonders why he instances Pindar and Anacreon rather than
Petrarch.

Jonsonus Virbius and other complimentary verses establish Jonson
in a corresponding position. The majority of the Cavaliers had been
admitted to the 'Tribe of Ben', and liked to call themselves his 'Sons';
Suckling celebrates rather disrespectfully a *Session of the Poets*. In their
poems the tribe naturally take his work as a whole, or his dramatic
work in particular and, as he had taught them, stress its moral value.
Once more, out of poems by Falkland, May, Habington, Waller,

Cleveland, Mayne, Cartwright, Carew, Lord Herbert, Suckling, and
Randolph one selects Carew's for his fine verse, his tact in dealing
with an embarrassing situation – Jonson's *Ode to Himself*, which
Carew feels to be a tragic lapse of taste – and his exact reference to the
lyrics and their classical ancestry:

> Repine not at the Tapers thriftie waste,
> That sleekes thy terser Poems, nor in haste
> Prayse, but excuse; and if thou overcome
> A knottie writer, bring the bootie home. ...

The Cavaliers were following Jonson when they naturalized the
themes of Catullus and other Latin lyrists. His influence on them
was an example of careful art – 'no matter how slow the style be at
first, so it be laboured and accurate; seek the best, and be not glad
of ... first words ...' (*Timber*) – urbanity of tone and control of
emotion, rather than as a source of images and phrases. Rough as he
was in himself, he taught them how to put the tone of the gentleman
into poetry:

> Aske me no more where *Jove* bestowes,
> When *June* is past, the fading rose:
> For in your beauties orient deepe,
> These flowers as in their causes, sleepe

shows Carew combining both Metaphysical and Classical material
with courtly elegance. On the other hand, Lovelace's

> Strive not, vain Lover, to be fine,
> Thy silk's the Silkworms, and not thine;
> You lessen to a Fly your Mistris Thought,
> To think it may be in a Cobweb caught ...

restates 'Still to be neat ...' from the opposite side, and also gives it a
more solemn moral note.

If one takes the principal 'Sons of Ben' in approximate order of
seniority, one obtains a fairly clear picture of how Cavalier poetry
developed as the years went on. Lord Herbert (1583–1648) scarcely
qualifies for the rather vague title of 'Son of Ben' or, on account of
his seniority, as a Cavalier, but his lyrics, such as 'Come hither,
womankind', 'I am the first that ever lov'd' and

If you refuse me once, and think again
I will complain,
You are deceiv'd: love is no work of Art,
It must be got and born,
Not made and worn,
Or such wherein you have no part

decidedly have the tone and accent of the group, and he was associated with his 'witty Carew' in that his *A Description* was apparently
the occasion for the latter's *Complement*, and in the disputed authorship of 'Now you have freely given me leave to love.'

Herrick (1591–1674) belongs much less to the tradition, though he
was a member of the 'Tribe' and celebrated its meetings in verse.[4]
He also wrote a fine portrait of *His Cavalier*:

> Give me that man that dares bestride
> The active sea-horse, and with pride,
> Through the huge field of waters ride:
> Who, with his looks too, can appease
> The ruffling winds and raging seas,
> In mid'st of all their outrages.
> This, this a virtuous man can doe,
> Saile against rocks, and split them too;
> I! and a world of pikes passe through.

But the Metaphysical manner is beyond Herrick's powers of imagination and he lacks Jonson's polished technique and emotional
discipline. *Upon Julia's Clothes*:

> When as in silks my Julia goes,
> Then, then (me thinks) how sweetly flowes
> The liquefaction of her clothes

has some of their strength and elegance. 'Gather ye rosebuds' is a
pleasant version of the '*Carpe diem*' theme, but it lacks complexity.
His epitaphs and poems on children are, if placed beside Jonson's,
sentimental. Herrick is a poet of a charmingly fanciful but simple
sensibility. *Corinna's going a-Maying* is in the sixteenth-century convention, with its mass of flowery imagery and naïve medley of

classical allusions and colloquial phrases. Its virtue is in its very lack of discipline:

> Get up, get up for shame, the Blooming Morne
> Upon her wings presents the god unshorne.
> See how *Aurora* throwes her faire
> Fresh-quilted colours through the aire.
> Get-up, sweet-Slug-a-bed, and see
> The Dew bespangling Herbe and Tree.
> Each Flower has wept, and bow'd towards the East
> Above an houre since; yet you are not drest,
> Nay! not so much as out of bed?
> When all the Birds have Mattens seyd,
> And sung their thankfull Hymnes: 'tis sin,
> Nay, profanation to keep in,
> When as a thousand Virgins on this day
> Spring, sooner than the Lark, to fetch in May.

Herrick undoubtedly had a real feeling for flowers and trees and for country customs and beliefs, as one sees them in *Night-piece to Julia*, *Fairies*, *A Country Life*, and *The Hock Cart*, despite his complaints at 'banishment' from London.

One finds the great house and the idealized patriarchal community again in Carew's *To Saxham* and *To my friend, G.N.* Both these poems are heavily dependent on Jonson's *Penshurst*, but the fact that a man like Carew could write them at all shows, I think, that Charles I's courtiers – Carew is one of the most urban as well as urbane – had not entirely forgotten their social responsibilities and the quality of life outside London. *In Answer of an Elegiacall Letter upon the death of the King of Sweden* puts the Court before us – and a pastoral masque. If Carew is perhaps not a major poet, he has certainly been under- as much as Herrick has been over-rated. He has, as Sir Herbert Grierson says, a deeper vein of thought than one might expect from a gay and frivolous Court official; the two influences of Donne and Jonson are fused in him by a considerable native talent. Borrowings from Donne are comparatively rare in his work, but imitations of Marino and other continental poets show the width of his culture. His poems on Donne and Jonson show not only his immense admiration for them but also his critical intelligence and power of sustained thinking in verse. This intelligence is the controlling force in his lyrics.

Let us examine his *To my Inconstant Mistris*:

> When thou, poore excommunicate
>   From all the joyes of love, shalt see
> The full reward, and glorious fate,
>   Which my strong faith shall purchase me,
>   Then curse thine owne inconstancie.
>
> A fayrer hand than thine, shall cure
>   That heart, which thy false oathes did wound;
> And to my soule, a soule more pure
>   Than thine, shall by Loves hand be bound,
>   And both with equall glory crown'd.
>
> Then shalt thou weepe, entreat, complaine
>   To Love, as I did once to thee;
> When all thy teares shall be as vaine
>   As mine were then, for thou shalt be
>   Damn'd for thy false Apostasie.

We begin with a characteristic religious conceit to express with suitable force his rejection of his mistress for her infidelity; it is worth noting that Roman Catholic practices were respected at the Court of Henrietta Maria. Faith, in fact, connotes both his religion of love and his own constancy in it which contrasts with the lady's lack of that quality. But the blasphemous exaggeration together with the sarcastic note of line 1, and the angry off-hand last line of the stanza, give an undertone of mockery to the whole. Carew has a critical anti-Petrarchan attitude, but he is not writing a solemn denunciation. He continues his attack in the next stanza with a closely argued statement, in firm sinuous rhythms, of his relationship to his new mistress; he is polite but delicately ironical ('a soule more pure Than thine'). The new mistress is canonized in glory along with him, and the old is 'damn'd', both according to the convention of worship and also by Carew's real anger. The first three and a half lines of the last stanza have the accent and manner of the man speaking his mind. Though the poem's solemnity may be mock solemnity, a deeper seriousness seems to emerge at this point. Such complexity is typical of Carew at his best. His lyrics are conventional verse in the best sense; that is, the convention really corresponded to an actual way of thinking and feeling, and the lyrics had their accepted and recognized place in the relationship between men and women. 'Give me more love, or more disdaine ...' loses nothing from the fact that Godolphin and Lovelace, and no doubt others, followed out its argument exactly or that Petrarch or Jonson ('Or scorne or pittie on me take ...') may have given the hint. *To a Lady that desired I would love her*, if it be his, is both more conversational and slangy and more serious:

> Then give me leave to love, and love me too,
>   Not with designe
> To rayse, as Loves curst Rebells doe,
>   When puling Poets whine,
> Fame to their beautie, from their blubbr'd eyne.
>
> Griefe is a puddle, and reflects not cleare
>   Your beauties rayes,
> Joyes are pure streames, your eyes appeare
>   Sullen in sadder layes,
> In chearfull numbers they shine bright with prayse.

It is a highly individual lyric, using, later, 'Wounds, flames and darts' with an air of freshness and almost of originality.

The wit of Carew includes, besides his Metaphysical scope of imagery and intellectually critical discipline, this urbanity or sense of social fitness. His attitude is related to chivalry, but is more sophisticated and more egalitarian as between the sexes. Though he is often critical and even angry with Celia, whoever, or however many, the name represents, he is not cynical or coarse – *A Rapture* is frankly luxurious and sensual – or familiar; there is always present something of the respect with which he regards the Countess of Anglesey, while there is at the same time a certain freedom in his attitude to her:

> You, whose whole life
> In every act crown'd you a constant Wife,
> May spare the practice of that vulgar trade,
> Which superstitious custome onely made;
> Rather a Widow now of wisedome prove
> The patterne, as a Wife you were of love:
> Yet since you surfet on your griefe, 'tis fit
> I tell the world, upon what cares you sit
> Glutting your sorrowes; and at once include
> His story, your excuse, my gratitude.

Carew looks forward to the manners of the Augustans, but he is not so formal as they tend to be and he has a more intimate personal delicacy. His elegies have this poise and balance of phrase and emotion. *Maria Wentworth* is in the great tradition of seventeenth-century elegies and exemplifies particularly a well-known feature of wit not yet dwelt on, the blending of the light and even humorous with the solemn:

> And here the precious dust is layd;
> Whose purely-tempered Clay was made
> So fine, that it the guest betray'd.
>
> Else the soule grew so fast within,
> It broke the outward shell of sinne,
> And so was hatch'd a Cherubin.

Finally, *To my worthy friend Master Geo. Sand* must be mentioned to show the full range of Carew's poetic achievement. Written near the end of his life and the end of an epoch, it has an urbane reverence:

> I presse not to the Quire, nor dare I greet
> The holy place with my unhallowed feet;
> My unwasht Muse ...

and 'a holy mirth' and a profound sense of sin and penitence are realized in magnificent Metaphysical imagery and solemn, emphatic Donnean rhythms:

> Though nor in tune, nor wing, she reach thy Larke,
> Her Lyrick feet may dance before the Arke.
> Who knowes, but that her wandering eyes that run,
> Now hunting Glow-wormes, may adore the Sun,
> A pure flame may, shot by Almighty power
> Into her brest, the earthy flame devoure.
> My eyes, in penitentiall dew may steepe
> That brine, which they for sensuall love did weepe.
> So (though 'gainst Natures course) fire may be quencht
> With fire, and water be with water drencht.

The biographical background of this does not concern us here. It is enough that Carew has a sense of values and has written a great poem. Something that one may risk calling the poetic spirit of the age, its richly imaginative sensibility, has inspired him to write above his usual self without, at the same time, borrowing from his masters.

Sir John Suckling (1609–42) needs less attention. The double influence shows itself again, but Suckling is far less urbane and civilized than Carew and, though he wrote a prose work on religion, far less serious as a poet. His delicacy of imagination, such as it is, his fluency – he criticized Carew as laboured – and his uninhibited and boisterous cynicism come out in:

> Hast thou seen the down in the air,
>   When the wanton blasts have toss'd it?
> Or the ship on the sea,
>   When the ruder waves have cross'd it?
> Hast thou mark'd the crocodile's weeping,
>   Or the fox's sleeping?
> Or hast view'd the peacock in his pride,
>   Or the dove by his bride,
>   When he courts for his lechery?
> O, so fickle, O, so vain, O, so false, so false is she?

'Out upon it, I have lov'd ...' turns the attitude on himself. His language is racier and more careless than Carew's.

> 'Tis not the meat, but 'tis the appetite
>   Makes eating a delight,
>   And if I like one dish
> More than another, that a Pheasant is ...

shows how thoughtlessly he can throw off a conceit to express his feeling about a woman. In Dryden's *Essay of Dramatic Poesy* Lord Buckhurst as Eugenius is made to say that none of his contemporaries in drama 'expresses so much the conversation of a gentleman, as Sir John Suckling'. The spirit of his poetry, the controlling wit, is a good sense or horse sense, and the social tone belongs to a masculine company – his most urbane poem is probably 'My dearest rival ...'. *A Ballad upon a Wedding* is a charming dramatic achievement. Suckling knows just how to assume the manner of the 'awe-struck' yeoman without being patronizing, and he gives an ironic glance at good society at the end. Perhaps the poem implies the kind of underlying sympathy with the rural community that caused Carew to write *To Saxham*.

His forthright Royalist *Answer*, quoted at the beginning of this chapter, reminds us of the Cavalier exemplar, Richard Lovelace (1618–58). He is a very uneven poet and often seems both careless and amateurish. His finer sensibility, however, redeems the clumsiness of his syntax, and he is a poet of very varied interest. His famous lyrics to Lucasta and Althea, *A Mock Song* and, with them, Montrose's 'My dear and only love ...' voice the Cavalier attitude at its best to life and to the war. We find here the surviving code of chivalry and the public values of the seventeenth-century country gentleman expressed with great clarity and with intellectual ingenuity and sophistication of tone. Lovelace is not on Marvell's level of intelligence, but he is not a simpleton – he is a courtier and a soldier of European culture; beside his work, the revolutionary and nationalist ardours of the Romantics of his class seem crude. One sees the more private interests of the Kentish squire, and once again the rural roots of the Cavaliers, in another interesting group of poems, *The Ant, The Snail, The Toad and the Spider, The Falcon*, and *The Grasshopper*. These combine first-hand observations of nature with superstition, and traditional knowledge of field sports with literary allusion and inoffensive moralizing in a manner very characteristic of the early seventeenth century. The following examples must suffice:

> Look up, then, miserable Ant, and spie
>   Thy fatal foes, for breaking of her law,
> Hov'ring above thee, Madam, *Margaret Pie*,
>   And her fierce servant, Meagre – Sir *John Daw*;
> Thy Self and Storehouse now they do store up,
> And thy whole Harvest too within their Crop.

> Thus we unthrifty thrive within Earths Tomb
>   For some more rav'nous and ambitious Jaw:
> The *Grain* in th' *Ants*, the *Ants* in the *Pie's* womb,
>   The *Pie* in th' *Hawk's*, the *Hawk's* i' th' *Eagle's* maw:
> So scattering to hord 'gainst a long Day,
> Thinking to save all, we cast all away.

and the deservedly famous

> O thou that swing'st upon the waving haire
>   Of some well-filled Oaten Beard,
> Drunke ev'ry night on a delicious teare,
>   Dropt thee from Heav'n where now thou art rear'd. ...

It must not, incidentally, be forgotten that *The Grasshopper* is an invitation to conviviality of which the insect is supposed to set an example. *A Loose Saraband* is even more bacchanalian:

> Lord! What is man and sober?

Poetry of this quality on themes of all these kinds would seem to end with Lovelace and his friends, such as Charles Cotton. Charles II's 'mob of gentlemen' are inferior even in drinking songs.

Lovelace's love poetry has similar qualities – freshness and exuberance, a delicacy and strength of fancy, and a courtly tone. He is not often vulgar like Suckling, but sometimes has a deeper cynicism that surprises one. *The Scrutinie* is tough and detached in the manner of Donne's *Communitie*. He has some brilliant contracted conceits, such as:

> Like the Sun in's early ray,
> But shake your head and scatter day.
> > *To Amarantha*

or :

> Not yet look back, not yet; must we
> Run then like spoakes in wheeles eternally,
> And never overtake?

from *A Forsaken Lady to her False Servant*, a fine dramatic monologue in couplets. *Ellinda's Glove* is equally brilliant at greater length:

> Thou snowy Farm with thy five Tenements!
> > Tell thy white Mistris here was one
> > That call'd to pay his dayly rents;
> But she a-gathering Flowers and Hearts is gone,
> And thou left void to rude Possession. ...

Gratiana Dancing and Singing, another large-scale conceit, is at once ingenious, rhythmically subtle, and also a little clumsy:

> See! with what constant Motion,
> Even and glorious as the Sun,
> > *Gratiana* steers that Noble Frame,
> Soft as her breast, sweet as her voyce
> That gave each winding law and poiz,
> > And swifter than the wings of Fame.

She beat the happy Pavement
By such a Starre made Firmament,
   Which now no more the Roofe envies,
But swells up high with *Atlas* ev'n,
Bearing the brighter, nobler Heav'n,
   And, in her, all the Deities. ...

Lovelace was never a 'Son of Ben', and there seems to be a lack of his disciplining influence over the suns and flowers that burst forth a little too brightly in this poetry. The gentle, courtly tone is Lovelace's own contribution, and owes nothing directly to others. But this sometimes lapses badly; the vital elements of irony and humour fall into abeyance and exaggeration effects get out of control. I think that this is the defect, rather than mere indecency as Dr Johnson and the nineteenth-century critics thought, of such things as:

   Heere wee'll strippe and cool our fire
   In Creame below, in milke-baths higher;
     And when all Wells are drawne dry,
    I'll drink a teare out of thine eye.

or *Lucasta taking the Waters at Tunbridge* or *Love made in the First Age*; there is also the 'reverend lady cow' in *Amarantha*. If Suckling foreshadows the tone of Charles II's Court, Lovelace by these flaws in the quality of his wit gives an indication that the Donne-Jonson aristocratic synthesis was breaking up with the Court that had cherished it.

NOTES

1. See Part I and also Professor L. C. Knights' 'Social Background of Metaphysical Poetry' in *Scrutiny* XIII (1945) for further information and reflections on this theme.

2. There is a very interesting, and disagreement-provoking, article by Mr M. Bewley. 'The Colloquial Mode of Byron', in *Scrutiny* XVI (1949). He writes on Lovelace and more minor Cavaliers.

3. See chapter I of F. R. Leavis's *Revaluation* for a further discussion of this, and also Sir Herbert Grierson's Introduction to *Metaphysical Poetry* for a different point of view. Mr G. Williamson, in *The Donne Tradition*, handles the subject in more detail.

4. In *English Literature in the Earlier XVIIth Century*, chapter IV, Professor D. Bush describes Herrick's work in similar terms to mine, but places him in a relatively higher position – in fact, the conventional one.

MILTON'S RELIGIOUS VERSE

BY L. A. CORMICAN

Principal, St Patrick's College, University of Ottawa

OF all the great figures in English literature, Milton is in several ways the most controversial. No writer, except Shakespeare, has been so continuously admired; no teacher, except perhaps Bunyan, has been so revered by so many generations. Yet since Addison's famous remark in 1712 that our language 'sunk under him', there have been many derogatory criticisms not merely of details but of whole aspects of his work. It is impossible to read Milton without feeling that we are in the presence of a great mind; yet even critics who have praised him most highly have felt it was necessary to come devoutly and staunchly to his defence.

The reasons for this long-standing diversity of opinion form a useful introduction to his work. To both the general reader and the professional critic, Milton presents special difficulties which, if they cannot be overcome, must at least be recognized. In the first place, he has built lengthy works out of religious convictions which are widely discarded or despised today. Without a fair understanding of these convictions and a certain amount of (at least temporary) sympathy towards them, we are likely to misread him; in few poets in any language can we make less distinction between the doctrinal content and the literary art, or concentrate on the purely 'aesthetic' side of his poetry.

In the second place, his greatness and the nature of his topics invite comparisons with Shakespeare and Dante. As Mr Eliot has pointed out, the basic tools of criticism are analysis and comparison. The critical judgements we arrive at will depend on what we compare with what, and there is no doubt that Milton suffers by comparison not only with Shakespeare and Dante, but also with Donne and Hopkins; he has little of the latter poets' capacity for startling phrase and packed emotion, and neither Dante's vivid intimacy nor Shakespeare's profound psychological insight. Our effort must then be to see what special qualities he possesses and what special difficulties he faced.

Thirdly, the very nature of his themes and the great purposes he had in mind remove his poetry to a much greater extent than that of any others, even the Biblical poets, from the ordinary concerns and common experience of men. For his material he chose the fall of man,[1] the tempting of Christ by Satan, and the Lord's vengeance on His enemies through Samson. The existence of angels, the fall of a whole race in Adam, the restoration of that race in Christ, the deliberate destruction of God's enemies – these are ideas which, whether accepted or rejected, have little affinity with the mentality of the twentieth century, and are remote from the common experience even of the devout believer. Milton, then, presented himself with a particularly difficult task, a task faced neither by the Hebrew poets (who concentrate on the experience of the Israelites); nor by the Greeks (who, even in dealing with the gods, are constantly concerned with the human situation); nor by Dante (who expresses his theological material in terms of a human pilgrim progressing towards Heaven through a series of vivid encounters with human beings); nor by Shakespeare (who, in presenting a profound study of human character, abstains from personal moral judgements). Even the great bulk of medieval religious poetry (the anonymous hymns and lyrics, *Piers Plowman* and the medieval plays) does not attempt to elaborate the story of the early parts of Creation; it keeps religious beliefs and moral principles constantly in touch with the world we know. We might perhaps conclude that Milton's artistic judgement was at fault, that what he attempted was beyond the reach of human language, that he should, as he had first intended, have dealt with some more 'human' story such as the legend of Arthur. But that conclusion could reasonably be based only on great critical ability, on a precise estimate of his difficulties, and on a very wide and exact grasp of the theology which exerts so deep and so pervasive a pressure on his verse. Milton was guilty of some hyperbole in describing his 'adventrous Song' as pursuing 'things unattempted yet in Prose or Rhime'; but the hyperbole may stand as a reminder of the great difficulties he entered into with such deliberate choice and after so long and so careful a preparation. Unless we see his difficulties, we cannot fairly estimate his success or his failure.

The difficulties are further aggravated by Milton's intense conviction that his poetry must teach. And the influence of the Old Testament is seen in his conception of teaching; he wishes not merely to instruct the mind but to purify and elevate the heart, and in this one word, 'heart' (*P.L.*, I. 18), he is supposing in the reader some knowledge of the Books of Wisdom in the Old, and the Epistles of the New, Testament. His great object, he says, is to

> ... assert Eternal Providence
> And justify the ways of God to men.
> (I. 25.)

The whole of *Paradise Lost* must be understood in the light of the exordium (lines 1–26), and the exordium in the light of the whole poem; we misunderstand the poem from the outset if we think of it as another seventeenth-century controversial tract. The criticism that Milton does not succeed in justifying God's ways is based on a mis-conception of what Milton meant by God and what he meant by justification. It should be clear from the whole poem that, to Milton, God always remains the Great Mystery whose inscrutable ways can be comprehended only in the 'light' which is as yet inaccessible to men. And by justification Milton did not mean a merely logical demonstra-tion which would prove an intellectual conclusion and bring God within the framework of the rational universe. He uses the word with the overtones it acquired from New Testament usage, where it im-plies a divine, not a human or logical, understanding, a supernal illumination from the Holy Spirit whom he invokes for special guidance in his difficult task.[2] Milton aspires to higher things than were possible through the Greek Muses or even through the inspira-tion of the Old Testament. If the ways of God can be justified, it must be through a purification of the heart rather than by the reason-ings of the intellect.[3] The poem is, among other things, a prayer addressed to the Deity from all mankind, a prayer in which he perse-veres even though he concludes, from his Biblical sources and his personal experience, that many would reject the divine revelation; hence the later form of his prayer (VII. 31) that his Muse, 'heavenly-born Urania' who 'with Eternal Wisdom didst converse', might 'fit audience find though few.' (The whole passage, VII. 1–39, should be closely connected with the opening of Book I.) We should then understand Milton as aspiring through his poem to prepare the hearts of men for the coming of the Spirit whose great office is to lead men into the truth about God and themselves.

The main question for the reader of Milton's poetry is not, indeed, the nature of his theological doctrine or his value as a moral teacher, but the extent to which theology and morality are transmuted into poetry. But no estimate of his poetry can be arrived at in complete abstraction from the discussion of his doctrinal content; the way in which his words 'work' – the definable effect they have on our minds – depends so largely on the religious connotations and suggestions they have for an individual reader. Different interpretations of the words 'Father' and 'sin do not necessarily result in different estimates of Donne's *Hymn to God the Father* because the experience within the poem does not depend on the technical meaning we assign to them. But disagreement on 'justify', 'Victor', and 'Mightiest' (*P.L.*, I. 26, 95, 99.) will deeply affect our understanding of Satan and our literary judgement of the poem. The two *Paradises* draw constantly on a doctrine no one point of which can be fully understood through the poems alone. Yet a certain amount of Milton can be enjoyed immediately with no reference to doctrine (e.g. II. 51–105, XII. 624–49, or – a good introduction to Milton – the passages in any good dictionary of quotations). Such passages (like Shakespeare's 'Friends, Romans, countrymen') should encourage the reader to go further in the endeavour to understand the presuppositions and qualities of the writer's art.

We can assist ourselves by noting a parallel between the opening of *Paradise Lost* and that of *Antony and Cleopatra*. However concerned both writers are with exposition, they are already, at the opening, supposing a great deal in the reader. To catch the many hints and overtones of Philo's speech, we need a knowledge of love, war, and politics; Shakespeare is drawing on forms of knowledge which have no necessary connexion with poetry. In somewhat the same way, to perceive Milton's meaning in the generalized 'Man', the implication of 'first' and of 'fruit' supposes our ability to bring what we know of Christianity to bear on the opening sentence.

> Of Man's First Disobedience, and the Fruit
> Of that Forbidden Tree, whose mortal tast
> Brought Death into the World, and all our woe,
> With loss of *Eden*, till one greater Man

Restore us, and regain the blissful Seat,
Sing Heav'nly Muse, that on the secret top
Of *Oreb* or of Sinai, didst inspire
That Shepherd, who first taught the chosen Seed,
In the Beginning how the Heav'ns and Earth
Rose out of *Chaos*: or if *Sion* Hill
Delight thee more, and Siloa's Brook that flow'd
Fast by the Oracle of God; I thence
Invoke thy aid to my adventrous Song,
That with no middle flight intends to soar
Above th' *Aonian* Mount, while it pursues
Things unattempted yet in Prose or Rhime.
And chiefly Thou O Spirit, that dost prefer
Before all Temples th' upright heart and pure,
Instruct me, for Thou know'st; Thou from the first
Wast present, and with mighty wings outspread
Dove-like satst brooding on the vast Abyss
And mad'st it pregnant: What in me is dark
Illumine, what is low raise and support;
That to the highth of this great Argument
I may assert Eternal Providence,
And justifie the wayes of God to men.

'Man', the second word of the poem, introduces us to one of the main themes – the unity of the human race whose sinfulness, woe, and hope of restoration are summed up in Adam. The *first* disobedience is thus not only the first in time; it is in a general manner (whose mysteriousness Milton does not claim to be able to clarify) the source of all other disobedience. All he can say about the disobedience for the moment is condensed in the word 'fruit', which is both the edible fruit itself and fruit in the biblical sense (i.e. the results which grow as naturally from decisions as fruit from a tree). In Milton's idiom (since he frequently uses a participle with a noun force), the 'Forbidded Tree' is equivalent to 'the divine command which forbade man to eat of the tree', the transgression of which had such vast results. He thus connects the 'Disobedience' with the whole plan of Divine Providence, and indicates that it was not the temporary trespass of an arbitrary command but a violation of that divine order which the Spirit drew from the 'vast Adyss'. The second half of the sentence suggests how, in spite of men's sins, divine inspiration followed the chosen race from Egypt to Jerusalem, from ancient to apostolic times. The key terms thus reinforce and clarify one another in a manner very similar to the theological shorthand so often employed by Dante. Milton draws on a different kind of knowledge from Shakespeare; but in either case, if the knowledge is not there, the verse will not 'work' properly.

Even the least experienced reader can easily see the marked difference between the jerky, flat language of the 'arguments' and the evocative language of the poem. An analysis of the differences between the two would elicit many points on Milton's verse style, but particularly the accumulative quality by which, though no one phrase is immediately felt as striking, the large scope of the poem, and the multiple inter-relation of its parts, gradually become evident. While this method carries with it a sometimes disconcerting shifting of focus and a lack of sensuous contact with reality, it is still fit for Milton's purpose, if we see how the verse is constantly reaching out in different directions – to Heaven, Hell, and earth; to sin, redemption, and Providence – and is thereby assimilating the human to the divine mind which sees all time and space at once. Some readers feel an hypnotic or incantatory quality in such sentences as this, and obviously it has not the brisk, curt quality of Philo's speech; but the endeavour to respond fully to the implications of the terms and see the ways in which they clarify each other should sharpen rather than dull the mind.

The second sentence (which concludes the introductory section) draws a parallel between the divine and the human work of creation, between producing the world and creating great poetry, a parallel which is intended to suggest the poet's scope and his (and the reader's) need for divine help. The idea of an analogy between art and divine creation was not, of course, original to Milton, but he gives it a particular relevance by speaking of the creative power as Spirit and Dove, that is, as combining in himself divine power, wisdom, and gentleness; it is because God has these qualities that Milton confidently addresses to him a prayer for help in his 'adventrous Song'. God is thought of not merely as a gentle dove, but as having wings wide enough to brood over the 'vast Abyss', and as having wisdom and power enough to draw order out of chaos; this God, gentle, wise, and powerful, is now besought to establish intellectual and moral order in the poet by cleansing, strengthening, and elevating his heart, by enlightening and making pregnant his mind. All the items in the exordium have an exact relevance to what Milton is doing at the moment and hopes to do in the poem as a whole. This degree of poetic condensation is not indeed maintained throughout the work; yet the opening gives some suggestions of the literary excellence we are to look for in the poem, particularly the power to keep central themes steadily, if loosely, in control of a multiplicity of details, the power to achieve a great sweep of meaning in a single sentence, and the occasional power to fuse apparent contradictories without incongruity. The passage on the Dove recalls the Metaphysicals; the Dove is both gentle and mighty; while remaining motionless ('sat'st brooding'), it became the source of all creation and movement by turning the 'vast' (i.e. 'waste' or 'lifeless') abyss into the womb of the whole universe. Every detail carries the parallel between creation and poetic inspiration a step further.

At the same time, Milton is not concerned with any mere theory of aesthetics; he appeals to the Dove-like Spirit because, to achieve his moral aspiration in poetry, he must have some share in the peace and width of the divine mind, in the divine wisdom and strength. The notion of the 'pregnant Abyss', with its suggestion of the analogy between the darkness of the abyss and that of the womb, and the contrast between the formless desert of the one and the organized life of the other, is a good example of Milton's occasional power to fuse disparate ideas without incongruity while fitting the language to the illustration of his main themes. If he turned from the Metaphysical style which he attempted in *The Passion* (1630), he did not discard all that could be learnt from the Metaphysicals. That he moulded rather than copied the Metaphysical style is evident from the fact that the 'pregnant Abyss' has none of the startling effect which we find (and rightly enjoy) in Donne's 'Busie old foole, unruly Sunne', or in Hopkins's 'May-mess'. Milton is not arousing us out of our ordinariness to see the human world through the eyes of a startlingly original mind, but is endeavouring to lift us to the peace of the divine vision. In such ways as these, Milton adapts his language to his moral purpose and his theological doctrine.

There is a minor point in Milton's treatment of religion which gives a disproportionate amount of trouble to many readers. All the important forms of religion and culture in seventeenth-century England were derived from the Continent, but were profoundly modified by the English mind. Thus Milton's mysticism is not merely Christian but English and Miltonic; it is coloured by the strongly controversial spirit of the times and by the exploratory and argumentative bent of Milton's mind. *Paradise Lost* was probably written while he was exploring Christian doctrine to decide what he should believe. The poem is not, consequently, based on a finally settled creed such as we find in Dante or Bunyan, and incidental blows are directed in it against such things as medieval beliefs about angels (V. 435), the Roman doctrine of indulgences (III. 478-93), and the Anglican hierarchy (XII. 515-24). Controversial asides and doctrinal discrepancies within the poem need not be given serious consideration by the critic, and can be completely overlooked by the general reader.[4] Once we are aware that we may find controversial asides and doctrinal discrepancies, we can afford to treat them with the passing interest they deserve, and concentrate on the main purpose, which is not to expound a theological thesis but to reinforce a mystical mood and habit of mind. The poem is a survey of the whole scheme of Providence by which he hopes to attune the human to the Divine Mind, and thus purify the human heart and elevate it to God. Milton wishes to present the Fall of Adam as a key incident that would lead men to a divine understanding of the larger story of the Creation and of the Fall and restoration of man. Theological doctrine he does suppose but, as in the poetry of the Old Testament (from which Milton drew so much inspiration), the emphasis falls not on speculative doctrine but on the practical task of inducing the right attitudes in both writer and reader. Unless we read the invocations (at the beginning of Books I, III, and VII) as Milton meant them – as prayers – we mis-read them. Every poet must produce the moods and attitudes by which his work is understood and enjoyed; the bulk of serious adverse criticism of Milton argues that he lacks this very important element of poetic ability. We should remember, however, that such failure may be due to the reading public as much as to the writer (the slow recognition of Wordsworth or Eliot is a case in point). Milton's failure has been due largely to two things: his deliberate choice of topics which preclude recurrence to common experience, and the unwillingness of the modern mind to have any precise demands made on its credence or its morals (and neither Wordsworth nor Eliot makes such demands). It is rather vain to hope (as Douglas Bush hopes in various places in '*Paradise Lost*' *in Our Day*) that the reading of Milton will help to restore high moral standards; for unless we are already willing to accept Milton's moral mysticism, either permanently or temporarily, we are unlikely to understand him. Poetry written in an age very different or distant from our own requires us to do what we can to recapture the mind and mood of those to whom it was addressed.

Here again the comparison with Shakespeare can be very misleading. For besides his own unique excellence in disentangling human situations from merely local conditions, and thereby giving them a universal appeal, Shakespeare has one advantage which Milton deliberately discarded, the advantage of confining himself to the temporal as contrasted with the eternal point of view. What Shakespeare aimed at in his audience is what any audience has in common with ourselves. But when we think of Milton's audience, with its definite religious convictions, its intense moral fervour, its willingness to apply religious principles to every phase of the national and individual life, we find a world which is mentally much farther from our own than Shakespeare's or even Homer's. From this point of view, the understanding of Milton is discouragingly difficult; but from another it is relatively easy, and consists in taking his prayers and mysticism with complete seriousness. It may be suggested that the best 'preface' to Milton is not a piece of scholarship or literary criticism, but the intense reading of the Psalms, which Milton could take for granted in his 'fit audience'. Hebrew poetry can, more effectively than scholarship or criticism, habituate the reader's mind to Milton's mood and purpose. To endeavour to read him without any close acquaintance with the Bible is to evade the kind of preparation which he assumed.

* * *

It will follow from the above that neither structure nor style in Milton can be discussed apart from his central preoccupation with a mystical vision. It is almost entirely irrelevant to adduce Greek or Latin epics, or Aristotelean principles, in order to examine the structure of either *Paradise Lost* or *Paradise Regained*, though Greek tragedy supplies some useful hints for *Samson Agonistes*. Since what he created is so specially Miltonic in both poetic excellence and religious purpose, parallels with other writers can mislead as well as guide. We may, however, find a useful approach through Hebrew and Shakespearian poetry, where the structure consists not so much of the concatenation of events or the logical development of an idea, but rather in the gradual exploration or 'explication' of an opening theme, such as 'the triple pillar of the world transformed into a strumpet's fool' (*Antony and Cleopatra*), or 'The Lord is my shepherd' (Ps. 23).

The arrangement of the incidents in Milton is determined, not by the desire to tell a good story (as in the *Iliad*) or by the narrative exposition of a theological system (as in *The Divine Comedy*), but by the gradual reinforcing and intertwining of four central themes – the universality of Divine Providence, the reality of evil, the hope of redemption from evil, and the unity of the human race.* It is the repetition and mutual clarification of these four themes, far more than any manipulation of the incidents, that gives the poem whatever structural unity it possesses. They are kept alive sometimes by explicit statement, but more often by reference and allusion. They are not dealt with separately in different parts of the poem because Milton is constantly aware of their close inter-connexion; his language is turned to the task of keeping them pervasively present and at times (e.g. III. 1–21, IV. 32–112) intensely felt. There is, for example, a nice adjustment of emphasis in Book I. The obvious emphasis falls on the vigour, independence, and resoluteness of Satan; but there is a subtler emphasis on the dedication of these powers to evil. Both emphases are expressed in a way which helps us to see the range of Satan's pride (the source of the first violation of divine order) and to see in Satan and his plans a parody (completely humourless but effective) of God and Divine Providence. If we avoid the mistake of understanding Milton's God through Satan's mind (as we should wish to avoid understanding King Claudius merely through Hamlet's mind), we can see Milton's purpose in Satan's reference to the 'Realms of Light' (line 96); the darkness of Hell is not merely exclusion from glory and happiness, but the darkness of uncertainty and error in which Satan must plot to defeat the designs of God. The reference to light comes

* It is probable that no poet would accept anyone else's summary of his themes; the four given above are offered merely as handy terms of reference.

not merely from the desire to present a portrait of Satan, but from the desire to keep the whole scheme of the poem in mind. Milton offers the exclusion from light as his own comment on the ultimate futility of Satan's plan:

> If then his Providence
> Out of our evil seek to bring forth good,
> Our labour must be to pervert that end,
> And out of good still to find means of evil;
> Which oft times may succeed, so as perhaps
> Shall grieve him, if I fail not, and disturb
> His inmost counsels from their destined aim.
>
> (162-8.)

In many other places do we find a similar inter-weaving of the main themes by which Milton explores the antecedents and the consequences of 'Man's first disobedience'. To knit so many large issues (each of them a complexity in itself) into one large pattern, to make them clarify and reinforce each other in so long a poetic work, is a major achievement in poetic structure.

The events are thus means to an end, not the main interest; similarly, the various shifts of attention (from the exordium to Hell, to Heaven, to Eden) are not the dramatist's or novelist's devices for keeping the various parts of the story abreast of each other, but rather a circular tour through the whole scheme of Divine Providence. Thus by the beginning of Book III, the Fall of Man (described in detail in Book IX) is yet a future event for Satan and Adam, but is spoken of (III. 86-131) as already present in God's manner of cognition and as already incorporated into the divine plan. The 'discussion' which follows on the method of redemption is not a heavenly council of deliberation, but Milton's way of affirming the ancient Christian teaching that God fulfils His design by the co-operation of free agents.[5] The problem of reconciling divine foreknowledge with human freedom is not a poetic but a religious one; Milton assumed (and expected his audience to assume) that it was one of the divine mysteries, discussible but not soluble. Similarly, the end of the poem is not (as it is with the multiple deaths of an Elizabethan tragedy) the end of the story; it does not conclude Milton's survey, but is rather the beginning of that long life of woe, the delivery from which is an integral part of the main poetic theme. The Redemption has already been presented in considerable detail in Books III, X, XI, and the early part of Book XII. Such telescoping of events is not, of course, peculiar to Milton; but it is used by him for a special purpose – to present the successive working out of what is eternally present in the Divine Mind. It is probable that Milton derived hints for such a treatment not only from the similar conspectus in Augustine's *City of God*, but also from Hebrew grammar which does not possess the Occidental distinctions of past, present, and future, and frequently speaks of future events in the Hebrew 'imperfect' to which the closest English equivalent is the past.

For much the same reasons, it is rather superfluous to discuss where the crisis or climax of *Paradise Lost* occurs. The poem is much too concentrated in many places, and much too long, for any one incident to carry an emphasis which is readily perceived as greater than that of others. Besides, the story is not a series of incidents but a circular contemplation of God's ways, and contemplation does not lend itself to crisis or climax. The poem contains a series of emphases (alternated with descriptive and reflective material); to decide which of these is the greatest is a highly personal or subjective question.[6] Milton's whole cast of mind (at least by the time he wrote the last three works) rather closely resembles Wordsworth's; both present incidents, but incidents 'recollected in tranquillity', not portrayed in dramatic evolution. It is not only the close of the stories, but the poems as a whole that we are to read in 'calm of mind, all passion spent' (*Samson*, 1758). The reader is expected to survey the actions of Satan, Adam, and Eve from the calm beatitude of Heaven, that is, with as close an approximation to God's own view as human nature, elevated by grace, permits. Miltonic structure must then be discussed, not in terms of 'plot' or arrangement of incidents, but through the careful reading of key passages which recall and reinforce the divine point of view. This will imply (among other things) the effort to understand such key words as 'Providence' (I. 25), 'Reason' (III. 108), and 'incensed Deity' (III. 187) as they were understood by the Puritan mind.

If the structure depends on individual passages, the latter also depend on the structure, and depend in a way which has been little discussed. Milton's style, like Shakespeare's, has various levels of meaning, the understanding of which comes, not so much from further literary training as from deepening and widening our experience. To increase our grasp of Hamlet's soliloquies or of the political situation in *Antony and Cleopatra* is a matter of becoming not more scholarly but more adult. In much the same way, no increase in critical ability or scholarship will by itself take us very far into Milton's meaning; while it may clarify individual points, it will leave the total effect or appeal of the poems very much where it stood before. But the re-reading of Milton presents another and special difficulty, the difficulty of deepening religious beliefs and of stabilizing religious moods. Without this deepening and stabilizing, scholarship fastens more and more on details, and critical ability may turn earlier pleasure into later distaste. Milton's complexity rather resembles that of the great passages in the Psalms or the New Testament; he cannot be read merely as literature since he is not re-living or re-enacting personal religious experiences in the manner of Herbert or Hopkins, but is inculcating a particular attitude towards God. The parallel between Milton and the Bible is true to this extent that it is only by an intensification of the religious spirit, as well as by expanding experience, that we can come to grasp the complexity of the great Psalm 22, the Lord's Prayer, or *Paradise Lost*; can come to see explicitly what was before only implicit to our less developed religious sensibility. It is probably only a man who has passed through what John of the Cross calls 'the dark night of the soul', or some analogous experience like that of Milton after the Restoration of the Stuarts to the throne, who could seize the full meaning of:

> Man therefore shall find grace;
> The other [Satan], none. In mercy and justice both,
> Through Heaven and Earth, so shall my glory excel;
> But mercy, first and last, shall brightest shine.
>
> (III. 131.)

If the reader considers the distinction made here between Satan and Adam to be the result of mere arbitrariness on God's part, if he does not find in the phrase, 'mercy first and last', a summary of Divine Providence and of the whole poem, it is because he is unaware of the commonplaces of theology in Milton's time and probably because he has had little religious experience. Without that experience, the last three poems will have as superficial a meaning as *Romeo and Juliet* to the youngster who has never been in love.

There is a good reason why Milton's peculiar complexity has been little discussed. In so far as religious growth occurs, it is a growth which almost defies formulation in words unless they be the words of the rare hymnographer like the author of the *Stabat Mater*, or the rare Dante or Milton, who possess the power of carrying the contemplation of Divine Providence a step further – a power which no critic of Milton has possessed, which cannot perhaps be expressed in criticism at all, and which has never yet been expressed but in great creative writing.

The conclusion can hardly be drawn that it is only the convinced Christian who can perceive the complexity of Milton, any more than it is only the Thomist who can perceive the complexity of Dante. The atheist or agnostic who is willing to re-create in himself something at least of the religious mentality Milton supposed, who is humble enough to keep his own pre-judgements out of the way, can do for Milton what he must, on a smaller scale, do for Donne or Hopkins. It is because Milton's verse so constantly demands our acceptance of his religious mood, because he is habitually so far from common experience, because he affords us so little opportunity to look at things from the merely human point of view (as he does in the felicitous description of Mulciber's fall, I. 738–46), because he so seldom allows us to enjoy beauty in a merely human manner (as he does in the description of Paradise, IV. 213–87), that we tend to refuse to Milton the 'willing suspension of disbelief' – the condition on which alone most people today can enjoy religious poetry. Even in such passages as those just cited, Milton is still mindful of his general scheme to which he quickly returns the reader's attention. When he adds a line of comment like 'Thus they relate erring' (I. 746), he is not tacking an extraneous ornament on to his main theme or apologizing for indulgence in luxurious poetry inappropriate to a Puritan. Having afforded a resting-place for the reader, he is contrasting the merely human or the pagan with the Christian conception of the universe; he is reinforcing the central interest. These resting-places (corresponding roughly in poetic function to the deliberately quieter passages in Shakespeare, e.g. the welcome to Duncan in *Macbeth*, I. vi) become rarer towards the end of the poem; a larger number of them, organically built into the structure, would have made it a better poem, or at least one better accommodated to the limitations of the ordinary reader. If Johnson voices a common impression in feeling that 'none ever wished the poem longer', it is because no other poem imposes so constant a strain, except perhaps *King Lear*, which is Shakespeare's greatest endeavour to lift the popular audience above its habitual self. The perusal of *Paradise Lost*, says Johnson, 'is a duty rather than a pleasure. We read Milton for instruction, retire harassed and over-burdened, and look elsewhere for recreation'. But before deciding whether this is a judgement on the weakness of the poem or on the limitations of the reader, we should remember that intense religious feeling (as in Psalm 91 or in the poetry of John of the Cross) is little concerned about the reader's convenience; and (since the poem is a prayer) we should recognize the common weakness of men who seldom desire their prayers to be longer or consider prayer as a form of recreation.

Johnson was nearer the mark when he quoted a Milton encomiast as saying that 'in reading *Paradise Lost* we read a book of universal knowledge'. For the poem is not, as Johnson hints, an encyclopaedia of natural history, ancient fable, and modern science; it is the last of the medieval attempts to write the history of Everyman, to survey the whole course of events from the Creation to man's final ascent into Heaven, and to relate this course to the universal plan of Divine Providence. It is the highest achievement of the Protestant mind looking at the whole created cosmos through faith purified and elevated till it coincides with the mind of God. Milton was incurring serious dangers when he made God a spokesman in the poem (though it is worth noting that God is a spokesman rather than a participant in the action); but if we argue (as Sir Herbert Grierson does in *Criticism and Creation*) that it would have been better to omit God, then we are arguing that the poem should have been radically different.

* * *

It is with a knowledge of Milton's scope and purpose that we can best discuss the vexed question of his style. Milton himself touches off the controversy (in his prefatory note on *The Verse*) by rejecting rhyme as the 'invention of a barbarous age'; and something of Milton's belligerent spirit of insensitive generalization has entered into the later discussion. Since it is impossible, except in a large book, to examine even the main critical positions on the style, what follows is merely a supplementary guide to the discussions listed in the bibliography in the Appendix.[7]

(a) We do not find in Milton either the constant sensuous contact with physical reality, or the frequent alternation of swift intensity with calm slowness, or the profound insight into character and motive which keep most people's interest in Shakespeare alive; and only rarely do we find the short, pregnant phrase which strikes us immediately because of its concrete, aphoristic, or poignant quality. Shakespeare and Pope excel in a kind of condensed poetic vitality, in packing so much meaning into a short passage that the poetic life survives when the phrase is separated from the total work of art to which in Shakespeare and Pope it is usually subordinated. Shakespeare, however, has also a number of phrases (e.g. 'Nothing will come of nothing' in *Lear*) which gather a great deal of meaning from the context, but are rather flat, lacking in rich suggestiveness or connotative power, when taken by themselves.

Much of Milton is like the second kind of Shakespearian language. As is suggested below, Milton was too concerned with an ideal audience, too careless of the reader's ease, approval, or delight. By a combination of indifference to the public and a certain hardening of his mind, he fails to condense his effects, to localize his main interests in short passages. As a result, the analysis of short passages of Milton, unless accompanied by an extensive and rather unwieldy body of exegesis and cross-references, tends to throw the emphasis on what is wrong with the verse – the grandiloquence, the cumbrous involution of phrases, the lack of focus, the remoteness from concrete experience. When we add to this that Milton, in spite of his love of music and in spite of the fact that he dictated the poems orally, had very little feeling for the cadences and emphases of the speaking voice, we find the source of most of the disapproval with which his verse has met. Milton's verse moves with relatively little variety of speed or emphasis. The main point of interest, instead of being precisely localized or standing in sharp relief from the rest, is often lost in the successive surge of clauses. In spite of his close attention to the Psalms and to the Latin periodic sentence, Milton learnt neither pointedness from the one nor strong emphasis from the other. The shifting of focus which enables him to achieve a wide survey in the better sentences leads him into diffusiveness and pointless piling up of effects in the worse. Occasionally, he smothers the main idea by prolonging the sentence too far; by the time we come to line 208 or 355 in *Paradise Lost*, Book I, the point of the comparison has been lost in rather wanton luxuriance. What is true of individual sentences is true of whole passages; it is not, however, so true of the poem as a whole; partly through, and partly in spite of, the accumulative style, the main themes of Providence, evil, redemption, and human unity are kept fairly steadily before our eyes. His own kind of preoccupation with God makes the essential themes sufficiently salient, but leads him into a neglect of the human means by which greater appeal and force could be given to them.

(*b*) While Milton had the well-instructed Christian in mind as his reader, the three great poems are not addressed to any particular public in the same sense as, say, Shakespeare's plays. He thought of himself as writing 'general' or 'catholic' works in the manner of the epistles of James and Peter in the New Testament (as contrasted with the 'local' epistles of Paul). It is from this, as well as from the special qualities of his character and genius, that the characteristics of his style derive. For example, he frees himself at once from any need to cater to low taste, to prejudices religious or literary in his readers, and, quite content to alienate the audience which is not 'fit', can treat his topic exactly in the manner which seems right to him. He thus achieves full scope for the use of Biblical references (and for a more technical use of them than Shakespeare employed) and for the long-sustained sentence in which he is often at his best. But the fact that he is engaging in so solitary a poetic effort and has no definite group of human beings in mind, encourages him also to indulge his own foibles (as when his love of argument reduces God to a seventeenth-century controversialist – III. 106–28; his views on women make Eve ridiculous and the verse naïve and tumid – VIII. 39–58; or his desire to remain dignified urges him into a pompous parody of his own style – VIII. 4–38).

Of the many penalties Milton paid for his poetic freedom, attention may be directed to one in particular. While he learnt much from earlier writers, he reversed the Renaissance tradition in England. Marlowe, Shakespeare, and Jonson had achieved new effects in drama largely by blending with classical seriousness and profundity the vigour, raciness, and earthiness of the folk mentality. Milton had shown an admiration for the blend in *The Nativity Hymn* (1629) and in *Comus* (1634); but by the time of writing the later poems, his ideas of seriousness, restraint, and religious decorum had narrowed and hardened. His Puritan solemnity eschewed the homely, familiar manner of speaking about divine things which is found in the Psalms and in the medieval plays. Milton marks the point at which reserve and respectability were becoming marked qualities of English life and religion. The arguments of Tillyard, Bush, and many others that the poet must be allowed to 'wear his singing robes' are not very convincing, since the Hebrew and medieval poets write of God with much less attention to literary decorum and in a much more conversational idiom than Milton.

In other words, Milton's implied theory of epic is not related to the concrete experience of men in the way in which the theory of epic in Homer or of tragedy in Shakespeare grows out of the way in which men actually feel and speak. Even the best equipped and most sympathetic reader is unable, except at rare moments, to feel himself involved in the story, to be deeply moved, or to find an echo of his own experiences. It is this removal from common experience which makes it so difficult for Milton to do what comes readily to Shakespeare – to create and maintain the mood in which the poetry is enjoyed. Unless we bring the mood to the poem (say, through previous partial readings of it), our impression is like that of an Englishman watching an Oriental ritual – admiring the splendour and the formal patterns of movement, but remaining an external spectator. In *Paradise Regained*, even more than in *Paradise Lost*, Milton's preoccupation with the divine point of view keeps the situations and the speakers at too great a distance from ourselves. And in *Samson Agonistes* it becomes quite apparent that the non-dramatic quality of the language results not only from the calmness of Milton's contemplation, but also from a rigidity of mind which does not accommodate itself sufficiently to the shifting moods of the story. We note, for example, how tenuous is the relation between the speaker and the immediate situation in Dalila's self-defence, and how easily the speech (841–70) could be turned into a messenger's impersonal account of her betrayal. In such respects *Samson* is inferior to the much earlier *Comus*. Milton's independence and artistic solitariness involved him in the loss or decay of powers which a surer critical instinct and a greater need for popular appeal might have led him to cultivate.

(c) There are three methods of language (three fusing qualities of the one style) which sustain Milton in the great task he set himself; alternate use of condensation and expansion, structural devices recalling the divine point of view, and a high degree of allusiveness. The three are found in the first eighty lines of *Paradise Lost*. The opening sentence (one of the most condensed in English) contains references to Greek mythology, some dozens of allusions to particular passages in the Old and New Testaments, and is intended to attune the reader's mind to the aspect under which all subsequent considerations are presented. It is not a mere opening flourish of trumpets, as Professor C. S. Lewis seems to consider it, but is the first statement of the mood and purpose which Milton wishes to pervade the whole poem. It has a markedly different rhythm from the following section (27–80), which fixes attention on Satan immediately after his fall. The first exchange between Satan and Beelzebub (81–191) is built around clear and varied but subtly appropriate repetitions of the opening theme; he then expands his vision till it includes the whole fallen army, the meaning of Hell, and the dedication of the devils to evil. After the more detailed description of Book II, he returns to another condensed passage on the central theme in the great address to 'Holy Light' (III. 1–21). Such is Milton's general method: to embrace everything in the opening, concentrate on a particular point, expand it, recall the opening, transfer the scene of the action, and expand again.

(d) The last three poems represent a kind of triumph of language which has no parallel elsewhere in English. Milton lived and worked in three worlds which were in conflict along various fronts: the medieval, the Renaissance, and the Puritan. It was Milton's great achievement to draw on all three, to harmonize the wide range of medieval beliefs with the intense seriousness and sense of responsibility of the Puritan mind and with the Renaissance discussions of the good life and the ideal state. If his psychological insight was weak, he at least shows some of the forces which were at work when modern England was coming into being. His verse is one of the great vehicles by which we come to know the cultural, religious, and political vitality of his times. If it has serious and disconcerting limitations, if it presents no vivid portrait of human beings, it does give a special insight into a religious doctrine and mentality without which we cannot understand what England then was or later became.

NOTES

1. It is worth noting, as one of the points of doctrine necessary to understand Milton, that the whole human race suffers from the Fall of one, while the angels fall individually – they are merely led by Satan who cannot involve others in his sin except by their free consent. This is one of the subtler points which complicates Milton's theology but which helps to shape his verse. It enables him, for example, to reinforce one of his main themes, the unity of the human race (united in one way by its fall in Adam and in another by its elevation in Christ), and to establish a strong contrast between human and angelic guilt, between the bitterness and recrimination in which Adam indulges, and the calmer, more intellectual fixation on evil which he makes so forceful in the devils (e.g. I. 105–9). Milton succeeds unobtrusively in making us feel that fixation, and thus reinforces another theme – the reality of evil.

2. *Paradise Lost* contains many echoes of St Paul's doctrine of the Spirit which Paul himself sums up in I Cor. ii. 6–16. It was a commonplace of Biblical theology that the Spirit was richer in gifts to the Christians of the New Testament than to the Israelites of the Old.

3. Cf. *Samson*, 322–5.

4. Milton's pneumatology hardly deserves all the space Professor C. S. Lewis gives it in chapter xv of *A Preface to 'Paradise Lost'*. His impressive array of theological authorities does not begin to answer the questions: How good is the poetry of Book vi? Is the humour successful? Is the invention of angelic artillery great epic or is it ludicrous?

5. The point would present little difficulty to Milton's contemporary reader; he would recall, for example, the passage in John's Gospel (vi. 5–6) where Jesus asks Philip, 'Whence are we to buy bread?' ... 'and this he said to prove him; for he himself knew what he would do.'

6. See, however, E. M. W. Tillyard's lengthy discussion of the question in 'The Crisis of *Paradise Lost*' in *Studies in Milton*.

7. See particularly J. H. Hanford's *A Milton Handbook*, Chapter vi, and F. R. Leavis's two essays, 'Milton's Verse' in *Revaluation* and 'Mr Eliot and Milton' in *The Common Pursuit*.

THE POETRY OF ANDREW MARVELL

BY F. W. BRADBROOK

DURING the nineteenth century Andrew Marvell (1621–78) was chiefly remembered as a public figure, a Puritan who was a defender of toleration as well as of individual liberty. The revival of interest in his poetry in this century coincided with the fashionable cult of John Donne and the Metaphysical school of poets. But Marvell was also the subject of one of the finest of T. S. Eliot's essays, a piece of criticism that remains the best introduction to the poems. Marvell's reputation depends upon a few lyrics, but within this small compass there is great range and variety. His quality is best seen in such poems as *A Dialogue between the Resolved Soul and Created Pleasure*, *To His Coy Mistress*, *The Definition of Love*, *The Garden*, and *An Horatian Ode upon Cromwell's Return from Ireland*.

The exact date of composition of the majority of Marvell's poems is not known. The first collected edition was not published until 1681, and except for two copies this omitted one of the finest of his poems, *An Horatian Ode*, which was not generally printed until 1776. Some of the best-known lyrics, including *The Garden*, were almost certainly written during the two years (1651–3) that Marvell was tutor to the daughter of General Fairfax at Nun Appleton House in Yorkshire. 'It was as the result of those years of uniquely peaceful and agreeable life, in his own country, and in such a setting of learning, piety, and rural privacy, that Marvell seems to have produced his best work'.[1]

A Dialogue between the Resolved Soul, and Created Pleasure is a soliloquy in which two opposing impulses debate with each other. The martial and Biblical imagery of the opening, based on Ephesians vi. 16–17, is common in the literature of spiritual struggle. It is to be found, for instance, in Bunyan's *Holy War*. But though there is an atmosphere of siege in Marvell's poem, the attitude of the poet towards his subject is ironical. The almost jaunty rhythm emphasizes the playfulness with which the theme is to be treated:

> Courage my Soul, now learn to wield
> The weight of thine immortal Shield.

Close on thy Head thy Helmet bright.
Ballance thy Sword against the Fight.

The sense of the poem appears to be simple and straightforward at first reading, though it depends for its final effect on delicately veiled puns and double-meanings, and on the subtle use of rhythm. The word 'ballance' suggests rhythmically its meaning. One can feel the swords crossing and sliding against each other, and the balance of the sword in the hand. With its further suggestion of delicately poised scales it is an image of the debate which is to follow between 'Pleasure' and 'Soul' (emotion and reason). The soul 'holds the balance' or has the power to decide, and its actions and opinions are 'weighed' by the demands of pleasure. Yet behind the antithesis there lies harmony. The replies of the soul are gentle and genial. There is a suggestion of the dance as well as of the debate. The battle is a battle of wits in which pleasure woos the soul and finally surrenders to it. Moreover, the pleasures with which the soul is tempted are the delicately sensuous ones of nature and of art. Its resistance to them is firm without being priggish, the firmness being implied in the terse epigrammatic replies which contrast with the generous expansiveness of the temptations. The detachment of the poet is also underlined by this neatness and by the slight air of exaggeration of the dialogue, the first part of which ends with an image of music and the paradoxical but stern reply of the soul:

Cease Tempter. None can chain a mind
Whom this sweet Chordage cannot bind.

'Chain' implies not merely 'fetter' but the chains used on board ship to fasten shrouds, and thus connects with 'thy stay' and the 'fall' referred to in the previous stanza by Pleasure. 'Chordage' re-emphasizes the imagery of music. But it also supports the nautical suggestion of 'chain', and appropriately rounds off the exchange with mathematical neatness. The power of Marvell's poetry is partly owing to this ability to use such an apparently simple word (a sixteenth-century refashioning of 'cord') with such different meanings as the harmonious combination of notes, the straight line joining the extremities of an arc, the string of a musical instrument (in this sense first used by Milton), a rope used for hanging, and in the figurative sense used in the Bible ('the cords of sin' and 'the cords of friendship').[2]

The chorus returns at the end of this section to the imagery of battle:

> *Earth cannot shew so brave a Sight*
> *As when a single Soul does fence*
> *The Batteries of alluring Sense,*
> *And Heaven views it with delight.*

The word *'fence'* refers back to the 'ballance' of the opening of the poem, but also includes the sense of the noun which meant not only 'a barrier' but 'a bulwark'. At the beginning of the poem the fight had been imagined as one between two armies: this first section of the poem ends with the imagery of a sea-battle.

Pleasure continues the contest with the temptations of sex, wealth, glory, and knowledge, and the Soul replies to these Mephistophelian baits with Socratic scepticism. The situation is dramatic, almost that of a morality play, and the rejection of knowledge in favour of humility finally clinches the argument. The completeness of the victory of the Soul is stressed with an almost burlesque exaggeration by the chorus at the end of the poem. The poet himself remains detached. The attitude towards the subject is very different from that in the much lengthier treatment of the theme by Milton in *Comus*.

The Soul is not allowed the same triumph in another poem of Marvell's entitled *A Dialogue between the Soul and Body*, where, on the contrary, it is the Body which has the last word. The imagery of chains and fetters reappears to describe the subjection of the Soul, and there is a similar use of paradox and exaggeration to create an effect verging on comedy. But in the second dialogue the Soul and Body reflect antithetically. Whereas the first reminds one of Milton, the couplets and personifications of the second look forward to Pope.

The use of paradox and exaggeration to produce an effect of comedy is one aspect of the wit that Mr Eliot pointed to in his essay as characteristic of the poetry of Marvell. He describes it as 'an alliance of levity and seriousness' by which the seriousness is intensified. 'Wit', he continues, 'is not erudition; it is sometimes stifled by erudition, as in much of Milton. It is not cynicism, though it has a kind of toughness which may be confused with cynicism by the tender-minded. It is confused with erudition because it belongs to an educated mind, rich in generations of experience; and it is confused with cynicism because it implies a constant inspection and criticism of experience. It involves, probably, a recognition, implicit in the expression of every experience, of other kinds of experience that are possible.' This quality of wit, defined elsewhere by Mr Eliot as 'a tough reasonableness beneath the slight lyric grace', was inherited by Marvell from his literary master Ben Jonson. It pervades all of his best poetry, and is found in a particularly concentrated form in his love lyric *To His Coy Mistress*.

The general idea on which this poem is based is classical: the belief in the virtue of enjoying oneself while one is still young ('*Carpe diem*') has been so often made the subject of lyric poetry as to be in some danger of becoming commonplace. Like Ben Jonson's *Song to Celia* ('Come my Celia let us prove'), Marvell's *To His Coy Mistress* derives directly from the well-known theme of the Latin poet Catullus ('*Vivamus, mea Lesbia, atque amemus*'), though in its details it is original. The treatment of the theme of time is both witty and imaginative, the effect being gained, as so often in Marvell, by the combination of rhythm and ambiguity:

> My vegetable Love should grow
> Vaster than Empires, and more slow.

'Vegetable' means 'having the power of sense-perception' as well as 'like a plant' (the Latin *vegetabilis* actually suggests speed and is equivalent to 'animating', 'enlivening', 'lively', 'quickening'). The anti-climax is gained by the contrast between the size of the love and the time it takes to grow, and rhythmically this is given in the verse by the sudden pause in the middle of the second line, and the three dead, heavy monosyllables, emphasized by the long-drawn-out vowels. The reader taking 'vegetable' in its Latin sense would meet a sudden contradiction and reversal of meaning.

The tone and movement of the verse both suddenly change in the second section of the poem, achieving that effect of surprise noted by Mr Eliot:

> But at my back I alwaies hear
> Times winged Charriot hurrying near: ...

Then, pausing again, the poet concentrates the thought of death into a single brief and vivid image:

> Desarts of vast Eternity.

The verse renders perfectly the feeling of desolation and the sense almost of betrayal that comes with death. The epigrammatic force of this line and the reflections on the horrors of the tomb which follow it could be parallelled in many of Donne's lyrics where he contemplates this subject. The description of the opening of his own tomb in *The Relique*, for instance, has the same epigrammatic force:

> And he that digs it, spies
> A bracelet of bright haire about the bone. ...

Marvell treats the theme rather more lightly. He is mainly concerned with death as a means of frightening his mistress and as a contrast with the invitation to love contained in the final section of the poem. Vital and dynamic, love is contrasted with the coldness and silence of the tomb where the only movement is that of the worms, and with the dullness and monotony of a humdrum passive life, the iron gates through which love must tear its way. Time and death, the theme of so much Elizabethan and seventeenth-century poetry, are conquered by love as they were conquered by nature in Marvell's other great lyric, *The Garden*. The means by which the poet reaches this climax after the leisurely and apparently digressive opening is a triumph of control and of organization. The verse gradually quickens, until at the end there is again a sudden pause, accentuating by contrast the momentum of the previous lines, giving the last two lines a note of finality:

> *Thus*, though we cannot make our Sun
> *Stand still*, yet we will make him run.

The Definition of Love shows Marvell at his most Metaphysical, and even closer to Donne in style and subject than in *To his Coy Mistress*. It consists of eight four-lined stanzas and deals with the subject in the formal manner befitting 'a definition'. Puns, ambiguities, paradoxes, and double-meanings are common to both poems, but whereas the subject of one is desire and fulfilment, the other deals with despair and the impossibility of desire ever being fulfilled. Despair is paradoxically described as 'magnanimous'. The lover is overwhelmed by the excellence of the person loved: to hope would be a sign of superficiality. The excellence of the loved person is matched by the despair of the lover. To complain at the impossibility of fulfilment would be a proof of petty-mindedness. This is a complete statement of platonic love. The soul is described as both 'extended', drawn out to unite itself with the other soul, and 'fixed', kept firm and stable because its attention is constantly directed towards the other. The soul is 'fixed in' the loved person so that they are both one and part. But events (the 'iron wedges' of fate) keep them separate. Their love would not be so perfect if this were not so. Moreover, if they could unite physically, fate, in the sense of death or destruction, would herself be destroyed. So fate separates them with her decrees of steel like the sword placed down the middle of the bed to ensure chastity. Though the whole world of love 'wheels' (or 'whirls') about them, they can never embrace. They are as distant as the two poles. To unite them the earth itself would have to be flattened as on a map. Here, again, there is a typical paradox. For the verb 'cramped' ('cramp'd into a Planisphere') suggests the noun. The world could be held flat only by a strong iron bar which would still separate the lovers. This image is continued in the next stanza with the mathematical figure of the oblique and parallel lines. Obtuse lovers, like obtuse angles, can meet anywhere, like 'the dull sublunary lovers' of Donne's *A Valediction: forbidding mourning*, which Marvell's lyric closely resembles. In Donne the communion of the two souls is compared to 'gold to ayery thinnesse beate' and to two arms of a compass, while their separation is like 'a trepidation of the spheares'. Both poems contrast ordinary worldly lovers, who are neither truly one nor separate, with the lovers who can be so united only because they are apart from each other, like the parallels of latitude on the globe. They are parallel, too, in the sense of spiritually corresponding to each other; their relationship is only so perfectly proportioned because they are analogous, two similar or identical spirits. Fate 'debarrs' the union, but by doing so 'unbars' their love (the Latin *debarrare* has the contrary sense to the English verb). The lovers may be poles apart physically, but mentally they are like two heavenly bodies in proximity to each other.

The great strength of Marvell is his ability to make poetry out of such paradoxical and complex material. He is much less slight and light than many other poets who self-consciously adopt an attitude of profundity. *The Definition of Love* is no mere display of intellectual fireworks, but a graceful and perfectly proportioned lyric. All the resources of rhythm are used, and emotion is generated by the very simplicity of the form. In such a poem of apparently bare statement, the slightest mistake in the choice of words would be disastrous. But there is an inevitability both in the detail and in the development and building up of the argument. The argument is not so much stated as embodied in the verse, as in the lines on hope in the second stanza, with their sensitive use of rhythm, rhyme, imagery, and alliteration.

There is a similar kind of philosophical argument, though with a much more strongly stressed natural background, in *The Garden*. The garden itself is a complex symbol. Marvell has a real garden in mind, the garden of Lord Fairfax at Nun Appleton House, and it is freshly and vividly described. But it is compared with the garden of Eden and hence represents symbolically the state of innocence, as Keats was much later to use autumn as a symbol of fruition and maturity. Philosophically the Garden is associated with the school of Epicurus, and the poet seems partly to share his view that the highest good is pleasure (particularly sensuous enjoyment). Pleasure is synonymous with virtue. From another point of view the garden is an indication of an ideal of human character. (In one of the early biographies of Sir Thomas More his personality is similarly described in terms of a garden, and his various characteristics in terms of flowers.[3]) This use of a symbol with layers of allegorical interpretation ends in poetry with Marvell. It was a literary tradition and a habit of mind that connected the Metaphysical poets with the Elizabethan dramatists and with medieval usage. It is to be found still later on in the century in prose in the work of Bunyan.

The Garden is opposed in every way to ambition and to the coarser worldly amusements. The palm, the symbol of victory and the prize for excellence, the oak, which was the civic crown, and the bay leaves, awarded as an honour to poets, are all rejected. That this should be done in a poem celebrating, among other things, the beauty of trees, is a characteristic paradox. The trees mock the human beings who use their leaves for such trivial and ridiculous purposes. Their mockery is prudent in case humanity retaliates by cutting them down. The poet, by implication, chides and reproaches too. As the home of innocence and quiet, the pleasures of the garden and the woods are reserved, as in Milton's *Il Penseroso* (a much lighter treatment of a similar theme) for the solitary and thoughtful man. Human love itself is rejected in the third stanza. The beauties of the garden excel those of any mistress; no woman could give such a constant love as nature. The gods themselves are shown finding solace in nature for frustrated sexual passion, and it is even hinted, in a characteristically witty paradox, that the quiet of nature was what they were really seeking:

> *Apollo* hunted *Daphne* so,
> Only that She might Laurel grow.
> And *Pan* did after *Syrinx* speed,
> Not as a Nymph, but for a Reed.

Then follows an impassioned and voluptuous wooing of the poet by nature. After the rejection of human love all the emotions associated with it are regained in the garden itself. To this extent the poet is like the gods. Nature, as here described, is very different from the rather languorous 'mellow fruitfulness' of Keats's autumn. It is active, almost in a state of revolt:

> What wond'rous Life in this I lead!
> Ripe Apples drop about my head;
> The Luscious Clusters of the Vine
> Upon my Mouth do crush their Wine;
> The Nectaren, and curious Peach,
> Into my hands themselves do reach;
> Stumbling on Melons, as I pass,
> Insnar'd with Flow'rs, I fall on Grass.

Marvell succeeds in conveying the tactile sense of the fleshy ripeness of the apples and the sound of their falling. The adjective 'luscious' gives both the smell and taste of the vine clusters which crush their wine on his mouth. The nectarine, though a kind of peach, naturally suggests by its sound and derivation 'nectar', the drink of the gods in Greek mythology. The peach itself is 'curious' in the Latin sense of 'full of care'. It is considerate, as well as strange, surprising, and odd. The poet may stumble and be ensnared, but his fall is a soft one.

In the sixth stanza the emphasis changes suddenly from the body and the senses to the mind itself. The mind 'withdraws' after all this activity of nature and in self-contemplation reaches a state of peace:

> Annihilating all that's made
> To a green Thought in a green Shade.

This means either 'reducing the whole material world to nothing material', i.e. to a green thought, or 'considering the whole material world as of no value compared to a green thought'.[4] Green was the colour for lovers,[5] so that the 'withdrawal' of the mind is not ego-istic or a mere absorption in its own perfections. It 'creates' as well as 'withdraws'. The poet now reaches the highest and most impersonal state of contemplation and of love. He regains the primal state of innocence and purity. Then his attention returns to the outside world and he sees in a floral sundial the symbol of nature's permanent con-quest over time that he himself had temporarily attained through nature. By its sweet smells and sounds the sundial measures time more effectively than the sun itself. Time has no power over the flowers, herbs, and industrious bees. On the contrary, without them time would not exist: they indicate and measure the passage of time. The garden and nature are not merely healthy influences in the Words-worthian sense – they are symbols of the triumph over decay and the other morbid influences of time.

The version of *The Garden* that exists in Latin is a reminder of Marvell's debt to the classical poets. In some of his minor pastoral poems there are resemblances to the Eclogues and Georgics of Virgil, themselves an imitation of the Greek pastoral poems of Theocritus. Marvell's debt here is shared by Spenser in his *The Shepheardes Calen-der*, Sidney, and many of the Elizabethan lyric poets through whom he assimilated the influence. *To his Coy Mistress*, on the other hand, treats themes common in the poetry of Catullus and Horace, and it is the Horatian influence that is the most important in Marvell's poetry, as it has been in that of Ben Jonson before him. The polished and graceful transitions from one state of mind or feeling to its opposite, the appreciation both of the countryside as a retreat and of the town and Court as providing standards of manners and behaviour, the mixture of gallantry and cynicism, the concern with the problems of death and time with its natural corollary of '*carpe diem*', are to be found in both Horace and Marvell. Of one of the greatest of Marvell's poems, *An Horatian Ode upon Cromwell's Return from Ireland*, Goldwin Smith remarked: 'Better than anything else in our language this poem gives an idea of a grand Horatian measure, as well as of the diction and spirit of an Horatian Ode.'[6] The resemblance to Ben Jonson's *Ode to Himself* ('Come leave the lothed Stage') has also been pointed out.[7]

while in parts of the poem, such as the passage praising Cromwell and the description of the death of Charles I, there are numerous verbal echoes from Lucan's *Pharsalia*.[8]

An Horatian Ode also provides a clear indication of the character of the poet himself. Marvell expresses sympathy with the king, but thinks that Cromwell is more efficient as a ruler. Viewing the conflict between them impartially, he is able to see the virtues of both men, and the human and dramatic situation interests him more than the clash between parties and principles. Cromwell is the man of the moment, 'moved by and yet driving [l. 12] a power which is above justice [l. 37]'.[9] But Charles is the more attractive as a person. The detachment and impersonality are typical both of the poet and the man, and are evident even at the climax of the Civil War. Marvell remains independent, and without being irresponsible is in a sense above the struggle.

The first few lines of the poem call upon the youth of England to reject poetry and take up arms. Marvell himself, however, had not yet given up poetry, and the poems composed at General Fairfax's residence were written during the next two years. The attitude towards Cromwell and the war is, from the beginning, one of tolerant approval rather than of enthusiasm.

Marvell admires Cromwell's past life more than his present triumphs, and the central passage praising him anticipates the mood of *The Garden*:

> Who, from his private Gardens, where
> He liv'd reserved and austere,
>   As if his highest plot
> To plant the Bergamot ...

The ideal way of life celebrated in *The Garden* is that lived by Cromwell himself in retirement. Just as 'th' industrious Bee' in the garden 'computes its time as well as we', so Cromwell with his 'industrious Valour', rifling the State as the bee rifles the flowers, climbs 'to ruine the great work of Time'. As the poet describes the struggle between Cromwell and Charles, the dramatic tension increases and the language becomes complex with puns:

> Where, twining subtile fears with hope,
> He wove a Net of such a scope,

> That *Charles* himself might chase
> To *Caresbrooks* narrow case.

'Subtile' is used partly in the old sense of 'finely woven', and 'case' means both 'plight' and 'cage'. Whether the cage in which Charles is trapped is that of a lion, a mouse, or a butterfly is left characteristically ambiguous, but there is no doubt of the sympathy expressed for the king when facing his death. While there is a suggestion of the flamboyant and theatrical in the picture of 'the Royal Actor' adorning 'the Tragick Scaffold', Charles is still capable of moving the armed bands of soldiers, and by the picture of them clapping their bloody hands the reader's sympathy is also drawn to him. At this point Charles compares favourably with Cromwell himself. His aristocratic poise and courage emphasize the crudity of 'the forced Pow'r'. His eye is sharper than the edge of the axe as he examines it ('axe' may recall Latin *acies* suggesting both sharpness of eyesight and the keenness of the blade).[10] The hard brutality is transformed by the dignity of Charles himself:

> *He* nothing common did or mean
> Upon that memorable Scene ...
> Nor call'd the *Gods* with vulgar spight
> To vindicate his helpless Right,
>   But bow'd his comely Head,
>   Down as upon a Bed.

Charles in his death has all the dignity of a martyr. The subtle placing and stress of the word 'down', the gradual slowing of the rhythm, and the contrast between the sharp and soft vowels of the last four lines, help to produce this effect. At the same time, the image of the handsome monarch dying with the same calm as he would put his head on a pillow contrasts with the force, power, and energy of his opponent. Marvell goes on to show, with a mixture of admiration and scepticism, how

> The same *Arts* that did *gain*
> A *Pow'r* must it *maintain*.

This analysis of a few poems reveals that Andrew Marvell had a range and depth out of all proportion to the amount that he wrote. The friend of Lovelace and Milton, he seems to combine in a unique synthesis the virtues of the Puritan and the Cavalier. The kind of reconciliation of opposing thoughts and feelings to be found in his best poetry would hardly have been possible if his style, and the general poetic tradition on which it was based, had not been extremely flexible. Writing in the middle of the seventeenth century his language is still Shakespearian in its complexity. The Restoration involved a radical change, and in many ways a deterioration and a coarsening. Although Marvell continued to write poetry, his best work belongs to the tradition initiated by Donne and Jonson. Dryden, the poet of the new age, was in some ways a greater poet than Marvell, but in Mr Eliot's opinion 'he lacked what his master Jonson possessed, a large and unique view of life: he lacked insight, he lacked profundity'. Marvell was more immediately and intimately the poetic heir of Jonson, and yet he was no mere imitator. What Marvell gained from his master can be seen by comparing his lyrics with those of 'the mob of gentlemen who wrote with ease' after the Restoration. Andrew Marvell was a gentleman but he did not belong to a mob, and from Ben Jonson he learned that one could write too easily. Marvell, with all his variety, was no mere facile versifier. His style is always deliberate and accurate, conforming to the ideal of the best writers mentioned in Ben Jonson's *Discoveries* who 'did nothing rashly; they obtained first to write well, and then custom made it easy and a habit'.

NOTES

1. M. C. Bradbrook and M. G. Lloyd Thomas: *Andrew Marvell*, p. 25.

2. These examples of the different senses in which the word could be taken in Marvell's time are given in *The Oxford Dictionary*.

3. The Epistle Dedicatory to *The Life of Sir Thomas More*, by Ro. Ba. (Early English Text Society), pp. 3-4.

4. H. M. Margoliouth: *The Poems and Letters of Andrew Marvell*, Vol. I, p. 226.

5. M. C. Bradbrook and M. G. Lloyd Thomas: *Andrew Marvell*, p. 59 (note).

6. H. M. Margoliouth: *op. cit.*, p. 237 (quoted from Ward's *English Poets*, II, 383).

7. F. R. Leavis: *Revaluation*, p. 21.

8. H. M. Margoliouth: *op. cit.*, p. 237 (quoting *The Times Lit. Supp.* of 29 Jan. and 5 Feb., 1920).

9. H. M. Margoliouth: *op. cit.*, p. 236.

10. This is pointed out by William Empson in *Seven Types of Ambiguity* (1947), p. 166.

POLITICAL DEBATE AND THOMAS HOBBES

BY D. H. PENNINGTON

Lecturer in History, University of Manchester

THE period covered by this volume was dominated by one great theme of conflict: who should hold power in the organized community and what relation had that community to the rights and duties of the individual? Under a feudal monarchy and a universal Church, the questioning had concerned only the few men at the top; under the Tudors it had been deliberately and on the whole successfully prevented from becoming too conspicuous; but between the accession of James I and the restoration of Charles II everyone became aware of it. The old State had already gone far to adapt itself to the new relations between men in the production and exchange of goods. The old Church had given way to creeds and organizations acceptable to men of widely differing outlooks. Now the fundamental assumptions of both Church and State were challenged, and into the argument went some of the greatest literary gifts of the age.

Much of the debate was inevitably conducted in religious terms. The Authorized Version was a contemporary work in which every writer could find common ground with his readers; and since the still accepted method of conducting a dispute was the competitive piling up of quotations from authorities, even those who had doubts about the universal relevance of every phrase of the Bible constantly cited it. Moreover the religious community – the Church or the independent congregation – was for most people a more real and comprehensible one than the State. Those who thought at all in abstract or philosophical terms could seldom move far from religious ones. But from the religious bondage in which political thought was held there now lay open two principal ways of escape. One was the appeal to English history, real or mythical, and to the embodiment of past wisdom in the Common Law, of which Sir Edward Coke[1] had become the acknowledged prophet. The other was the Law of Nature, a concept which in most of its various forms could produce a separation between questions of man's relations with his fellows and those of his relations with God. The Law of Nature was something perceptible to Reason. Often, as in the phrase 'Right Reason', the word meant the revelation to human understanding of a divine order. But it was an easy step from this to a purely human reason applying itself unfettered and uninspired to the solution of human problems.

Only a fraction of the great debate used the printed word as its medium. Most of it took place in churches and conventicles, in courts of law and in Parliament, in the Army and in countless outdoor gatherings.[2] There is no rigid line between the printed pamphlet and the printed speech; some of the best expositions of political ideas survive in the reports of debates at Westminster and at Putney. But we shall deal here only with material that is primarily literary in origin. Much of this was concerned more with vituperation than with argument. The broadsheet ballads[3] that were sold and sung in the streets of London; the newspapers,[4] legal and illegal, official and unofficial, that exchanged lively abuse and stories of heroism on their own side and atrocity on the other; the scandalous revelations like Clement Walker's exposure of the profits of war for the Independents[5] – such material had usually little literary merit. But occasionally scurrility rose to artistic heights. The dedication to Cromwell of *Killing No Murder*[6] – written to justify assassination of the Protector – is an ironical masterpiece:

> And if in the Black Catalogue of High Malefactors, few can be found that have lived more to the affliction and disturbance of mankind, than your Highness hath done; yet your greatest enemies will not deny but there are likewise as few that have expired more to the universal benefit of mankind than your Highness is like to do.

The outstanding best-seller among popular propaganda was unquestionably *Eikon Basilike*,[7] John Gauden's ornate version of the thoughts of the martyr-king, compounded from the unfinished manuscripts which Charles had left and from the author's imagination. It was at once accepted by Royalists as the king's authentic work, and despite attempts to suppress it, it ran through forty English editions and several translations before 1660.

From all this ephemeral controversy there emerge a few works in which the major topics of the great debate are seriously discussed. Some were as much a part of the struggle as anything that happened in Parliament or on the battlefield; others had no immediate relevance to it. The two sides in the main military conflict were not far removed from each other in their theoretical position. Parliamentarians proclaimed their loyalty to the king whom they were saving from his evil counsellors; Royalists paid tribute to the constitutional importance of Parliament. The Divine Right which James I[8] had upheld much on paper and little in practice was not in 1640 an urgent issue. The most unqualified defence of royal absolutism, Sir Robert Filmer's *Patriarcha*[9] was written before the war and circulated in manuscript among his friends, but was not printed until long after the Restoration, when it achieved notoriety through the attack on it by Locke. Even Filmer, though he bases his argument firmly on the Scriptures, offers a natural rather than a supernatural basis for royal absolutism. Obedience to a king is a moral duty because it is identified with obedience to a father. Adam exercised, by God's will, a father's authority over his children; Noah divided that authority among all his sons, from whom it descended to modern rulers. However fantastic his own arguments, Filmer sometimes scores in exposing the absurdities of those who justified obedience to limited monarchies by hypothetical consents and contracts. Logically, he insisted, the only alternative to absolutism is anarchy. But it was in a constitutional monarchy, however illogical, that the ordinary supporters of Charles I believed; they fought, not for the right of a monarch to do as he pleased, but for stability and against rebellion. Like their opponents, they believed that they were upholding the Rule of Law. The claims of this constitutional royalism were argued by such writers as Sir John Spelman,[10] Henry Ferne,[11] and Dudley Digges.[12] All these were involved in controversy with the one outstanding theorist of the moderate Parliamentarians, Henry Parker,[13] who expressed for the first time in clear and consistent terms the theory of political power that was afterwards tacitly accepted. Power was originally 'inherent in the people'; the king held his authority as a limited and revocable trust from the people as represented in Parliament. Parliament's sovereignty, though derivative, was absolute. It was subject to no overriding laws, but was itself the guardian of the law against the excesses of radical democracy, and must make the safety of the State its guiding principle. Yet since Parliament was in part an elected body, its absolutism could never be used for wrong purposes. Parker's conclusions are generally the commonplaces of our own time, and they are argued not on the basis of Scripture or bogus history but from the contemporary crisis and 'the charter of Nature'. The weakness of the argument is, of course, the easy assumption that Parliament did represent the people.

This was one of the assumptions challenged in the deeper struggle that began within the victorious side and ended in the triumph of Cromwell and the Protectorate constitutions. The theoretical defence of successive phases of the Interregnum was undertaken by the most distinguished, though hardly the most successful, of official propagandists. But John Milton[14] did not put aside his poetry to become a mere government hack. The pamphlets are full of his personal ideas and experiences – even of his personal doubts and spites. Their mood ranges from the inspired faith of *Areopagitica* to the thinly disguised disillusionment of *The Ready and Easy Way*[15]; their style from the heights of poetic prose to colloquial vilification. His contribution to the debate before 1649 had been his pamphlets against episcopacy and his *Areopagitica* (1644), which like many less nobly phrased pleas for liberty of speech and thought lays itself open today to the charge of restricting its high principles to those ideas with which its author does not disagree too much. Nevertheless, it goes much further towards altruistic toleration than the usual views of the sectaries. In *The Tenure of Kings and Magistrates* (1650), Milton volunteered a reasoned defence of the slaying of tyrants. 'All men naturally were born free', but when they fell into 'wrong and violence' they agreed to mitigate the evil by setting up a restraining authority. '... The power of Kings and Magistrates is nothing else but what is only derivative, transferr'd and committed to them in trust from the People, to the common good of them all, in whom the power yet remaines fundamentally, and cannot be taken from them without a violation of their natural birthright.' A few weeks after publishing this, Milton became Secretary of Foreign Tongues to the Council of State; and it was in a semi-official capacity that he produced, for European circulation, the two Latin pamphlets, the *Defences of the People of England*,[16] justifying successively the Commonwealth and the Protectorate. 'Nothing in the world', he says in the second, 'is more pleasing to God, more politically just, or more generally useful, than that the supreme power should be vested in the best and wisest of men.'

Cromwell had established his claim to this status by defeating not only the Royalists and the Presbyterians, but a third group whose importance he never underestimated – the Levellers,[17] who tried to start a democratic revolution within the Army. John Lilburne, Cromwell's only serious rival as a popular leader, had before 1640 made his extreme Puritanism and his sufferings in its cause well known. After the war he turned his two trials into personal triumphs that made him the hero of those 'common people' who felt they had been cheated of their victory. In 1645 he wrote in prison *England's Birthright Justified*,[18] proposing many of the reforms which became the standard Leveller programme – annual Parliamentary elections with universal suffrage, free speech, free trade, and publication of the laws in English. Lilburne's vigorous clarity avoids many of the common literary vices of the pamphleteers; but he was neither the best writer nor the most original thinker of the movement. *England's Birthright* shows him already under the influence of the two men from whom Leveller ideas chiefly originated – William Walwyn and Richard Overton. Walwyn had published in 1643 *The Power of Love*,[19] a sermon which set the tone of all his later writing – faith in and love for his fellow men, rational questioning, hatred of 'tyranny, oppression, cruelty, perjury, and deceit', and a gentle unassuming manner which contrasts sharply with Lilburne's self-advertisement.[20] His God was a God of love and reason, his Christianity a faith that must be shown in works. He wanted 'more of the deeds of Christians and fewer of the arguments'. Politically he based his devotion to liberty not on historical precedents or the text of Magna Carta (as Lilburne seemed to) but on 'reason, sense, and the common law of equity and justice'. His brilliance and lack of self-assertion made opponents label him as the secret and sinister influence behind the left-wing sectaries, a serpent whose craft and subtlety were 'seducing the indigent and poorer sort of men'.[21]

Overton's contribution is in some ways the counterpart of Walwyn's – satirical humour, a call to action, and a little bitterness. *Man's Mortality*, a highly heretical argument that the body and soul are inseparable, earned him an undeserved reputation for atheism and materialism.[22] *A Remonstrance of Many Thousand Citizens*,[23] written in support of the imprisoned Lilburne, calls on the House of Commons to assert its sole claim to sovereignty: 'Ye only are chosen by Us, the People; and therefore in you only is the power of binding the whole nation by making, altering, or abolishing of laws.' Afterwards, from prison, he developed his angry attacks on the House of Lords and on the unworthy element in the Commons, neatly linking his constitutional theory with denunciations of the grievances of the moment.

In later Leveller pamphlets the work of Lilburne, Walwyn, and Overton cannot always be disentangled with certainty. All three, together with Thomas Prince, were imprisoned for the second part of *England's New Chains Discovered*[24] (March 1649), though Walwyn was no longer closely associated with the others. Directly or indirectly all contributed to the final version of the *Agreement of the People*[25] (May 1649), in which Leveller theory was worked out as a written constitution. They had rejected Ireton's claim that political power was for those with a 'permanent fixed interest in this kingdom'. 'The people in generall are the originall sole legislators and the true fountain and earthly well-spring of all just power' (*Regal Tyranny Discovered*, 1647). But universal suffrage, which Rainsborough[26] had proclaimed at Putney as the Leveller faith, was modified in the third *Agreement* by the exclusion of 'servants' (i.e. wage-labourers) and recipients of alms. The elected chamber was to have sole legislative authority; but 'having by wofull experience found the prevalence of corrupt interests powerfully inclining most men once entrusted with authority' (*Article IX*), the Levellers bound the assembly by an irrevocable constitution. It could not restrict religious toleration, impose conscription, collect tithes, or levy any tax except 'by an equal rate in the pound upon every reall and personall estate' (*Article XIX*). Privilege of every kind was as far as possible to be eliminated, but the Levellers remained the spokesmen not of the destitute but of the lowest classes of property holders. There is nothing to justify the accusation that they would reduce all men to economic equality or would have property held in common

For ideas like this we have to listen to the almost unsupported voice of Gerrard Winstanley,[27] leader of the Digger community that tried to practise its economic creed on the commons of St George's Hill in Surrey. In him the doubts and qualifications of the Levellers are thrown aside. He calls for equality of power and possessions in prose whose passionate directness and moments of lyrical purity are un-equalled in any of the other pamphleteers. 'In the beginning of Time the great Creator Reason, made the Earth to be a Common Treasury, to preserve Beasts, Birds, Fishes, and Man, the lord that was to govern this Creation' (*The True Levellers' Standard Advanced*, 1649). But then selfishness and covetousness appeared, 'and the Earth that was made a Common Storehouse for all is bought and sold and kept in the hands of a few'. Private property brought in many other evils – war, the oppression of governments, the wiles of lawyers and clergy. With the abolition of property and the universal recognition of the Reason that Winstanley identifies with God, 'covetousness, pride and oppression' will disappear. Despite his faith in the inherent goodness of man, his Utopia[28] is not an anarchy, but a highly organized agrarian democracy, where 'overseers' planned economic affairs and filled the common storehouses from which all could draw according to their need.

The only writer who saw as clearly as Winstanley the dependence of political on economic power was James Harrington. He, too, thought of the connexion entirely in terms of land; but the *Common-wealth of Oceana*[29] is not so much a Utopia as a rational historical analysis of English politics, and a practical outline for a constitution to replace Cromwell's. Political authority, he thought, must, in a stable society, rest entirely in the hands of those who own the land. To distribute authority more widely he would therefore abolish primo-geniture and fix a limit of £2,000 to the annual value of land any individual might hold. His other reforms included an elaborate sys-tem of indirect elections and the separation of the task of debating legislation from that of deciding it. For Harrington accepted inequality of intelligence as well as of wealth: only a select few would be worthy to propose laws and argue their merits and defects. Like Aristotle, he tries to persuade himself and his readers that the rule of a propertied class is the same as the rule of the most intelligent. His system is at bottom an optimistic practical recognition of the victory of the gentry. The rulers of Oceana were the gentry as they idealized themselves.

Indeed, every theorist we have so far considered idealizes someone. For an analysis of the conflict that makes no concessions to ideals or to optimism, we have to turn to the one writer who with masterly realism draws together the themes of the great debate and sets them in the wider context of political philosophy. To say this of a man whose major works rarely mention the Civil War[30] may seem paradoxical. But the study of Thomas Hobbes[31] is beset by paradoxes. He was a Royalist and, when he wrote *Leviathan*, a refugee in Paris; yet the book was printed in London under the Commonwealth and bitterly attacked by Filmer and Clarendon.[32] His arguments defended the most extreme form of royal absolutism and denounced rebellion as the worst of crimes; but they made consent the basis of government, and were held to justify submission to Cromwell. He was a retainer of a great aristocratic family, and he exploded many of the cherished ideas of the Parliamentarians; but the terms in which he thought were those of the new society, with the interests and behaviour of competitive men mercilessly revealed. Most of the paradoxes are the product of Hobbes's greatest quality – his intellectual integrity. Where others tested existing society by imagined ideals, Hobbes, by reasoning from cause to effect, laid bare the realities of political power. He invoked neither moral condemnation nor visions of perfectibility; the most that political devices could do was to mitigate the evil consequences of human nature.

The *Leviathan* is the last of three main statements of Hobbes's political thought, in which, though the essentials remain the same, we can trace an increasingly confident rejection of orthodox ideas.[33] The *Elements of Law*, written in 1640 and printed in 1650, is no more than a pamphlet. *De Cive*, published in Latin in 1642 and in English in 1651, amplifies the argument, sometimes more clearly than *Leviathan*, which appeared in the same year. The three versions therefore became available in English almost simultaneously. They were all written when Hobbes was over fifty, and after the study of Euclid had drawn him to the methods of mathematics and natural science.[34] Politics became for him the highest and most complex part of a system of knowledge which started with the simple propositions of geometry and included in its scope the workings of the human body and the human mind.

His approach was a scientific and a materialist one, in which neither religion nor 'natural law' in the accepted sense had any place. But many traces of the discarded ways of thought remained. Hobbes was a scholar, brought up on the uneasy mixture of Christian and Aristotelian concepts that was the standard fare of his kind. Despite his cynicism, complete repudiation of the old apparatus never came easily to him, and it is from his attempts to adapt it to new purposes that many of his difficulties spring. Orthodox Christianity was clearly incompatible both with his method and with his conclusions. The Hobbesian State excluded any division of loyalties: neither a Church, national or universal, nor individual conscience must dispute the State's claim to absolute obedience. 'The law is the publique conscience, by which he hath undertaken to be guided.' Yet religion occupies a prominent place in his works. Nearly half of *Leviathan* is devoted to analysis of the Scriptures. He does not openly reject Christianity: having repeatedly led us to the brink of rejection, he indicates reasons for going no further. Religion is better than unresolved doubt, and it should be retained for reasons of State. Whatever subjects may think in private, they should outwardly conform; 'for the points of doctrine concerning the Kingdome of God have so great influence on the Kingdome of Man as not to be determined but by them that under God have sovereign Power' (*Leviathan*, ch. 38). The Laws of Nature, too, are accepted only to serve a purpose that reverses their traditional significance. They become merely the rules of behaviour that a reasonable man ought to arrive at in his own interests. Hobbes is concerned not with moral laws of superhuman origin, but with the practical problems of securing and reconciling individual interests and rights.

His system has its gaps and inconsistencies. It is not in flawless coherence that he triumphs, but in the sheer force of intellect with which he attacks his doubts. Despite his argumentative tone he grapples with problems rather than opponents – though his swift and fatal thrusts at muddle-headed idealists are a constant delight. His style is energetic and purposeful rather than immediately pleasing. He has not Milton's powerful range of language, nor Lilburne's passionate enthusiasm. The sentences are tightly packed with meanings and there is little room for ornament or elegance. Wit and dexterity are always evident; emotional eloquence comes only in occasional moments of anger or horror.

Hobbes was a materialist. He was also a determinist; for he held that the behaviour of the human mind was as predictable as that of any other part of the universe. But he was not an economic determinist. He recognized three main sources of action: greed, vanity, and fear. Men quarrel with each other for 'Gain' or for 'Reputation', or for 'Safety', and 'hereby it is manifest that during the time men live without a common power to keep them all in awe, they are in that condition which is called Warre' (*Leviathan*, ch. 13). Life is dominated by the fear of violent death, and material or cultural progress is impossible. Nor can there be morality: 'Where there is no common power there is no Law; where no Law, no Injustice. Force and Fraud are in Warre the two cardinall vertues' (*Leviathan*, ch. 13). The 'state of warre' is, in short, the worst possible evil, and to escape from it men turn to a lesser evil, the surrender of their freedom to an absolute sovereign. They make a covenant with each other 'to conferre all their power and strength upon one man, or upon one Assembly of men, that they may reduce all their Wills by plurality of voices unto one Will' (*Leviathan*, ch. 17). Hobbes admits that the 'state of Warre' is not historical. 'I believe it was never generally so, all over the world.' But he has some cogent answers to this objection. The condition exists at all times between nations; and consider the citizen who locks his doors at night: 'does he not as much accuse mankind by his actions as I by my words?' Similarly the covenant is not a historical one, but a symbol of the fact that the power of the sovereign rests not on Divine Right but on consent, given because it is expedient.

The covenant is of course irrevocable. It is a contract between subject and subject, not between sovereign and subject. Once the sovereign exists he must not be resisted merely because he behaves badly – and he probably will – for that would mean a return to the 'State of Warre'. He does not forfeit his power by breaking any body of law, such as a written constitution or the Common Law, for laws proceed only from him and can be made or unmade as he chooses. Only when he fails to maintain his sovereignty, or to preserve the life of the subject, are disobedience and rebellion justified.

So far there are no doubts or qualifications. But on one of the main questions of the contemporary debate Hobbes's answer is equivocal and incomplete. He always admitted the possibility that the sovereign might be an Assembly. He accepts Aristotle's classification of governments as monarchies, aristocracies (meaning any form of representative government), and democracies (where the sovereign body is an assembly of the whole people). He has no doubt about the superiority of monarchy, but the reasons he gives hardly ring true. In *De Cive* he is afraid that the meetings may be so infrequent and irregular as to endanger the existence of the State. In *Leviathan*, though he admits that monarchy has its dangers, he tries to show that a monarch is less likely than an Assembly to subordinate public to private benefits. He gets in some shrewd blows at the smugness of Parliamentarians: the counsellors of a democracy or aristocracy will be 'for the most part those who have been versed more in the acquisition of Wealth than of Knowledge'; an Assembly has more friends and relations than a monarch; secrecy may produce better decisions than publicity. But behind all this there lies the fear that dominates his political thought – the fear of disagreement and strife. Hence it is one of the duties of the sovereign 'that he judge what opinions and doctrines are enemies unto peace, and also that he forbid them to be taught'. He insists that a condition of any government other than monarchy is the acceptance by the minority of the will of the majority; and in monarchy itself there must be no doubts about the succession. When the subject's life is threatened he may, to protect it, resist the sovereign – for the preservation of life comes before all other considerations. Otherwise he should not even protest against the sovereign's decisions. It is not surprising, therefore, that Hobbes rejects the comfortable compromise of a 'limited monarchy' or a 'mixed constitution' – everything, in fact, for which both moderate Royalism and Presbyterianism stood. Political activity for the subject should be in the subordinate 'bodies politic' within the State rather than in matters of sovereignty. Individual liberties 'depend on the Silence of the Law', and their extent is for the sovereign to determine. A Hobbesian State could equally well mean rigid totalitarianism or *laisser-faire*. Stability, he feels, requires that the sovereign must act rationally and justly for the welfare of his subjects. He never fully solves the problem that arises when the sovereign manifestly fails in this.

Both his omissions and his assertions disqualified Hobbes from being the accepted theorist of the new order. He leaves his readers with little sense of hope, or of satisfaction, or even of complete understanding, but rather with the feeling that Leviathan is an ugly and elusive monster who never reveals the whole of himself above the deep waters. Yet, despite his hatred of muddle and compromise, he was on the side that won in the end. Peace with security; protection of property; the keeping of covenants; conformity in great things and tolerance in small – his demands are what the propertied classes reconciled at the Restoration needed, however repellent they found the price he asked them to pay. Hobbesian society lay below the smooth surface of Whig society. Hobbesian politics are the politics of the nation State with the hypocrisy removed. No wonder he was not popular reading.

NOTES

1. Sir Edward Coke: *Institutes of the Laws of England*, vol. I, pp. 35–40; vol. III, pp. 383–6.

2. Reports of the debates in the early months of the Long Parliament are reprinted, with introductions and notes, in *The Journal of Sir Simonds D'Ewes* (Yale Historical Publications No. VII, edited by W. Notestein, 1923, and No. XVIII, edited by W. H. Coates, 1942). Sir Ralph Verney's *Notes of Proceedings in the Long Parliament* is reprinted in the Camden Society No. 31. For the Army Debates, see A. S. P. Woodhouse, *Puritanism and Liberty* (London, 1938).

3. H. E. Rollins: *Cavalier and Puritan* (New York, 1923) gives a selection of ballads with an introduction and woodcuts.

4. Extracts from the principal Royalist newspaper, *Mercurius Aulicus*, are reprinted with an introduction by F. J. Varley (Oxford, 1945).

5. Originally included in his *History of Independency*, they were reproduced and brought up to date in the popular Restoration pamphlet, *The Mystery of The Good Old Cause*, which is reprinted in *Cobbett's Parliamentary History*, vol. III, col. 1591.

6. By Edward Sexby and perhaps Silius Titus; the dedication is reprinted in Orwell and Reynolds, *British Pamphleteers*, vol. I (London, 1948). This also contains extracts from one of the best of the anonymous pamphlets – *Tyranipocrit*.

7. For the history of the pamphlet, see F. F. Madon: *A New Bibliography of Eikon Basilike* (London, 1951), and the article by Professor H. R. Trevor-Roper in *History Today* (1951).

8. *The Political Works of James I*, edited, with introduction, by C. H. McIlwain (Cambridge, Mass., 1918).

9. *Patriarcha and other Political Works*, edited, with introduction, by P. Laslett (London, 1949). See also J. W. Allen in *Social and Political Ideas of Some English Thinkers of the Augustan Age* (ed. by F. J. C. Hearnshaw, London, 1928).

10. His pamphlet, *Certain Considerations upon the Duties both of Prince and People*, is reprinted in Somers Tracts, vol. IV, p. 316.

11. In *The Resolving of Conscience* (1642).

12. In *The Unlawfulness of Subjects Takyng up Armes against their Soveraigne* (1647).

13. W. K. Jordan: *Men of Substance* (Chicago, 1942) is a comparative study of Parker and Henry Robinson.

14. The Yale edition of *The Complete Prose Works of John Milton* is now in progress. Vol. I, 1624–42 (New Haven, 1953) has an introduction by D. M. Wolfe. Most of the political writings are in *Milton's Prose* (Oxford World's Classics series, 1925). See also D. M. Wolfe, *Milton in the Puritan Revolution* (New York, 1941).

15. *The Ready and Easy Way to Establish a Free Commonwealth* (1660) contains detailed proposals for a republican constitution.

16. There are translations in *The Prose Works of John Milton* (Bohn's Standard Library), vol. I. Several passages show that he did not altogether conceal his doubts about some aspects of Cromwellian government.

17. For the movement as a whole see Perez Zagorin, *A History of Political Thought in the English Revolution* (London, 1954), chapters 2 and 3; W. Schenk, *The Concern for Social Justice in the Puritan Revolution* (London, 1948); W. Haller, *Liberty and Reformation in the Puritan Revolution* (New York, 1951); Joseph Frank, *The Levellers* (Cambridge, Mass., 1955). The Leveller pamphlets in the last of these and in D. M. Wolfe, *Milton in the Puritan Revolution* (New York, 1941), pp. 469–83.

18. In W. Haller, *Tracts on Liberty in the Puritan Revolution* (New York, 1934), vol. III, p. 257.

19. In W. Haller, *op. cit.*, vol. II, p. 271.

20. The manner is suggested by the titles of some of his other writings: *A Whisper in the ear of Mr Thomas Edwards*; *A Still Soft Voice*.

21. See *Walwyn's Wiles*, in W. Haller and G. Davies, *The Leveller Tracts* (New York, 1944), p. 285.

22. For a discussion of his materialism see W. Schenk, *op. cit.*, appendix A.

23. In W. Haller, *op. cit.*, vol. III, p. 349, and D. M. Wolfe, *Leveller Manifestoes of the Puritan Revolution* (New York, 1944), p. 109.

24. In D. M. Wolfe, *Milton in the Puritan Revolution* (New York, 1941), p. 197, and W. Haller and G. Davies, *The Leveller Tracts* (New York, 1944), p. 171.

25. All three *Agreements* are in D. M. Wolfe, *Leveller Manifestoes of the Puritan Revolution* (New York, 1944), pp. 223, 291, 397. The first and second are also in S. R. Gardiner, *Constitutional Documents of the Puritan Revolution* (3rd edition, London 1906), pp. 333, 359. A. S. P. Woodhouse, *Puritanism and Liberty* (London, 1938), p. 342, prints the second *Agreement* with the amendments made by the Council of Officers and Lilburne's account of its origin.

26. There is an essay on Rainsborough in H. Ross Williamson, *Four Stuart Portraits* (London, 1949).

27. For reprints of his works see G. H. Sabine, *The Works of Gerrard Winstanley* (New York, 1941), and *Selections from the Works of Gerrard Winstanley* ed. by L. D. Hamilton with introduction by Christopher Hill (London, 1944).

28. *The Law of Freedom in a Platform* (1651).

29. Published in 1656. See also *A System of Politics*, which sets out his ideas in the form of 'short and easy aphorisms'.

30. *Behemoth*, which gave Hobbes's interpretation of the origins of the war, was written about 1668, but its publication was forbidden and it did not appear until 1682.

31. In addition to the works listed in Part IV there are short accounts of Hobbes in Perez Zagorin, *A History of Political Thought in the English Revolution* (London, 1954), chapter 13, and G. H. Sabine, *A History of Political Theory* (London, 1937), chapter 23.

32. For an account of these and other criticisms, see J. Bowle, *Hobbes and his Critics* (London, 1951).

33. See L. Strauss, *The Political Philosophy of Hobbes* (Oxford, 1936), especially chapter 5.

34. Compare the views of this in Strauss and in Michael Oakeshott's introduction to *Leviathan*.

THE HUMANISM OF JOHN BUNYAN

BY MAURICE HUSSEY

Lecturer in English, Cambridgeshire Technical College and School of Art

As the technique of popular religious composition evolved in the Middle Ages, it came to embrace a wide range of thought and emotion; soon, all human experience was involved in the oral and written explanation of theology. Religious and political ordinances at the Reformation could not banish traditional ideas from the English mind, so that when John Bunyan came to print his *Pilgrim's Progress* in 1678 he was still unconsciously in touch with the ideas of medieval Catholicism acknowledged by Geoffrey Chaucer and William Langland, to say nothing of the tenets of the Anglican Church accepted and taught by George Herbert. But the conventions which dominate successful religious fiction are not entirely theological. There are practical considerations, and an author is obliged, before embarking upon anything which he visualizes as popular literature, to recognize the nature and sophistication of his audience. It became necessary to him not only to make use of the tone and accent of current speech, but also to reduce the philosophical circumference of his work. Chaucer, Langland, Herbert, Jonson, and Shakespeare all share with Bunyan this linguistic qualification; they may at times employ concentrated imagery, but they are equally skilful in the direct colloquial expression of truth. Bunyan has precisely these qualities, and his work, while employing an allegorical method of great integrity, is charged with language pre-eminently suitable for telling legends, fables, and romances besides teaching the faith of Christianity. *Pilgrim's Progress*, with its spiritual subtlety and its popularity of idiom, is at once excellent Puritan propaganda and fine adventure writing; it offers much to literary criticism and to childhood wonderment as well.

A study of the work of John Bunyan reveals not only the religion of an old dispensation but also the predestinarian philosophy of John Calvin. The most insistent of this theologian's demands upon his followers is a scrupulous examination of conscience for signs and proofs of salvation and damnation. Predestination is apparent in

Pilgrim's Progress, which for this reason cannot be satisfactorily interpreted as another version of the Catholic Morality *Everyman*, whose protagonist indeed is a symbol of mankind as a whole. Christian is one of the Lord's elect, and an individual Christian; those that oppose him are reprobated and consigned to eternal damnation. In Calvin there is an insistence also upon two covenants for two classes of man: the Covenant of Grace for the saved which was the effectual sacrifice of Christ and an immediate passport to paradise; and the Covenant of the Law for the damned which was the standard of the Ten Commandments, a rule of life which was impossible for anyone who lacked direct divine guidance. Symbols of both covenants appear in *Pilgrim's Progress*; without accepting these symbols of the author's intention, no reading of the text can be complete.

Finally, in this preview of Bunyan's art, one needs to notice its heavy debt to reality and the dependence upon autobiography for so many incidents. The author's experience in the Civil War, in lawcourts, in prison, and in the countryside all appear; more important than these, however, are episodes which depict spiritual striving. This striving is dramatized and given a convincing and objective public form in what may be regarded as a crucial literary experiment. An innocent desire for diversion was admitted at the same time, and all these sources of the author's art enabled him to contribute largely to the growth of the classical novel in this country.

Pilgrim's Progress (1678–84) is an amalgam of religious aspiration and rustic life. Several similarities may be detected between earlier Catholic writings and this allegory, which has influenced all subsequent generations of readers and writers: Langland's *Piers Plowman* (c. 1360–90), Walter Hilton's *Scale of Perfection* (c. 1390), and Guillaume Deguileville's *Pilgrimage of the Soul* (c. 1330). In fact, a strong case has been made that *Pilgrim's Progress* is unconsciously the culmination of a long sequence of ideas and compositions communicated orally from preacher to congregation and from parent to child down the centuries.[1]

Although much can be established through a study of folk-idiom, we should not use verbal classification as anything more than a starting-point in literary criticism. There is often a danger that we may relegate the language and imagery of a popular writer to the folk-museum along with the metal fiddle and the tinker's irons still preserved in the Bunyan Museum in Bedford. We know, coming to his language, that Bunyan made a deep impression upon sinners precisely by calling them *breeders of lice*, *dirty sows*, or *greedy dogs*, but such colloquiality has little value unless it permeates longer moral passages with aphorisms. The language of the present subject is popular and agricultural, and we find all manner of unusual terms and single words in it: *slithy rob-shop, pick-pocket men; all on a dung sweat; would a had him; she all-to-be-fooled me;* the almost Joycean *to get a thing by root of heart; made shift to wag along;* short animal tales and farming metaphors and sayings: *loses his sheep for a halfpennyworth of tar* and the ubiquitous *make hay while the sun shines.* From these phrases and the completely frank descriptions of such things as pregnancy and bodily disease, we realize that Bunyan wrote as a man rather than as a gentleman and that his sensibility was of a practical nature. Abstractions seem to have come to his mind first in concrete or personal form, as the next quotation will show. One finds this most strongly in his spiritual autobiography, *Grace Abounding to the Chief of Sinners* (1666). It is a first statement in words of ideas which, as personification, allegory, and symbolism, carried the artistic perfection of the religious genre to its height. The book itself is surprisingly lacking in external event, since it makes the most of the growth of mind and spirit with its fluctuations of temptation and resistance. As a Calvinist, Bunyan abases himself and his pretensions in order to glorify the undeserved mystery of election and reconciliation with God which became his happy lot. This personal element is lost when Bunyan shaped the Pilgrim as a universally intelligible though not applicable symbol; ideas which are elaborated in *Pilgrim's Progress* make a first appearance in simpler state here, as in this passage:

> There came flocking into my mind an innumerable company of my sins and transgression, amongst which were at this time most to my affliction, namely my deadness, dulness and coldness in holy duties; my wanderings of heart, of my wearisomeness in all good things, my want of love to God, his ways and people, with this at the end of all, Are these the fruits of Christianity? are these the tokens of a blessed man?

Here we have the identification of sins with people, of the whole of life with allegorical fragments or 'wanderings of the heart'. The concrete style is developed for a simple and illiterate audience, which was expected to observe personifications and identify them in real life, much perhaps as had been the development inside the author's mind when he himself apprehended before realizing their significance; biblical texts emerge as factual imagery and physical experience in this book, rather than as thoughts. A whole gallery of portraits might spring out of this passage, which ends with the characteristic demand for fruits and tokens of salvation, from which a state of spiritual certainty can be achieved when the heart wanderings and the equivocal situations are over.

One of the finest short passages to exemplify the amalgam of rustic and moralist in *Pilgrim's Progress* follows, in the dialogue between Mr Talkative and the Pilgrims. Christian remarks upon the danger of his empty words in these terms:

> His House is as empty as the white of an egg is of savour. There is neither prayer, nor sign of repentance for sin; yea, the brute in his kind serves God far better than he. He is the very stain, reproach and shame of religion, to all that know him; it can hardly have a good word in all that end of the town, where he dwells through him. Thus say the common people that know him, A saint abroad, and a devil at home.

The first analogy here is essentially domestic, yet advanced as a permanent criterion. The words 'kind' and 'shame' retain early connotations, of creation and personal repentance respectively; the culminating epigram is a succinct idiom with a long literary history, to be found in several authors of the century, and clearly indebted for its sharp visualization of the hypocrite to folk-tradition. Discussions of this nature in *Pilgrim's Progress* provide effective drama, and they are the result of the author's experience of moral teaching and of popular taste.[2] They represent the summit of Bunyan's Puritan artistry.

It is not necessary to categorize *Pilgrim's Progress* as novel, belated morality, or theological allegory. It is hard to do more than touch upon the qualities of this book in limited space; from such a survey no idea of the vitality of the whole can be conveyed. In places the book is most vigorously related to dramatic speech with its informal movement and sinuous inflexion; while in others it rises to didacticism of permanent validity, its tone suggestive of a more academically trained mind. The places of rest in the pilgrimage, such as the halt by the River of Life, are carefully contrived and proclaim artistry as much as any rhetoric or skill in narrative:

> Besides on the banks of this river, on either side, were green trees, that bore all manner of fruit; and the leaves of the trees were good for medicine; with the fruit of these trees, they were also much delighted; and the leaves they eat to prevent surfeits, and other diseases that are incident to those that heat their blood by travels. On either side of the river was also a meadow, curiously beautified with lilies, and it was green all the year long.

A halt of this nature offers spiritual refreshment and creates a store of potential energy; in its use of Biblical 'green pastures' there is an artist's handling of light and shade, of tension and relief. The poetic evocation of grace, 'curiously beautified with lilies', is significant also, for it reminds us that the beauties of Puritan literature were never simply aesthetic ones; they always disclose connexions with the practical or didactic. They exist to do good, 'to prevent surfeits' or to cure those that 'heat their blood' in experiencing the world. Had this not been the case, a Puritan artist would not have dwelt at length upon them.

At the opening of the narrative Christian (then called Graceless, it should be noticed) deserts his home in the City of Destruction in order to avoid the snares of worldly experience, symbolized by the townsfolk present in the early scenes of both parts of the allegory. Two important incidents may be discussed together: the Slough of Despond and that of the Wicket-Gate.* The former recapitulates Christian history in the familiar manner later adopted by Jonathan Swift – an admirer of Bunyan – in his *Tale of a Tub*, and is a fine example of a verbal wit rare in one lacking formal education:

> It is not the pleasure of the King that this place should remain so bad; his labourers also have, by the direction of his Majesty's surveyors, been for above these sixteen hundred years, employed about this patch of ground, if perhaps, it

---

* Mr Worldly Wiseman, who separates them, was a later addition.

might have been mended; yea, and to my knowledge, said
he, [Help] here have been swallowed up at least twenty
thousand cart-loads; yea, millions of wholesome instructions
... but it is the Slough of Despond still.

This has the concreteness of the descriptions one reads of the state of
the roads in medieval England, and the handling of God under the
title 'King' and elsewhere the 'Lord of the Manor' brings the allegory
down to the life of the seventeenth-century parish most vividly.

The episode which follows is evidence of Bunyan's retention of
Catholic formulas. To negotiate the Wicket-Gate successfully demands the same humble submission on the part of the pilgrim as the
confessional-box, and the time Christian spends here can legitimately
be interpreted as a reference (perhaps unconscious) to that Catholic
sacrament:

> ... He knocked therefore, more than once or twice. ... At
> last there came a grave person to the gate, named Good-will,
> who asked who was there? and whence he came? and what
> he would have?
> CHRISTIAN. Here is a poor burdened sinner. I come from
> the City of Destruction, but am going to Mount Zion, that I
> may be delivered from the wrath to come.

Just outside the Wicket-Gate the armies of the devil are massing;
as in *The Holy War* they lay siege to Mansoul, and are prepared for a
fatal attack upon those who seek to enter with a wrong disposition –
the Catholic analogy need not be extended further. The sack of sin
becomes more oppressive as the true nature of its contents is realized
by the penitent[3]; the manner of its final disappearance is so economically described that it deserves separate discussion.

Between the episodes stands Mr Worldly Wiseman, the first hypocrite to attempt to impose an alien pattern of life upon Christian and
the nearest of them all to success. He indicates a turning, where

> ... dwells a gentleman whose name is Legality* a very judi-
> cious man, and a man of very good name, that has skill to
> help men off with such burdens as thine are from their

* Legality is synonymous with formal social behaviour, with Morality but
not Religion – 'he always goes to the town of Morality to church'.

shoulders ... and that which will make thy life the more happy is, to be sure, that thou shalt live by honest neighbours, in credit and good fashion.

Almost all the terms of reference are ambivalent: 'gentleman', 'judicious', 'good', 'honest', and 'happy' have different meanings for a Christian and a tempter, and the pilgrim is too inexperienced to realize the nature of this difference. He accepts the appearance and the name of reality, and turns away until, reaching the foot of Mount Sinai which emits flames as he passes, he finds himself face to face with Evangelist. His mentor upbraids him for deserting the path at the virtual cost of his soul – for the symbol of Sinai with the pressure of the Covenant of the Law behind it would be so interpreted within the theology of Calvin. But for Christian there is better news; as he passes the place of the cross and sepulchre, his sack of sin is taken away and the roll of election is borne to him by the angels:

> ... upon that place stood a cross, and a little below, in the bottom, a sepulchre. So I saw in my dream, that just as Christian came up with the cross, his burden loosed from off his shoulders, and fell from off his back. ... He looked, therefore, and looked again, even till the springs that were in his head sent the waters down his cheeks. Now, as he stood looking and weeping, behold, three Shining Ones came to him and saluted him with 'Peace be to thee'.

The Shining Ones are related to the Angels that stood with Abraham and were accepted in the medieval Church as symbols of the Trinity; here they affirm election which accompanies true grief for sin. Christian is not released from the possibility of error even now; had this been so the book would stop, as would *Hamlet* if Claudius were instantly killed. Both to maintain the narrative and to teach further lessons of humiliation, Bunyan continues to draw spiritual torments from his own experience and clothe them in the external properties of the Valley of Humiliation, the Valley of the Shadow of Death, Vanity Fair, and Doubting Castle.

The Flesh is slow to learn, although the spirit within Christian rapidly appreciates the sinful suggestion in the words of the wayside interlopers. The greatest ordeal to which his weakness leads him, the

Valley of the Shadow of Death, is directly related to Bunyan's blasphemous verbal automatism which he described in *Grace Abounding*:

> No sin would serve but that; if it were to be committed by speaking such a word, then I have been as if my mouth would have spoken that word, whether I would or no; and in so strong a measure was this temptation upon me that often I have been ready to clap my hand under my chin, to hold my mouth from opening; and to that end also I have had thoughts at other times, to leap with my head downward into some muck-hill hole or other, to keep my mouth from speaking.

The effect of the writing was cathartic, for later he was able to present a similar state impersonally:

> I took notice that now poor Christian was so confounded, that he did not know his own voice; and thus I perceived it. Just when he was come over against the mouth of the burning pit, one of the wicked ones got behind him, and stepped up softly to him, and whisperingly suggested many grievous blasphemies to him, which he verily thought had proceeded from his own mind.

From these passages there can be no doubt of the intensity of Bunyan's experience, nor of the relief from the Devil which was necessary before he could 'place' this situation in calm words: 'I took notice.'

There are other trials ahead, and I would single out the meeting with the lions which are chained, although Christian does not (as one of the elect) need to know this. He goes past, though two others, Timorous and Mistrust, have fallen back most dramatically:

CHRISTIAN. Whither are you going?
MEN. They said, Back! back! and we would have you do so too, if either life or peace is prized by you.

'Life' and 'peace' acceptable to these men would not satisfy Christian; if he accepted their advice – such is the stylization of the writing – he would have identified himself with their retrogressive qualities. As it is, he lives to further his pilgrimage and yet to reach Doubting Castle in which he suffers severely for the capitulation to doubts and despairs which are more terrible because they are so late in the pilgrimage. Giant Despair, his keeper, is a fine comic creation, the product of folk-tales and ballads, and a high tempo is sustained throughout the episode which he dominates. The imprisoned pilgrims escape after a period in which Christian forgets the key of the promises and shows the measure of his despair. The key, when it is finally recalled, goes into the lock 'damnable hard'. At first sight this adjective is another impetus to the narrative, perhaps an imprecation which fell from Christian's lips; on closer inspection it is a grimly ironic pun playing upon the fate from which it releases them, the 'everlasting nay' of damnation; and through one bare word a universe of sinister implication is given to the whole episode.

The allegory is not complete without insistence upon the punishments in store for those who are too full of themselves to attend to God. In Mr By-Ends we meet a more astute member of the tribe of Talkative, whose dialogue repays the closest attention as a perfect revelation of the *parvenu*.[4] Then there is the most plausible Mr Ignorance, whose error lies in demanding the ends without bothering about the means, and who presents himself unqualified at the Celestial City, only to be thrown out like the man without the wedding-garment in the parable (Matt. xxii). There is no occasion to resent Bunyan's handling of him,[5] for the dialogue which passes between Christian and Ignorance is most convincing in its analysis of reprobate error. The submission of Christian already quoted should be compared with the empty prose of this:

> I know my lord's will and I have been a good liver; I pay every man his own; I pray, fast, pay tithes, and give alms, and have left my country for whither I am going.

The parable of the Pharisee and the Publican (Luke xviii) foreshadows this statement. A further source of it was a religious dialogue written in 1601 by the Essex minister Arthur Dent, *The Plain Man's Pathway to Heaven*. In this book – well known to Bunyan – the hero is the Plain Man and the villain a caviller named Antilegon, and as a pair they show a close resemblance to Christian and Ignorance, even down to the dramatic inanity of Antilegon's spiritual disposition:

> I have always served God duly and truly, and had him in my mind. I do as I would be done to. If I go to hell, I shall have fellows and make as good shift as others.

There is no doubt of Dent's displeasure at this, and Ignorance no less deserves his particular punishment for presumption, described with monosyllabic simplicity and finality when angels 'took him up, and carried him through the air to the door that I saw on the side of the hill and put him in there'. Thus the pilgrimage of the two estates of man is concluded. In the process of self-knowledge that Bunyan was steadily inculcating the comparison is vital, and it sums up what the author was seeking to offer when he put a commentary upon his private experience into the hands of the public.

In 1684 there appeared a sequel which brings the deserted wife and family to the Celestial City also. The greater romance-nature of this book suggests a simpler, non-didactic purpose. Dancing and music are more frequent, both folk-song and the art-music of the keyboard, and the rigours of the original journey figure in the sequel only in the manner of some military reminiscence. Its great liveliness extends to the final pages where the last embarkation, in the manner of a happier sixth book to Virgil's *Aeneid*, takes place. From the sequel, most of all, we may refute the arguments of the inhumanity of the Puritans,[6] for in making his own happiness explicit Bunyan has dwelt upon the great joy of the divine presence rather than upon the theological minutiae which in the first pilgrimage tend to predominate.

It must not be thought that Bunyan is the author of a single book; *The Life and Death of Mr Badman* (1680) is the most 'modern' of all his writings and is most likely to attract new admirers for them. It is a colloquy on urban life and a detailed examination of the habits of Vanity Fair, a counterpart to *Pilgrim's Progress* which studies the progress of reprobation in the soul of the protagonist. Mr Badman is a trader whose life is a conglomeration of the rusts of sin. The atmosphere is appropriately changed from that of *Pilgrim's Progress*; false weights, bankruptcy, persecutions, the sordidness and lechery of a market-town are the subjects of an extended homily given by Wiseman to his friend Attentive in the form of a dialogue enlivened by crisp narrative and satirical writing of great fluency and economy.

All the sins of childhood are fathered upon Badman at his arrival in the world, and as he grows more knowledgeable and cunning, his range of sin widens at the same time. The position of apprentices in the mercantile system and the theological justification of that system are the major concerns of conscience in this book. Good masters and bad are equal to young Badman, for his choice is inescapably wrong. The novel proceeds with the birth of illegitimate children and the hypocritical courtship of a religious girl which ends in their unhappy marriage. The consequences are described with devastating plainness:

> Well, to be short, in little time, Mr Badman obtains his desire, gets this honest girl, is married to her, brings her home, makes a feast, entertains her royally, but her portion must pay for all.

The pages in which he brings whores home, with his wife sitting patiently by longing for death, contain further lessons in feminine conduct and are handled with conviction and restraint.

At each turn in the story additional tales, recounted to the joy of the narrators, are introduced to point the moral. One of these, on fornication, will show the fierce pace of sin. In it, a debauchee is faced with his latest bastard child:

> Now there was made in a room hard by a very great fire; so the gentleman* took up the babe, went and drew the coals from the stock, cast the child in and covered it up, and there was an end of that.

More elaborately presented than this is the story of Dorothy Mately, a perjurer who stole a sum from a fellow worker in a sand-pit, and on denying the charge was sucked into the ground and suffo-cated. The description is comic – the lad had opportunely 'laid his breeches by and was at work in his drawers' – and is accompanied with a wealth of circumstantial evidence, exact sums, depths and lengths of time; such verification, in fact, as to compel belief among Dissenters, who distrusted fiction and needed the citation of respon-sible witnesses to overcome their innate suspicion†. By this realistic reportage the nonconformist middle-classes were brought to accept the novel as a legitimate device of self-improvement, and they clung to it for two hundred years. Mr Badman, as a contribution to the development of the novel, was perhaps of greater importance than Pilgrim's Progress. The point can be made by referring briefly to the work of Defoe. Robinson Crusoe is an account of a physically

---

* The satirical inflexion, damning to courtly society, should be noticed.
† The incident is authenticated from independent sources.

and spiritually isolated man, and, like many later novels, it depends upon the Calvinist interpretation of the individual conscience displayed in fictional form. *Moll Flanders* and *Roxana* owe most to *Mr Badman*, though they lack the traditional firmness of moral character, which Bunyan's novel might have taught his first distinguished successor; as slight compensation they possess the accuracy of detail which commands attention though it cannot replace moral evaluation.

Badman's end displays the working-out of the plan for reprobates. He had shown temporary repentance as the result of an accident, but after the death of his good wife he marries an old whore and sinks still lower in esteem. The ending of this career of loose living is as gentle as that of his wife's: 'Mr Badman died like a lamb, or as they call it, like a chrisom-child, quietly and without fear.' This departure from convention – made more prominent by the juxtaposition in the text of the quiet and holy death of his wife and the flanking description of an account of self-evisceration by one in despair – is made in order to point out the dichotomy between appearance and reality and to provide a final and startling example of it. Nobody could doubt the fate of the dead man; nothing, therefore, can be deduced from a deathbed scene. Bunyan's everyday discernment and his formal theology enrich jointly this most realistic of his writings.

Mr Badman may, finally, be seen as a social document, relevant to the study of the rule of conscience in commercial ethics and practice. Bunyan was in no sense an apologist of capitalist enterprise, although he was no social leveller. The phrase 'grinding the faces of the poor' is employed, and all manner of cheating and oppression from trader and landlord are severely condemned. Nowhere did he speak out more forcibly against Restoration society than in the preface to this novel. A long scholastic section is devoted to bankruptcy, since Badman declared himself broken prematurely in order to reserve stock and a 'hatful of money'. The positive advice offered is that a bankrupt must make honest statements and attempt prompt restitution. The creditor, for his part, must not forget the duty of all men to support their dependants. The bankrupt must in 'Reason, Conscience, and Nature' maintain them. These three terms sum up Bunyan's demands of the whole of society and its intercourse; they comprehend his standards of ethical conduct. In spite of certain similarities, they are further in spirit from the key-words of the age of Pope that ensued – Reason, Truth, Nature, Use, and Sense – than the mere letter admits. A permanent belief in conscience and an insistence upon following all its dictates characterizes Bunyan's advice to mankind. Whether it was in the isolation of the heart or in the traffic of the market-place his instruction was the same, and in two very different books he gave similar advice.

There are many other writings by John Bunyan; they fill three large folio volumes and several more of them are allegorical in method. Only one of these, *The Holy War* (1685), is ever reprinted. It is a work of great ingenuity, and maintains the allegorical form in a manner more complex than in *Pilgrim's Progress*, describing the waxing and waning of grace in Mansoul through encounters between heavenly and diabolical armies for the possession of the fortified city of the soul. A classic like *Pilgrim's Progress* it cannot ever be; it lacks the feeling for 'character' which Bunyan shows at his best, and its procedure admits of no single interpretation. But it shows the author's preoccupation with artistic problems; he was too scrupulous to repeat past successes.

Since his death, the Bunyan tradition has not ceased to grow; many writers have responded imaginatively to the suggestiveness of *Pilgrim's Progress*. Two New Englanders, Nathaniel Hawthorne in *The Scarlet Letter*, *The Blithedale Romance*, and his story *Young Goodman Brown*, and Herman Melville, in *Benito Cereno* and his posthumous *Billy Budd*, have owed their assurance ultimately to the English Calvinists of the seventeenth century. In our own time the most distinctive allegory to stem from the tradition has been *Mr Weston's Good Wine* by T. F. Powys, a great admirer of John Bunyan. All these – and there are many more books which employ the allegorical outline in a mechanical and imitative fashion – are reminders of the power of this long tradition. They are also proof that the Puritanism of the early generations was in accord with the culture, the vigorous speech, and living belief of the country, a belief which had existed for centuries and which was no deterrent to the production of works whose humanism we commonly think to be essentially repugnant to the name and nature of Bunyan's religious persuasion.

NOTES

1. *Literature and the Pulpit in Medieval England* (1933), by G. R. Owst.

2. For further analysis, see *Introduction to the English Novel* (1951), by Arnold Kettle, pp. 42–5.

3. Cf. 1 above.

4. Further discussion will be found in *Drama and Society in the Age of Jonson* (1937), by L. C. Knights.

5. *Fiction and the Reading Public* (1932), by Q. D. Leavis, is invigorating on the Puritan literary conscience in general, though her account of the death of Mr Badman is simpler than the one offered here. Cf. also the article by the present author, 'Mr Ignorance', in *Modern Language Review*, December 1949, for further material on reprobation and hypocrisy in Puritan literature.

6. The conflict between Puritanism and Humanism in the seventeenth century is analysed in *Cross Currents in the Literature of the Seventeenth Century* (1929), by Sir Herbert Grierson.

ABRAHAM COWLEY

BY GEOFFREY WALTON

BY his extraordinary versatility as poet and prose writer, Cowley (1618–67) forms a living connexion between the literature of the early seventeenth century and that of the age of Dryden. An infant prodigy among poets, he began his career as probably the youngest of all the 'sons' of Ben Jonson. In mid career he borrowed extensively from Donne's love poetry.[1] He ended it as a founder of the Royal Society, the leader, though characteristically in retirement, of the literary world and a rival of Butler as a best-seller.[2] It is usual to bracket him with Waller and Denham, or even Dryden, to whom his authority was 'almost sacred', as a reformer of poetry.[3] 'He forsook the conversation, but never the language of the city and the court', says that typical Restoration divine, Bishop Sprat, in his *Life of Cowley*.[4] He was the effective if not the actual creator of the Pindarique ode.[5] He began the first Neo-Classic epic in English.[6] His prose and his more classical verse continued to be admired until well into the eighteenth century for what Sprat calls 'the unaffected modesty, the natural freedom and easie vigour, and chearful passions and innocent mirth that appeared in all his manners'. Dr Johnson, after all, thought him 'undoubtedly the best' Metaphysical poet;[7] he wrote the kind of Metaphysical poetry that the gentleman in the coffee-house and the eighteenth-century common reader could enjoy without undue effort. As Coleridge said, he was a very fanciful poet. In his own way Cowley has notable qualities, especially of tone and accent, and it was largely through him – though Cleveland (1613–58) and Butler (1612–80) contributed to the process – that a stimulating infusion of Metaphysical wit was passed on into Neo-Classic poetry.[8]

His *Ode; Of Wit* provides a series of pointers to the extent of his imaginative range and the quality of his sensibility. He begins with a brief introduction:

> Tell me, O tell, what kind of thing is *Wit*,
>> Thou who *Master* art of it.
> For the *First matter* loves *Variety* less;

> Less *Women* lov't, either in *Love* or *Dress*.
>> A thousand different shapes it bears,
>> *Comely* in thousand shapes appears.
> Yonder we saw it *plain*; and here 'tis now,
> Like *Spirits* in a *Place*, we know not *How*.

Clearly wit implies a mass of varied material in the poet, viewed somewhat frivolously as for ornament or amusement. It is also a mysterious and pervasive spirit in the background. Cowley then proceeds to define wit mainly by negatives:

> 'Tis not a *Tale*, 'tis not a *Jest*
> Admir'd with *Laughter* at a feast,
> Nor florid *Talk* which can that *Title* gain. ...

> Rather then *all things Wit*, let *none* be there.

> 'Tis not when two like words make up *one noise*;
>> Jests for *Dutch Men*, and *English Boys*.
> In which who finds out *Wit*, the same may see
> In *An'grams* and *Acrostiques Poetrie*.
>> Much less can that have any place
>> At which a *Virgin* hides her face. ...

> 'Tis not such *Lines* as almost crack the *Stage*
>> When *Bajazet* begins to rage.*
> Nor a tall *Meta'phor* in the *Bombast way*,
> Nor the dry chips of short lung'd *Seneca*.†
>> Nor upon all things to obtrude
>> And force some odd *Similitude*.

These imply standards of correctness and decorum, literary and social – certain things are 'not done' in poetry – and when Dryden quotes the second passage in the Preface to *An Evening's Love*, the context is strongly social. No serious critic thinks that Donne is characterized by puns and odd similitudes, but nevertheless this disciplined, tidy, and sensible notion seems a long way from Donne's 'giant phansie' which almost burst the bonds of language and was 'longer a knowing than most wits do live', to quote Carew and Jonson. The positive account of wit is equally revealing:

* Turkish ruler as he appears in Marlowe's *Tamburlaine*.
† Latin model for epigrammatic style in prose.

The *Proofs* of *Wit* for ever must remain.

All ev'ry where, like *Mans*, must be the *Soul*,
And *Reason* the *Inferior Powers* controul.

In a true piece of *Wit* all things must be,
    Yet all things there *agree*.
As in the *Ark*, joyn'd without force or strife,
All *Creatures* dwelt; all *Creatures* that had *Life*.
    Or as the *Primitive Forms* of all
    (If we compare great things with small)
Which without *Discord* or *Confusion* lie,
In that strange *Mirror* of the *Deitie*.

The main emphasis is on 'Reason', 'agree', 'without *Discord* or *Confusion*'; we have also been told that the judgement is like a '*Multiplying Glass*', or telescope, to give greater clarity of vision. One now feels that intellectual discipline has been added to the definition, and one may compare Cowley's poem with the severely analytic definition of Hobbes and the later and more genial and discursive definition of Dryden. On the other hand, one has been told that wit is 'like *Spirits* in a *Place*' and later it is compared to 'the *Power Divine*'. Cowley's conception of the poetic imagination would therefore seem to combine the ideas of inspiration and variety of material with those of selection and conscious art. By a certain superficiality and looseness of texture – for none of the ode requires close textual analysis – one sees that he himself lacks the imaginative concentration and tension of the great Metaphysicals and, in fact, exemplifies the type of wit he is describing. In this way he is a representative transitional poet.[9]

Cowley did not, however, progress simply from one style to another. His *Hymn to Light*, an impressive but not entirely satisfactory Metaphysical work, was written at the end of his life, the *Davideis*, Metaphysical in imagery but Neo-Classic in form, at Cambridge immediately before the Civil War.[10] Much of his best poetry was written about this early time when, as he says in the extremely interesting preface to his folio of 1656, he was 'in the good humour' and had the 'serenity and chearfulness of *Spirit*' necessary 'for a man to write well'. The chief poem of this period is *On the Death of Mr Crashaw*, written in couplets. Cowley celebrates his friend's double character, literary and religious, with sustained and calculated hyperbole. The manner and mood vary considerably paragraph by paragraph from the satiric to the elegiac and the matter-of-fact argumentative. At the end Cowley salutes Crashaw with Neo-Classic magniloquence and Metaphysical ingenuity of analogy:

> Thou from low earth in nobler *Flames* didst rise,
> And like *Elijah*, mount *Alive* the skies.
> *Elisha*-like (but with a wish much less,
> More fit thy *Greatness*, and my *Littleness*)
> Lo here I beg (I whom thou once didst prove
> So humble to *Esteem*, so Good to *Love*)
> Not that thy *Spirit* might on me *Doubled* be,
> I ask but *Half* thy mighty *Spirit* for Me.
> And when my *Muse* soars with so strong a *Wing*,
> 'Twill learn of things *Divine*, and first of *Thee* to sing.

It is the most emotional, not to say rhapsodic, poem that Cowley wrote – far more so than any of his odes, but the lack of irony in the attitude to his main theme and the simple stately organization show him to be a contemporary of Waller and already practising the kind of literary decorum that one finds in the grandiose elegies and complimentary poems of the Restoration. The elegy *On the Death of Mr William Hervey* is scarcely Metaphysical at all except in a few slight touches; it combines a polite, quiet tone and discursive manner with poignant personal feeling. The dramatically ominous and pathetic scene with which Cowley opens the poem illustrates the personal directness of treatment:

> It was a dismal, and a fearful night,
> Scarce could the Morn drive on th' unwilling Light,
> When *Sleep*, *Death's Image*, left my troubled brest,
>   By something *liker Death* possest.
> My eyes with Tears did uncommanded flow,
>   And on my Soul hung the dull weight
>   Of some *Intolerable Fate*.
> What Bell was that? Ah me! Too much I know.

He gives a (for the time) unusually intimate account of the friendship:

> Ye fields of *Cambridge*, our dear *Cambridge*, say,
> Have ye not seen us walking every day?
> Was there a *Tree* about which did not know
>   The *Love* betwixt us two?

> Henceforth, ye gentle *Trees*, for ever fade;
>   Or your sad branches thicker joyn,
>   And into darksome shades combine,
> *Dark* as the *Grave* wherein my *Friend* is laid.

It is worth drawing attention to the fact, as a sign of the movement of poetic taste in Cowley, that Johnson admired the poem for its naturalness, and that Gray seems to have drawn upon it for an important phrase in the *Elegy*. Compared with both the early Metaphysical elegies and the formal elegies of Dryden, informality is its salient quality.

Cowley's *The Mistress* brought him his first contemporary fame and seems to have been considered a kind of *ars amatoria*. He himself eschews any responsibility other than poetic for the collection. These poems belong with the Cavalier lyric; they depend heavily on Donne in dealing with the themes of body and soul and union and separation, but never have the tautness of rhythm and precision of phrase which give these themes realization. There is also an explicit aspiration to emulate Waller. Many of the poems are characterized by mere exaggeration and ingenuity with nothing alive behind them. The successful and amusing ones are – unexpectedly – in the manner of Suckling when he most resembles the Dorsets and the Sedleys who succeeded him. *Discretion*, *The Frailty*, *The Waiting-Maid*, *Honour*, *The Dissembler*, *My Dyet* are all in this racy, carefree, conversational manner. *The Rich Rival* has probably the finest management of rhythm and tone:

> They say you're angry, and rant mightilie,
>   Because I love the same as you;
>   Alas! you're very *rich*; 'tis true;
> But prithee Fool, what's that to *Love* and *Me*.
>   You have *Land* and *Money*, let that serve;
> And know you have more by that than you *deserve*.

Thus the intellectual love lyric petered out. The taste in poetry represented by Dryden's jibe that Cowley imitated Donne to a fault in affecting the 'metaphysics' instead of writing of the 'softnesses' of love is not very different from that of his admirer, Sprat, who thought that 'in every copy, there is something of more useful knowledge very naturally and gracefully insinuated'. In both cases conceits and ideas are thought of as something extraneous to the poetry, which expresses – or fails to express – sentiment. Later Johnson remarked in this connexion that *The Mistress* might have been 'written by a hermit for penance'. One feels of these poems that it is Cowley's wit in the narrow senses of fanciful ingenuity and humour that survives.

The odes in which Cowley thought he was nearest to Pindar's 'way and manner of speaking' seem, as he himself feared of a translation, little more than a jumble of words. But certain Pindariques, such as *Destinie*, *Life*, and *The Resurrection*, which are really Metaphysical poems in loose irregular stanzas, have the same kind of conversational liveliness as the love lyrics and a great virtuosity in conceits, for example:

> We're ill by those *Grammarians* us'd;
> We are abus'd by *Words*, grossly abus'd;
>   From the *Maternal Tomb*,
>   To the *Graves* fruitful *Womb*,
>   We call here *Life*; but *Life's* a *name*
>   That nothing here can truly claim:
> This wretched *Inn*. ...

Dryden learnt much from these as well as from the more solemn odes. The following stanza from the ode *To the Royal Society* will illustrate Cowley's representative position as thinker as well as the later development of his style:

> Autority, which did a Body boast,
> Though 'twas but Air condens'd, and stalk'd about,
> Like some old Giants more Gigantic Ghost,
>   To terrifie the Learned Rout
> With the plain Magick of true Reasons Light,
>   He chac'd out of our sight,
> Nor suffer'd Living *Men* to be misled
>   By the vain shadows of the Dead:
> To Graves, from whence it rose, the conquer'd Phantome
>   fled;
>   He broke that Monstrous God which stood
> In the midst of th' Orchard, and the whole did claim,
>   Which with a useless Sith of Wood,
>   And something else not worth a name.
>   (Both vast for shew, yet neither fit

Or to Defend, or to Beget;
    Ridiculous and senceless Terrors!) made
Children and superstitious Men afraid.
    The Orchard's open now, and free;
Bacon has broke the Scar-crow Deitie;
    Come, enter, all that will,
Behold rip'ned Fruit, come gather now their Fill.
    Yet still, methinks, we fain would be
    Catching at the Forbidden Tree,
    We would be like the Deitie,
When Truth and Falsehood, Good and Evil; we
Without the Sences aid within our selves would see;
    For 'tis God only who can find
    All Nature in his Mind.

This is poetry with the prose virtues, a vigorous and vivid paragraph. Scholasticism is seen as an absurd and obscene, but still dangerous, Idol of the Tribe which has been overthrown by the great intellectual image-breaker and liberator. The interpretation of the Tree of Knowledge story comes straight from Book I of the *Advancement of Learning*. Cowley like his master felt that for the present enough time and energy had been devoted to the study of Final Causes and the ultimate truths – which still remained true – and that the learned should concentrate on experimental philosophy.[11] The Royal Society was doing this.

Cowley was living in retirement in the country when he wrote this ode at the request of Sprat and Evelyn. There he felt himself, and was felt by others, to be the Horace of his time, and he composed his last work, his *Essays, in Verse and Prose*. The verse, whether in couplets or stanzas, represents a further refinement, in every sense, of his conversational style; the prose is moving towards a lucid modern medium, polite but intimate. In fact, Cowley in his latest work, which earned the admiration of both Pope and Gray, was almost more of a minor Augustan than a seventeenth-century Metaphysical, and his attack on '... The Great Vulgar, and the Small'[12] became widely current in eighteenth-century society.

1. See Mr John Sparrow's preface to his edition of *The Mistress*.

2. Contemporary references to Cowley can be studied in Mr Nethercot's 'Cowley's Reputation in England, 1660–1800' (Section I), P.M.L.A. XXXVIII.

3. Dryden's comments and their context are often illuminating. See *Essays*, ed. W. P. Ker.

4. Sprat's *Life*, *Critical Essays of the XVIIth Century*, ed. Spingarn. Vol. II gives an extremely interesting and valuable survey of his work and personality – one must allow, of course, for the obituary eulogy.

5. For his position in the history of the ode, see Robert Shafer, *The English Ode to 1660*.

6. For his position in the history of the epic, see E. M. W. Tillyard's *The English Epic and its Background*.

7. Metaphysical poetry was not congenial to Dr Johnson, but his severe, reasoned criticism should be considered.

8. For a fuller treatment of this, see *Metaphysical to Augustan* by the present author (chapter II).

9. T. S. Eliot interprets the ode rather differently in 'A Note on Two Odes of Cowley' in *XVIIth Century Studies presented to Sir H. Grierson*. Chapter II of my *Metaphysical to Augustan* contains a comparison with the relevant passages of Hobbes and Dryden.

10. For the date of the *Davideis*, see Professor F. Kermode, *Review of English Studies*, 1946.

11. See Professor Willey's *Seventeenth Century Background*, especially chapter II, for a fuller treatment of this topic.

12. Bishop Hurd's *Select Works of Cowley*, 1772, contains a note that this phrase had become part of the language and gives other interesting indications of eighteenth-century taste in Cowley.

PART
IV

APPENDIX

COMPILED BY MARGARET TUBB

FOR FURTHER READING AND REFERENCE

LIST OF ABBREVIATIONS

C.H.E.L.	Cambridge History of English Literature	rev.	revised
Ec.H.R.	Economic History Review	repr.	reprinted
		b.	born
E.L.	Everyman's Library	d.	died
ed.	edited, edition	c.	circa
fl.	flourished	?	probably

Space has not always been allotted to authors according to their importance, but according to the amount of relevant facts available or the amount of information already given in the text. In a few cases, where authors are barely mentioned in the text, details have been given of their works rather than of their lives.

Under each author, the aim has been to list first a standard biography (if any), second a standard edition, and third a selection of books and articles for further study.

FOR FURTHER READING AND REFERENCE

The Social Setting

HISTORIES: POLITICAL AND GENERAL

Hyde, Edward, Earl of Clarendon. *History of the Rebellion* (1702–4; ed. W. D. Macray, 6 vols., Oxford, 1888)

Ashley, M. *England in the Seventeenth Century* (Pelican, 1952)

Brunton, D. and Pennington, D. H. *Members of the Long Parliament* (London, 1954)

Bush, D. *English Literature in the Earlier Seventeenth Century* (ch. i; Oxford, 1945)

Cheyney, E. P. *A History of England, 1588–1603* (2 vols., London, 1926)

Davies, G. *The Early Stuarts, 1603–60* (Oxford, 1937)

Feiling, K. *History of the Tory Party, 1640–1714* (Oxford, 1924)

Firth, Sir Charles. *The Last Years of the Protectorate, 1656–8* (2 vols., London, 1909)

Gardiner, S. R. *A History of England, 1603–42* (10 vols., London, 1883–4)

Gardiner, S. R. *A History of the Great Civil War, 1642–49* (4 vols., London, 1893)

Gardiner, S. R. *A History of the Commonwealth and Protectorate* (4 vols., London, 1903)

Hexter, J. *The Reign of King Pym* (Cambridge, Mass., 1941)

Hill, C. *The Century of Revolution, 1603–1714* (London, 1961)

Neale, J. E. 'The Elizabethan Political Scene' in *Proceedings of the British Academy* XXXIV (1948)

Notestein, W. 'The Winning of the Initiative by the House of Commons' in *Proceedings of the British Academy* XI (1924)

Plucknett, T. *A Concise History of the Common Law* (4th ed., London, 1948)

Trevelyan, G. M. *England under the Stuarts* (London, 1904)

Wedgwood, C. V. *The King's Peace* (London, 1955)

Wedgwood, C. V. *The King's War* (London, 1958)

THE SOCIAL AND ECONOMIC BACKGROUND

Bland, A. E., Brown, P. A., and Tawney, R. H. *English Economic History, Select Documents* (London, 1919)

Gardiner, D. *The Oxinden Letters, 1607–42* (London, 1933)

Hill, C., and Dell, E. *The Good Old Cause* (extracts from contemporary sources; London, 1949)

McClure, N. E. *The Letters of John Chamberlain* (Philadelphia, 1939)

Peachem, H. *The Compleat Gentleman* (1622; ed. G. S. Gordon, Oxford, 1906)

Schofield, B. *The Knyvett Letters* (Norfolk Record Society, 1949)

Smyth, J. *The Berkeley Manuscripts* (c. 1618; ed. Sir John Maclean, 3 vols., London, 1883)

Wilson, T. (the younger) *The State of England, A.D. 1600* (ed. F. J. Fisher, Camden Miscellany xvi, 1936)

Albion, G. *Charles I and the Court of Rome* (London, 1935)

Campbell, M. *The English Yeoman under Elizabeth and the Early Stuarts* (New York, 1942)

Chesney, H. E. 'The Transference of Lands in England, 1640–60' in *Transactions of the Royal Historical Society*, 4th series, xv (1932)

Clark, G. N. *The Wealth of England* (London, 1946)

Coate, N. *Social Life in Stuart England* (London, 1924)

Dodd, A. H. *Studies in Stuart Wales* (Cardiff, 1952)

Finch, M. *The Wealth of Five Northamptonshire Families* (Northants Record Soc. xix, 1956)

Firth, Sir Charles. *Cromwell's Army* (London, 1902)

Fisher, F. J. 'The Development of London as a Centre of Conspicuous Consumption in the 16th and 17th Centuries' in *Transactions of the Royal Historical Society*, 4th series, xxx (1948)

Friis, A. *Alderman Cockayne's Project and the Cloth Trade* (Copenhagen, 1927)

Hill, C. *The English Revolution, 1640* (London, 1940)

Hill, C. *Puritanism and Revolution* (London, 1958)

James, M. *Social Problems and Policy during the Puritan Revolution, 1640–60* (London, 1930)

James, N. G. Brett. *The Growth of Stuart London* (London, 1935)

Jordan, W. K. *Philanthropy in England 1480–1660* (Oxford, 1959)

Knights, L. C. *Drama and Society in the Age of Jonson* (London, 1937)

Knights, L. C. 'The Social Background of Metaphysical Poetry' in *Scrutiny* xiii (Cambridge, 1945)

Laslett, P. 'The Gentry of Kent in 1640' in *Cambridge Historical Journal* ix (1947)

Lee, Sir Sidney, and Onions, C. T. *Shakespeare's England* (2 vols., London, 1916)

Lipson, E. *Economic History of England* ii–iii (London, 1943 ed.)

Mathew, D. *The Jacobean Age* (London, 1938)

Mathew, D. *The Social Structure in Caroline England* (Oxford, 1948)

Mathew, D. *The Age of Charles I* (London, 1951)

Newton, A. P. *The Colonising Activities of the English Puritans* (New Haven, 1914)

Notestein, W. *The English People on the Eve of Colonisation, 1603–30* (London, 1954)

Petegorsky, D. *Left Wing Democracy in the English Civil War* (London, 1940)

Pickel, M. P. *Charles I as Patron of Poetry and Drama* (London, 1936)

Rowse, A. L. *The England of Elizabeth: the Structure of Society* (London, 1951)

Schenk, W. *The Concern for Social Justice in the Puritan Revolution* (London, 1948)

Sheavyn, P. *The Literary Profession in the Elizabethan Age* (Manchester, 1909)

Stone, L. 'The Anatomy of the Elizabethan Aristocracy' in *Ec.H.R.* XVIII (1948)

Stone, L. 'The Elizabethan Aristocracy: a Restatement' in *Ec.H.R.* 2nd series, IV (1952)

Stoye, J. *English Travellers Abroad, 1604–67* (London, 1952)

Summerson, J. *Georgian London* (chs. i and ii; London, 1945)

Tawney, R. H. *Religion and the Rise of Capitalism* (London, 1936 ed.)

Tawney, R. H. *The Agrarian Problem in the 16th Century* (London, 1912)

Tawney, R. H. 'Harrington and the Interpretation of his Age' in *Proceedings of the British Academy* XXVII (1944)

Tawney, R. H. 'The Rise of the Gentry' in *Ec.H.R.* XI (1941)

Tawney, R. H. 'The Rise of the Gentry: a Postscript' in *Ec.H.R.*, 2nd series, VII (1954)

Tawney, R. H. *Business and Politics under James I* (Cambridge, 1958)

Thirsk, J. 'The Sales of Royalist Land during the Interregnum' in *Ec.H.R.*, 2nd series, V (1952)

Thomson, G. Scott. *Life in a Noble Household, 1641–1700* (London, 1937)

Trevelyan, G. M. *English Social History* (London, 1944)

Trevor-Roper, H. R. 'The Elizabethan Aristocracy: an Anatomy Anatomized' in *Ec.H.R.*, 2nd series, III (1951)

Trevor-Roper, H. R. 'The Gentry, 1540–1640' in *Ec.H.R. Supplement* I (1953)

Unwin, G. *The Gilds and Companies of London* (London, 1938 ed.)

Wedgwood, C. V. *Poetry and Politics Under the Stuarts* (Cambridge, 1960)

Willcox, W. B. *Gloucestershire: a Study in Local Government, 1590–1640* (New Haven, 1940)

MEMOIRS AND BIOGRAPHIES

Aubrey, John. *Brief Lives* ed. A. Clark (2 vols., Oxford, 1898)

Bacon, Francis. *The Letters and the Life of Francis Bacon* ed. J. Spedding (7 vols. London, 1861–74)

Bamford, F. (ed.) *A Royalist's Notebook, The Commonplace Book of Sir John Oglander of Nunwell, 1622–52* (London, 1936)

Baxter, Richard. *The Autobiography of Richard Baxter* (1696; abr. ed. by J. M. Lloyd Thomas, London, 1925; repr. E.L., 1931)

Bottrall, M. *Every Man a Phoenix* (London, 1958)

Cavendish, Margaret. *The Life of William Cavendish, Duke of Newcastle* (1667; ed. C. H. Firth, London, 1886; repr. E.L., 1915)

D'Ewes, Simonds. *The Autobiography and Correspondence of Sir Simonds D'Ewes* ed. J. O. Halliwell (London, 1845)

Evelyn, John. *Diary* ed. A. Dobson (London, 1906)

Fox, George. *The Journal of George Fox* (1694; E.L., 1924)

Herbert of Cherbury, Edward, Lord. *Autobiography* (ed. Sir S. Lee, London, 1886; rev. ed. 1906)

Holles, Gervase. *Memorials of the Holles Family* (Camden Series, 1937)

Hutchinson, Lucy. *Memoirs of the Life of Colonel Hutchinson* (E.L., 1908)

Hyde, Edward, Earl of Clarendon. *Life* (2 vols., Oxford, 1859)

Smith, D. Nichol. *Characters from the Histories and Memoirs of the 17th Century* (Oxford, 1918)

Verney, F. P. and M. M. *Memoirs of the Verney Family during the 17th Century* (4 vols., London, 1892–9)

Warwick, Sir Philip. *Memoirs of the Reign of King Charles I* (London, 1813)

Walton, Izaak. *Lives* (1640–78; ed. G. Saintsbury, World's Classics, 1927)

Airy, O. *Charles II* (London, 1901)

Ashley, M. *Oliver Cromwell: the Conservative Dictator* (London, 1937)

Firth, Sir Charles. *Oliver Cromwell* (New York, 1900; repr. World's Classics, 1953)

Gibb, M. *John Lilburne the Leveller* (London, 1947)

Hervey, M. *Life of Thomas Howard, Earl of Arundel* (Cambridge, 1921)

Higham, F. M. G. *Charles I* (London, 1932)

Huxley, G. *Endymion Porter* (London, 1959)

Marriott, J. *Life and Times of Lucius Cary, Viscount Falkland* (London, 1907)

Notestein, W. *English Folk* (London, 1938)

Oman, Carola. *Henrietta Maria* (London, 1936)

Ralph, P. L. *Sir Humphrey Mildmay, Royalist Gentleman* (New Brunswick, 1947)

Scott, E. *The King in Exile* (London, 1905)

Smith, L. P. *Life and Letters of Sir Henry Wotton* (2 vols., Oxford, 1907)

Trevor-Roper, H. R. *Archbishop Laud, 1573–1645* (London, 1940)

Wedgwood, C. V. *Strafford* (London, 1961)

Williamson, H. Ross. *Four Stuart Portraits* (for the life of Sir Balthazar Gerbier; London, 1949)

Willson, D. H. *King James VI and I* (London, 1956)

Wormald, B. H. G. *Clarendon, Politics, History, Religion* (Cambridge, 1951)

Wormald, B. H. G. 'How Hyde became a Royalist', in *Cambridge Historical Journal* VIII (1945)

THE RELIGIOUS AND INTELLECTUAL BACKGROUND

Haller, W. *Tracts on Liberty in the Puritan Revolution, 1638–47* (3 vols., New York, 1934)

Haller, W., and Davies, G. *The Leveller Tracts, 1647–53* (New York, 1944)

Henson, H. H. *Selected English Sermons* (World's Classics, 1939)

Miller, P., and Johnson, T. H. *The Puritans* (an anthology of Puritan writing; New York, 1938)

More, P. E., and Cross, F. L. *Anglicanism: The Thought and Practice of the Church of England, Illustrated from the Religious Literature of the 17th Century* (London, 1935)

Bacon, Francis. *Essays* (1597–1625; World's Classics, 1902)

Bacon, Francis. *The Advancement of Learning* (1605; World's Classics, 1906)

Browne, Sir Thomas. *Religio Medici* (1642; ed. C. H. Herford, E.L., 1906)

Browne, Sir Thomas, *Pseudodoxia Epidemica (Vulgar Errors)* (1646; Bohn's Standard Library ed. of Works I, London, 1894)

Burton, Robert. *The Anatomy of Melancholy* (1621; ed. H. Jackson, E.L., 1932)

Filmer, Sir Robert. *Patriarcha* (1680; ed. P. Laslett, London, 1949)

Herbert, Edward, Lord. *De Veritate* (1624; trans. M. Carré, Bristol, 1937)

Hobbes, Thomas. *Leviathan* (1651; ed. M. Oakeshott, Oxford, 1946; and E.L., 1914)

Milton, John. *Areopagitica and other Prose Works* ed. C. E. Vaughan (E.L., 1927)

Ralegh, Sir Walter. *History of the World* (1614; *Works* II ed. Oldys and Birch, Oxford, 1829)

Selden, J. *Table-Talk* (1689; ed. Sir F. Pollock, Selden Society, 1927)

Allen, J. W. *English Political Thought, 1603–60* I (London, 1938)

Babb, L. *The Elizabethan Malady* (East Lansing, 1951)

Bethell, S. L. *The Cultural Revolution of the 17th Century* (London, 1951)

Bosher, R. S. *The Making of the Restoration Settlement* (London, 1951)

Braithwaite, W. C. *The Beginnings of Quakerism* (London, 1912, 2nd rev. ed. by H. J. Cadbury, Cambridge, 1955)

Brown, J. H. *Elizabethan Schooldays* (Oxford, 1933)

Burtt, E. A. *The Metaphysical Foundations of Modern Physical Science* (London, 1925)

Butterfield, H. *The Origins of Modern Science, 1300–1800* (London, 1951)

Clark, G. N. *The Seventeenth Century* (rev. ed., Oxford, 1947)

Costello, W. T. *The Curriculum at Seventeenth Century Cambridge* (Harvard, 1958)

Craig, H. *The Enchanted Glass* (New York, 1936)

Curtis, M. *Oxford and Cambridge in Transition 1558–1642* (London, 1959)

Dampier, Sir W. C. *A History of Science and its Relations with Philosophy and Religion* (3rd ed., Cambridge, 1942)

Firth, Sir Charles. 'Sir Walter Raleigh's *History of the World*' in *Proceedings of the British Academy* VIII (1919)

Frere, W. H. *The English Church in the Reigns of Elizabeth and James I* (London, 1904)

Gooch, G. P., and Laski, H. *English Democratic Ideas in the 17th Century* (Cambridge, 1927)

Hall, A. R. *The Scientific Revolution, 1500–1800* (London, 1954)

Haller, W. *The Rise of Puritanism, 1570–1642* (New York, 1938)

Harris, V. *All Coherence Gone* (Chicago, 1949)

Hill, C. *Economic Problems of the Church from Archbishop Whitgift to the Long Parliament* (Oxford, 1956)

Hutton, W. H. *The English Church from the Accession of Charles I to the Death of Anne* (London, 1903)

Hutton, W. H. Chapter on the Caroline divines in *C.H.E.L.* VII (1911)

Jones, R. F. *Ancients and Moderns* (Washington, 1936)

Jones, R. N. *Mysticism and Democracy in the English Commonwealth* (Cambridge, Mass., 1932)

Jordan, W. K. *The Development of Religious Toleration* II–IV (London 1932–40)

Knights, L. C. *Drama and Society in the Age of Jonson* (with an Appendix on Melancholy; London, 1937)

Leavis, Q. D. *Fiction and the Reading Public* (London, 1932)

Lovejoy, A. O. *The Great Chain of Being* (Harvard, 1936)

Lyons, Sir H. *The Royal Society* (London, 1944)

Mallet, Sir C. *History of the University of Oxford* II (3 vols., Oxford, 1924-7)

Miller, P. *The New England Mind: The Seventeenth Century* (New York, 1939)

Mitchell, W. F. *English Pulpit Oratory from Andrewes to Tillotson*, (London, 1932)

Mullinger, J. B. *The University of Cambridge* II and III (Cambridge, 1884)

Nicholson, M. *The Breaking of the Circle* (Evanston, 1950)

Notestein, W. *The History of Witchcraft in England* (Washington, 1911)

Ornstein, M. *The Role of Scientific Societies in the Seventeenth Century* (Chicago, 1938)

Powicke, F. J. *The Cambridge Platonists* (London, 1926)

Spencer, T. *Shakespeare and the Nature of Man* (Cambridge, 1943)

Stimson, D. *The Gradual Acceptance of the Copernican Theory of the Universe* (New York, 1917)

Tatham, G. B. *The Puritans in Power* (Cambridge, 1913)

Tillyard, E. M. W. *The Elizabethan World Picture* (London, 1943)

Usher, R. G. *The Reconstruction of the English Church* (2 vols., London, 1910)

Watson, F. *The English Grammar Schools to 1660* (Cambridge, 1908)

Weld, C. R. *History of the Royal Society* (2 vols., London, 1848)

White, H. C. *English Devotional Literature* (Prose, 1600-40) (Wisconsin, 1931)

Whitehead, A. N. *Science and the Modern World* (London, 1925)

Wiley, M. L. *The Subtle Knot* (London, 1952)

Willey, B. *The Seventeenth Century Background* (London, 1934)

Williams, A. T. P. *The Anglican Tradition* (London, 1947)

Woodhouse, A. S. P. *Puritanism and Liberty: Being the Army Debates (1647-9)* (London, 1938)

Wright, L. B. *Middle-Class Culture in Elizabethan England* (Chapel Hill, 1935)

Reference and Criticism

GENERAL STUDIES

Brooke, Tucker. 'The Renaissance, 1485-1660' in *A Literary History of England* ed. A. C. Baugh (New York, 1948)

Bush, D. *English Literature in the Earlier Seventeenth Century* (Oxford, 1945)

C.H.E.L. VI-VIII (1910-12)

de Sola Pinto, V. *The English Renaissance, 1510–1688* in 'Introductions to English Literature' II ed. B. Dobrée (London, rev. ed., 1950)

Grierson, Sir Herbert. *Cross Currents in English Literature of the Seventeenth Century* (London, 1929)

Grierson, Sir Herbert. *The First Half of the Seventeenth Century* (Edinburgh, 1906)

Knights, L. C. *Explorations* (London, 1946)

Seventeenth Century Studies presented to Sir Herbert Grierson (Oxford, 1938)

Wedgwood, C. V. *Seventeenth Century English Literature* (London, 1950)

Willey, B. *The Seventeenth Century Background* (London, 1934)

Wilson, F. P. *Elizabethan and Jacobean* (Oxford, 1945)

The Year's Work in English Studies (annual survey of literary research published by the English Association since 1919)

POETRY AND THE ARTS

Bennett, J. *Four Metaphysical Poets* (Cambridge, 1934)

Brooks, C. *Modern Poetry and the Tradition* (London, 1948)

Brooks, C. *The Well-Wrought Urn* (London, 1949)

Brooks, C., and Warren, R. P. *Understanding Poetry* (New York, 1938)

Bush, D. *Science and English Poetry* (New York, 1950)

Courthope, W. J. *History of English Poetry* II and III (London, 1897)

Cruttwell, P. *The Shakespearean Moment* (London, 1954)

Davis, Herbert, and Gardner, Helen (eds.) *Elizabethan and Jacobean Studies Presented to F. P. Wilson* (Oxford, 1959)

de Mourgues, Odette. *Metaphysical, Baroque and Précieux Poetry* (Oxford, 1953)

Eliot, T. S. 'The Metaphysical Poets' in *Selected Essays* (London, 1932)

Empson, W. *Seven Types of Ambiguity* (London, 1947)

Empson, W. *Some Versions of Pastoral* (London, 1935)

Freeman, R. *English Emblem Books* (London, 1948)

Grierson, Sir Herbert. Introduction to *Metaphysical Lyrics and Poems of the Seventeenth Century* (Oxford, 1921)

Leavis, F. R. 'The Line of Wit' in *Revaluation* (London, 1936)

Leishman, J. B. *The Metaphysical Poets* (Oxford, 1934)

Mahood, M. M. *Poetry and Humanism* (London, 1950)

McEwen, K. A. *Classical Influence upon the Tribe of Ben* (Cedar Rapids, Iowa, 1939)

Martz, Louis, *The Poetry of Meditation* (New Haven, 1954)

Mellers, W. H. *Music and Society* (London, 1946)

Pattison, B. *Music and Poetry of the English Renaissance* (London, 1948)

Praz, M. *Studies in Seventeenth Century Imagery* (London, 1939)

Sharp, R. L. *From Donne to Dryden: The Revolt against Metaphysical Poetry* (Chapel Hill, 1940)

Smith, J. 'Metaphysical Poetry' in *Determinations* ed. F. R. Leavis (London, 1934)

Summerson, J. *Architecture in Britain, 1530–1830* (Harmondsworth, 1953)

Walton, G. *Metaphysical to Augustan* (Cambridge, 1955)

Waterhouse, E. K. *Painting in Britain, 1530–1790* (Harmondsworth, 1953)

Welsford, E. *The Court Masque* (Cambridge, 1927)

White, H. C. *The Metaphysical Poets* (New York, 1936)

Williamson, G. *The Donne Tradition* (Cambridge, Mass., 1930)

Williamson, G. *Seventeenth Century Contexts* (London, 1960)

SEVENTEENTH-CENTURY CRITICISM

Atkins, J. W. H. *English Literary Criticism: the Renascence* (London, 1947)

Gregory Smith, G. (ed.) *Elizabethan Critical Essays* (2 vols., Oxford, 1904)

Jones, E. D. (ed.) *English Critical Essays: 16th–18th Centuries* (London, 1922)

Saintsbury, G. *History of English Criticism* (London, 1911)

Spingarn, J. E. *History of Literary Criticism in the Renaissance* (New York, 1899)

Spingarn, J. E. (ed.) *Seventeenth Century Critical Essays* (3 vols., Oxford, 1908–9)

Tuve, R. *Elizabethan and Metaphysical Imagery* (Chicago, 1947)

Wallerstein, R. *Studies in Seventeenth-Century Poetic* (Wisconsin, 1950)

PROSE

Daiches, D. *The King James Version of the English Bible* (Chicago, 1941)

de Sola Pinto, V. *English Biography in the Seventeenth Century* (London, 1951)

Eliot, T. S. 'Lancelot Andrewes' in *Selected Essays* (London, 1932)

Krapp, G. P. *The Rise of English Literary Prose* (New York, 1915)

Mitchell, W. F. *English Pulpit Oratory from Andrewes to Tillotson* (London, 1932)

Nichol Smith, D. *Characters of the Seventeenth Century* (Oxford, 1918)

Phelps, G. 'Prose Literature' in *Life under the Stuarts* (London, 1950)

Stauffer, D. *English Biography before 1700* (Cambridge, Mass., 1930)

Wedgwood, C. V. 'Practical Prose' in *Seventeenth Century English Literature* (London, 1950)

Willey, B. *The Seventeenth Century Background* (London, 1934)

Williamson, G. *The Senecan Amble* (London, 1951)

AUTHORS AND WORKS

Collections and Anthologies

Ault, N. (ed.) *Seventeenth Century Lyrics* (2nd ed., London, 1950)

Fellowes, E. H. (ed.) *English Madrigal Verse* (Oxford, 1920)

Gardner, Helen (ed.) *The Metaphysical Poets* (Penguin, 1957)

Grierson, Sir Herbert (ed.) *Metaphysical Lyrics and Poems of the Seventeenth Century* (Oxford, 1921)

Grierson, Sir Herbert and Bullough, G. (eds.) *The Oxford Book of Seventeenth Century Verse* (Oxford, 1934)

Hebel, J. W. and Hudson, H. H. (eds.) *Poetry of the English Renaissance, 1509–1660* (New York, 1932)

Howarth, R. G. (ed.) *Minor Poets of the Seventeenth Century* (E.L., 1931)

Judson, A. C. (ed.) *Seventeenth Century Lyrics* (Chicago, 1927)

Marshall, L. B. (ed.) *Rare Poems of the Seventeenth Century* (Cambridge, 1936)

Massingham, H. J. (ed.) *A Treasury of Seventeenth Century Poetry* (London, 1919)

Muir, Kenneth (ed.) *Elizabethan and Jacobean Prose 1550–1670* (Pelican, 1956)

Saintsbury, G. (ed.) *Minor Poets of the Caroline Period* (3 vols., Oxford, 1905–21)

Ure, Peter (ed.) *Seventeenth-century Prose 1620–1700* (Pelican, 1956)

Aldington, R. (ed.) *A Book of 'Characters'* (London, 1924)

Coffin, R. P. T. and Witherspoon, A. M. (eds.) *A Book of Seventeenth Century Prose* (New York, 1929)

Craik, H. (ed.) *English Prose Selections* II: *Sixteenth Century to the Restoration* (London, 1894)

Miller, P. and Johnson, T. H. *The Puritans* (New York, 1938)

Moore, C. A. and Bush, D. (eds.) *English Prose, 1600–1660* (New York, 1930)

Morley, H. (ed.) *Character Writings of the Seventeenth Century* (London, 1891)

Ward, A. C. *A Miscellany of Tracts and Pamphlets, XVI–XX Centuries* (World's Classics, 1927)

Authors

BROWNE, SIR THOMAS (1605–82): Author and physician; Winchester and Oxford; M.A., 1629; took M.D. at Leyden, 1634; *Religio Medici* written during period of leisure in Yorkshire village, published without his permission, 1642, and re-issued with his sanction, 1643; settled as doctor in Norwich, 1637; published *Pseudodoxia Epidemica* (*Vulgar Errors*), 1646; inspired by discovery of funeral urns near Norwich to write *Urne Burial*, 1658; knighted on royal visit to Norwich, 1671.

The Works of Sir Thomas Browne ed. G. L. Keynes (6 vols., London, 1928–31; vols. 5 and 6, *Miscellaneous Works and Correspondence*, reprinted with corrections, 1946)

The 'Religio Medici' and Other Writings of Sir Thomas Browne ed. C. H. Herford (E.L., 1906)

Religio Medici ed. J. J. Denonain (Cambridge, rev. ed. 1955)

Urne Burial; and The Garden of Cyrus ed. John Carter (Cambridge, 1958)

See M. Bottrall, *Every Man a Phoenix: Studies in Seventeenth Century Autobiography* (London, 1958)

E. Gosse, *Sir Thomas Browne* (London, 1905)

F. L. Huntley, *Sir Thomas Browne: The Relationship of 'Urne Burial' and 'The Garden of Cyrus'* (*Studies in Philology*, vol. 53, 1956)

O. Leroy, *Le Chevalier Thomas Browne (1605–82), médecin, styliste, et métaphysicien* (Paris, 1931)

E. S. Merton, *Science and Imagination in Sir Thomas Browne* (New York, 1949)

Leslie Stephen, *Hours in a Library, 2nd Series* (London, 1876)

B. Willey, *The Seventeenth Century Background* (London, 1934)

BUNYAN, JOHN (1628–88): Author and preacher; b. Elstow, Bedfordshire; son of tinker; educated for short time at Bedford Grammar School or Elstow; followed father's trade from early age till enlisted in Parliamentary army; married c. 1648 and returned to trade as tinker; made acquaintance of Gifford, head of Baptist community of Bedford, 1653; after death of wife c. 1656 achieved reputation as preacher throughout Bedfordshire; remarried c. 1659; imprisoned as unlicensed preacher, 1660, and spent most of next twelve years in prison, where made an intensive study of Bible and of Foxe's *Book of Martyrs* and other Puritan works; wrote many books and tracts during imprisonment, including *Grace Abounding* (1666) and *Pilgrim's Progress* (Part I published 1678, Part II published 1684); on release from prison preached all over country, particularly in London area.

Life by J. Brown, *John Bunyan* (London, 1885; rev. by F. Harrison, 1928)

Grace Abounding (E.L., 1953)

The Pilgrim's Progress (World's Classics, 1902; and E.L., 1954)

The Pilgrim's Progress, ed. J. B. Whaley, 2nd ed. rev by R. Sharrock (Oxford, 1960)

The Life and Death of Mr Badman (World's Classics, 1929; and E.L., 1953)

See Sir Charles Firth, *Essays, Historical and Literary* (Oxford, 1938)

F. R. Leavis, *The Common Pursuit* (London, 1951)

J. W. Mackail, Essay in *Studies in Humanism* (London, 1938)

R. Schlatter, *Social Ideas of Some Religious Leaders, 1660–88* (London, 1940)

R. Sharrock, *John Bunyan* (London, 1954)

H. Talon, *John Bunyan, The Man and his Works* (London, 1951)

CAREW, THOMAS (1595?–1640?): Poet; son of lawyer; Merton College, Oxford, 1608; B.A., 1611; Middle Temple, 1612; favourite of Charles I; became one of court poets; friend of Lovelace, Suckling, Davenant; reputation for dissipation; secretary to Sir Dudley Carleton, ambassador to Italy, 1613–15; accompanied Lord Herbert of Cherbury to France, 1619; wrote masque in collaboration with Inigo Jones, 1634.

Poems ed. R. Dunlap (Oxford, 1949)

See Edward I. Selig, *The Flourishing Wreath* (New Haven, 1958)

G. Williamson, *The Donne Tradition* (Cambridge, Mass., 1930)

CARTWRIGHT, WILLIAM (1611–43): Poet, dramatist, and preacher; b. near Tewkesbury; Westminster; Christ Church, Oxford, 1628; M.A., 1635; took holy orders; literary work much admired by contemporaries, including Ben Jonson; performed *Royal Slave* before court at Christ Church, Oxford, 1636; best poems are elegy on Sir Bevil Greville and poem on Jonson which contributed to *Jonsonus Virbius*, 1638; favourite of Charles I, who wore mourning for him when he died of fever.

R. C. Goffin, *The Life and Poems of William Cartwright* (Cambridge, 1918)

COWLEY, ABRAHAM (1618–77): Poet and essayist; b. London; son of stationer and bookseller; wrote first volume of poetry at age of fifteen while at Westminster; Cambridge; became Fellow of Trinity College, but was ejected by Puritans, 1644; cipher secretary to Henrietta Maria c. 1647; won contemporary reputation by publication of love poems *The Mistress*, 1647; worked for Royalist cause at Oxford and Paris; imprisoned by Cromwell as spy; in later years, lived in retirement in country, studying medicine and botany and writing *Essays in Verse and Prose* (published 1668); one of the first members of Royal Society, regarded as leader of literary world, even in retirement.

Life by S. Johnson, in *Lives of the English Poets* I ed. G. B. Hill (Oxford, 1905)

J. Loiseau, *Abraham Cowley* (Paris, 1931)

A. H. Nethercot, *Abraham Cowley* (Oxford, 1931)

English Writings ed. A. R. Waller (2 vols., Cambridge, 1905–6)

See T. S. Eliot, 'Note on two Odes of Cowley', in *Seventeenth Century Studies presented to Sir Herbert Grierson* (Oxford, 1938)

G. Walton, *Metaphysical to Augustan* (Cambridge, 1955)

G. Williamson, *The Donne Tradition* (Cambridge, Mass., 1930)

CRASHAW, RICHARD (1612–49): Poet; b. London; son of Puritan rector; Charterhouse; Pembroke, Cambridge; Fellow of Peterhouse,

1637 – expelled as Anglican, 1643; became Catholic c. 1645; friend of Cowley, to whom wrote two poems; went to Paris c. 1645 and to Italy c. 1648; at death held minor post at Cathedral of Holy House of Loreto.

Works ed. L. C. Martin (Oxford, 1927)

See M. Praz, *Secentismo e Marinismo in Inghilterra* (Florence, 1925)

    R. Wallerstein, *Richard Crashaw* (Madison, 1959)

    A. Warren, *Richard Crashaw; a Study in Baroque Sensibility* (Louisiana, 1939)

    H. C. White, *The Metaphysical Poets* (New York, 1936)

    B. Willey, *Richard Crashaw: a memorial lecture* (Cambridge, 1949)

    G. Williamson, *The Donne Tradition* (Cambridge, Mass., 1930)

DAVENANT, SIR WILLIAM (1606–68): Poet and dramatist; b. Oxford; son of tavern keeper; Oxford; in service of Duchess of Richmond and later of Fulke Greville; many friends at court, including Henry Jermyn and Endymion Porter; succeeded Ben Jonson as poet laureate, 1638; also wrote several plays produced before Civil War; knighted at Siege of Gloucester, 1643; after Royalist defeat accompanied court to France where began most important non-dramatic poem *Gondibert* and published *Discourse on Gondibert* with Hobbes' *Answer*, 1650; captured while sailing to America on royal mission, 1650, and imprisoned in Tower till 1654; wrote and produced plays for semi-private performance during Protectorate, including *The Siege of Rhodes* (first British opera), 1656; after Restoration became manager of own company.

Selected Poems ed. D. Bush (Cambridge, Mass., 1943)

Preface to *Gondibert* repr. in J. E. Spingarn's *Seventeenth Century Critical Essays* II (Oxford, 1908)

See C. M. Dowlin, *Sir William Davenant's Gondibert; Its Preface and Hobbes' Answer* (Philadelphia, 1934)

    A. Harbage, *Sir William Davenant, Poet Venturer* (Philadelphia, 1934)

DENHAM, SIR JOHN (1615–69): Poet; b. Ireland, where father was chief Baron of Exchequer; Oxford; Lincoln's Inn; loyal Cavalier; friend of Charles I; poetry, like that of Davenant, anticipates Restoration period, though most of it written before 1660; most famous poem, *Cooper's Hill*, 1642, pays tribute to Charles I and to Waller, gives an account of a stag hunt and describes places of historical interest such as Windsor Castle; regarded by Restoration critics as one of pioneers of new versification.

Works ed. T. H. Banks (New Haven, 1928)

DIGBY, SIR KENELM (1603–65): Autobiographer, poet, and philosopher; member of wealthy Catholic family; son of Sir Everard Digby, who was executed for his part in Gunpowder Plot against James I; imprisoned in Winchester House for activity against Parliament, 1642;

one of Sir Thomas Browne's first readers and published *Observations* on *Religio Medici*, 1643; autobiography, 1628, which was first published as Private Memoirs, 1827, is interesting as social history and as illustration of development of prose fiction; also wrote two philosophical *Treatises* (1645); great admirer of Spenser, on whom wrote essay *Concerning Spenser*.

Private Memoirs ed. Sir N. H. Nicolas (London, 1827)

See E. W. Bligh, *Sir Kenelm Digby and his Venetia* (London, 1932)

J. F. Fulton, *Sir Kenelm Digby, Writer, Bibliophile and Protagonist of William Harvey* (New York, 1937)

R. T. Peterson, *Sir Kenelm Digby* (London, 1956)

DONNE, JOHN (1572–1631): Poet and priest; son of prosperous iron-monger; educated as Catholic; Oxford, 1584; Lincoln's Inn, 1592; known in London as 'a great visitor of ladies, a great frequenter of plays, a great writer of conceited verses'; possibly travelled abroad, 1594–6; in Essex's expedition to Cadiz, 1596 and to the Azores, 1597; friend of Sir Henry Wotton and of Jonson; wrote most of *Satyres and Elegies* and probably many of *Songs and Sonets*, 1592–8; became Anglican c. 1598; private secretary to Lord Keeper Egerton, 1598; dismissed by Egerton, 1601, because of marriage to Anne More, niece of Egerton's wife; spent next ten years in poverty, with no regular occupation, at Mitcham, writing many of verse-letters, the rest of the *Elegies* and *Songs and Sonets* and the first religious poems, including *The Litany*, 1609; published two *Anniversaries*, 1611 and 1612, and wrote some of prose works, including *Biathanatos* about this time; ordained, 1615; chaplain to James I, 1615; Divinity Reader at Lincoln's Inn, 1616, preaching sermons which represent some of best prose of period; Dean of St Paul's 1621–31; during this last period wrote most of *Holy Sonnets* (? some earlier), rest of *Divine Poems*, sermons and other religious writings.

Life by I. Walton in *Walton's Lives* ed. G. Saintsbury (World's Classics, 1927)

E. Gosse, *Life and Letters of John Donne* (2 vols., 1899)

Sir Herbert Grierson in Introduction to his 1929 ed. of the *Poems*

Poems ed. Sir Herbert Grierson (2 vols., Oxford, 1912; abr. ed. 1 vol., Oxford, 1929)

ed. J. Hayward, *John Donne; Complete Poetry and Selected Prose* (London, 1929)

ed. T. Redpath, *Songs and Sonets* (London, 1956)

See A. Alvarez, *The School of Donne* (London, 1961)

R. C. Bald, *Donne and the Drurys* (Cambridge, 1959)

J. Bennett, *Four Metaphysical Poets* (Cambridge, 1934)

C. M. Coffin, *John Donne and the New Philosophy* (London, 1958)

P. Cruttwell, *The Shakespearean Moment* (ch. iii; London, 1954)

T. S. Eliot, 'The Metaphysical Poets' in *Selected Essays* (London, 1932)

H. Gardner, *John Donne: The Divine Poems* (Oxford, 1952)

K. W. Gransden, *John Donne* (London, 1954)

F. Kermode, *John Donne* (London, 1957)

F. R. Leavis, 'The Line of Wit' in *Revaluation* (London, 1936)

J. B. Leishman, *The Monarch of Wit* (London, 1951)

M. M. Mahood, 'Donne: The Progress of the Soul' in *Poetry and Humanism* (London, 1950)

M. Praz, *The Flaming Heart* (New York, 1958)

J. Smith, 'Metaphysical Poetry' in *Determinations* ed. F. R. Leavis (London, 1934)

T. Spencer, *A Garland for John Donne* (Harvard, 1931)

H. C. White, *The Metaphysical Poets* (New York, 1936)

Sermons ed. G. R. Potter and E. M. Simpson (10 vols., California, 1953–)

Devotions upon Emergent Occasions ed. J. Sparrow (Cambridge, 1923)

Donne's Sermons; Selected Passages ed. L. P. Smith (Oxford, 1919)

Ten Sermons ed. G. Keynes (London, 1923)

See E. M. Simpson, *A Study of the Prose Works of John Donne* (Oxford, 1924)

The Poetry and Prose of John Donne; with Izaak Walton's 'Life' (appreciations by Ben Jonson, Dryden, Coleridge and others, with an Introduction by H. W. Garrod; Oxford, 1946)

DRUMMOND, WILLIAM (1585–1649): Poet, aristocratic background; M.A., Edinburgh University; travelled on Continent; good linguist; led leisured and cultured life at estate of Hawthornden; death of fiancée and influence of Petrarch probably responsible for note of melancholy in his writing; leader of 'literary' life in Edinburgh and wrote courtly poem *Forth Feasting* to commemorate visit of King James to Scotland, 1617; visited by Ben Jonson, 1619, and made notes of their conversation.

Conversations ed. in *The Works of Ben Jonson* ed. C. H. Herford and P. Simpson I (Oxford, 1925)

Poetical Works ed. L. E. Kastner (2 vols., Manchester, 1913)

EARLE, JOHN (c. 1601–65): Character-writer, poet, scholar, and clergyman (bishop); Merton College, Oxford; Fellow, 1619; won fame by publication of *Microcosmographie*, 1628, which drew many of its 'characters' from university life; one of Falkland's circle at Great Tew; chaplain to Lord Chamberlain, tutor to Prince of Wales and adviser to Charles I; after Restoration became Dean of Westminster, then Bishop of Worcester and finally Bishop of Salisbury.

Microcosmographie ed. P. Bliss (Cambridge, 1811)

Mod. ed. H. Osborne (London, 1933)

FILMER, SIR ROBERT (d. 1653): Political writer; Trinity College, Cambridge, 1604; knighted by Charles I; imprisoned in Leeds Castle, Kent, 1644; involved in controversy with Henry Parker; *Patriarcha*, written before war in defence of absolutism and divine right, and published 1680, attacked by Locke.

> *Patriarcha and other Political Works* ed. P. Laslett (London, 1949)
>
> See J. W. Allen in *Social and Political Ideas of some English Thinkers of the Augustan Age* (London, 1926)

FLETCHER, GILES (c. 1588–1623): Poet; b. Cambridge; son of Dr Giles Fletcher, poet-ambassador, cousin of John Fletcher, dramatist; made first literary appearance with his brother in Cambridge Miscellany, *Sorrow's Joy*, 1603; disciple of Spenser; B.A. Trinity College, Cambridge, 1606; Reader in Greek, 1615; published most important poem, *Christ's Victorie and Triumph*, 1610; became rector of Alderton, Suffolk, 1619.

FLETCHER, PHINEAS (1582–1650): Poet and clergyman; son of Dr Giles Fletcher, brother of poet, Giles Fletcher; Eton and King's College, Cambridge; B.A., 1604; M.A., 1608; rector of Hilgay, Norfolk, 1621–50; on publication of most important poem, *The Purple Island*, 1633, was described by Francis Quarles as 'The Spenser of this age'; works of both Fletchers very fashionable when Milton went to Cambridge and had some influence on him.

> *The Poetical Works of Giles Fletcher and Phineas Fletcher* ed. F. S. Boas (2 vols., Cambridge, 1908–9)
>
> See A. B. Langdale, *Phineas Fletcher, Man of Letters, Science and Divinity* (New York, 1937)

FULLER, THOMAS (1608–61): Clergyman and writer; b. Aldwinkle, Northamptonshire; son of rector; took M.A. Cambridge, 1628, and became clergyman; published *The History of the Holy War*, 1639, and *The Holy State and the Profane State*, 1642; joined Charles I's court at Oxford and was chaplain to Royalist troops; after Royalist defeat, lost all clerical appointments and retired to Exeter where wrote *Good Thoughts in Bad Times*, 1645, and *Good Thoughts in Worse Times*, 1647; one of most popular writers of time and one of first English writers to support himself by pen; published *Church History*, 1655, and *History of the University of Cambridge*, 1659; after Restoration published *Mixed Contemplations in Better Times*, 1660, and became chaplain to Charles II; greatest work, *The History of the Worthies of England*, published posthumously, 1662; praised by Coleridge for his wit, 'surpassing that of the wittiest in a witty age' and for his 'sound, shrewd good sense and freedom of intellect'.

Life by J. E. Bailey (London, 1874)

D. B. Lyman, *The Great Tom Fuller* (California, 1935)

The Holy State and the Profane State ed. M. G. Walten (2 vols., Columbia, 1938)

The History of the Worthies of England ed. R. A. Nuttall (3 vols., London, 1840)

Selections ed. E. K. Broadus (Oxford, 1928)

See W. E. Houghton, *The Formation of Thomas Fuller's Holy and Profane States* (Cambridge, Mass., 1938)

GODOLPHIN, SIDNEY (1610–43): Poet; member of distinguished Cornish family; Oxford; M.P.; knew Donne, Hobbes, and Jonson; wrote obituary poems to Jonson and Donne; mainly wrote love poems; praised by Hobbes; translated fourth book of Aeneid.

Poems ed. G. Saintsbury in *Minor Poets of the Caroline Period* II (Oxford, 1906)

The Poems of Sidney Godolphin ed. W. Dighton (Oxford, 1931)

HABINGTON, WILLIAM (1605–54): Poet; b. Worcestershire; Catholic gentleman; educated in France; wrote one play *The Queen of Aragon* and one vol. poetry, *Castara*, composed in honour of Lucy Herbert, who became his wife; final version of *Castara* included four prose 'characters'; poem *In Praise of the City Life in the Long Vacation* gives interesting glimpses of contemporary life.

Poems ed. K. Allott (Liverpool and London, 1948)

HALL, JOSEPH (1574–1656): Character-writer, poet, and clergyman; b. Ashby-de-la-Zouch; Emmanuel, Cambridge, 1589; Puritan leanings; verse satires, 1597; published first English collection of 'characters', *The Characters of Virtues and Vices*, 1608; Bishop of Exeter, 1627; defended episcopacy against Milton, 1641.

Character Writings of the Seventeenth Century ed. H. Morley (London, 1891)

See D. Nichol Smith, *Characters of the Seventeenth Century* (Oxford, 1918)

HARRINGTON, JAMES (1611–77): Republican political theorist; aristocratic background; Trinity College, Oxford; spent some time in service of Elector Palatine; visited Rome and Venice; in service of Charles I at Holmby and in Isle of Wight; published *The Commonwealth of Oceana*, 1656, outlining a plan for an ideal republic in opposition to Hobbes' *Leviathan*; also wrote *Aphorisms Political . . .*, 1659, and *Political Discourses tending to the introduction of a free commonwealth in England*, 1660; formed 'Rota' club for political discussion, 1659–60; imprisoned in Tower, 1661.

The Commonwealth of Oceana ed. H. Morley (1883)
See I. Grimble, *The Harrington Family* (London, 1957)
    C. Hill, 'James Harrington and the People' in *Puritanism and Revolution* (London, 1958)
    A. E. Levett in *Social and Political Ideas of the Great Thinkers of the 16th and 17th Centuries* (London, 1926)
    H. F. R. Smith, *Harrington and his Oceana* (Cambridge, 1914)
    R. H. Tawney, *Harrington's Interpretation of his Age* in 'Proceedings of the British Academy XXVII' (London, 1941)

HERBERT OF CHERBURY, EDWARD, LORD (1583–1648): Poet, philosopher, historian and diplomat; b. Eyton-on-Severn, nr Wroxted; son of Sir Richard Herbert and eldest brother of George Herbert; University College, Oxford, 1596, where became proficient as linguist, rider, fencer and musician; at court, 1600; travelled abroad, 1608–10 and returned to England 'in great esteem both in court and city', according to autobiography; friend of Jonson, Carew and Donne; employed on diplomatic missions, 1619–24; published *De Veritate*, 1624; baron of Cherbury, 1629; began History c. 1632; aimed at neutrality during war and wrote autobiography during war years, submitted to Parliament and received pension, 1645.

Autobiography ed. C. H. Herford (London, 1928)
See Sir L. Stephen, 'Autobiography' in *Hours in a Library* III (London, 1907)
Poems ed. G. C. Moore Smith (Oxford, 1923)
    ed. R. G. Howarth in *Minor Poets of the Seventeenth Century* (E.L., 1931)
See P. Cruttwell, *The Shakespearean Moment* (London, 1954)
    G. Williamson, *The Donne Tradition* (Cambridge, Mass., 1930)

HERBERT, GEORGE (1593–1633): Poet and priest; b. Montgomery Castle; son of Sir Richard Herbert and brother of Lord Herbert; early contacts with Donne who was one of mother's friends; Westminster School; Trinity College, Cambridge; wrote Latin verses at Cambridge; distinguished scholar and able musician; Public Orator at Cambridge, 1619–27; abandoned worldly ambitions to become deacon, 1625, and priest, 1630; rector of Bemerton, nr Salisbury, 1630–3; most of poetry written during period of doubt before taking orders and during three years at Bemerton; prose work, *A Priest to the Temple*, published 1652, indicates state of mind in which wrote poems.

Life by A. G. Hyde, *George Herbert and his Times* (London, 1906)
Works ed. F. E. Hutchinson (Oxford, 1941)
Selected Poems, ed. Douglas Brown (London, 1960)
See J. Bennett, *Four Metaphysical Poets* (Cambridge, 1934)
    M. Bottrall, *George Herbert* (London, 1954)

T. S. Eliot, 'The Metaphysical Poets' in *Selected Essays* (London, 1932)

T. S. Eliot, essay repr. in *Spectator's Gallery* (London, 1932)

F. E. Hutchinson, essay in *Seventeenth Century Studies presented to Sir Herbert Grierson* (Oxford, 1938)

L. C. Knights, 'George Herbert' in *Explorations* (London, 1946)

J. B. Leishman, *The Metaphysical Poets, Donne, Herbert, Vaughan, Traherne* (Oxford, 1934)

J. H. Summers, *George Herbert* (London, 1954)

Rosemond Tuve, *A Reading of George Herbert* (London, 1952)

G. Williamson, *The Donne Tradition* (Cambridge, Mass., 1930)

HERRICK, ROBERT (1591–1674): Poet and clergyman; b. Cheapside, London; son of goldsmith; apprenticed to uncle, Sir William Herrick, prosperous London goldsmith, 1607–13; took two degrees at Cambridge; friend of Jonson and the court wits; became rector of Dean Prior, Devonshire, 1629, dismissed by Puritan government, 1647, and restored, 1662; poems which are said to have been handed down orally among country people of Dean Prior, not rediscovered till end of eighteenth century.

Poetical Works ed. L. C. Martin (Oxford, 1956)

See F. W. Moorman, *Robert Herrick, A Biography and Critical Study* (London, 1910)

F. Delattre, *Robert Herrick* (Paris, 1912)

HOBBES, THOMAS (1588–1679): Philosopher; b. Malmesbury; son of Wiltshire parson; learnt Latin and Greek at age of six; Magdalen Hall, Oxford, 1603; B.A., 1608; tutor and companion to second and third Earls of Cavendish family; friends included Harvey, Bacon, Cowley, Davenant, Jonson, Waller and Selden; travelled on Continent and made friends with Gassendi and Galileo; fled to Paris after meeting of Long Parliament, 1640; after publishing *Leviathan*, 1651, was accused of atheism and returned to England where similar charges made; was involved for many years in religious controversies and in controversies with John Boyle, John Wallis and Seth Ward; protected from Clarendon and church party by Charles II who made him pension of £100; retired to country estates, 1675.

Life by Sir L. Stephen, *The Life of Thomas Hobbes* (London, 1904)

Leviathan ed. M. Oakeshott (Oxford, 1946); and B.L. (London, 1914)

The Elements of Law Natural and Politic and *Behemoth* ed. F. Tonnies (1889)

See J. Bowle, *Hobbes and his Critics* (London, 1951)

C. Hill, 'Thomas Hobbes and the Revolution in Political Thought' in *Puritanism and Revolution* (London, 1958)

J. Laird, *Hobbes* (London, 1934)

M. Oakeshott, 'Thomas Hobbes' in *Scrutiny* IV (Cambridge, 1935)

L. Strauss, *The Political Philosophy of Hobbes* (Oxford, 1936)
H. Warrender, *The Political Philosophy of Hobbes: his theory of obligation* (Oxford, 1957)

HYDE, EDWARD, EARL OF CLARENDON (1609–74): Historian and statesman; Magdalen College, Oxford, 1626; barrister of Middle Temple, 1633; one of Falkland's circle at Great Tew; friend of Falkland, Jonson, Digby, Carew, Selden and Waller; one of opposition leaders till 1641, when refused to go whole way with Parliamentarians; Chancellor to Charles I, 1643; one of guardians of Prince of Wales (later Charles II) and followed him to Scilly and Channel Islands where began *History*, c. 1646, and wrote most of character studies of Falkland, Charles I, John Hampden, *et al.*, which were later incorporated in *History*; organizer and policy maker of exiled court; became Lord Chancellor at Restoration but was dismissed, 1667, and went to France where completed *History* and wrote *The Life of Edward, Earl of Clarendon*.

Life by Thomas Lister (3 vols., London, 1838)
History of the Rebellion ed. W. D. Macray (6 vols., Oxford, 1888)
Selections from *History of the Rebellion and Civil Wars* and *The Life . . .* ed. G. Huehns (World's Classics, 1955)
See Sir Charles Firth, *Essays, Historical and Literary* (Oxford, 1938)
    B. H. G. Wormald, *Clarendon, Politics, History and Rebellion* (Cambridge, 1951)

JONSON, BEN (1572–1637): Poet, dramatist and critic; b. Westminster; son of minister; Westminster School; bricklayer till enlisted; returned to England c. 1592; working for Henslowe c. 1597; leader of gatherings of writers held at Mermaid Tavern; great admirer of Shakespeare and Donne; friend of Selden, Bacon, Chapman and Fletcher; patrons included Countess of Bedford, Countess of Rutland, Sir Robert Sidney and the Earl of Pembroke; published poems with masques and plays, 1616; from 1616 granted pension by James I as 'King's poet'; visited William Drummond at Hawthornden, 1619 – recorded in Drummond's *Conversations*; withdrew from court after quarrel with Inigo Jones, 1630, and returned to stage; wrote last laureate verses, 1635; regarded as leader among London poets until his death when they extolled his memory in *Jonsonus Virbius*.

Life by M. Castelain, *Ben Jonson; L'Homme et l'œuvre, 1572–1637* (Paris, 1907)
Works ed. C. H. Herford and P. Simpson (Oxford, 1925–52); VIII contains Poems and Prose Works, XI contains the commentary on the poems.
Poems ed. G. B. Johnston (London, 1954)

See *The Jonson Allusion-book* ed. J. F. Bradley and J. Q. Adams (New Haven, 1922)

J. B. Bamborough, *Ben Jonson* (London, 1959)

T. S. Eliot, 'The Metaphysical Poets' in *Selected Essays* (London, 1932)

G. B. Johnston, *Ben Jonson; Poet* (New York, 1945)

F. R. Leavis, *Revaluation* (London, 1936)

H. A. Mason, *Humanism and Poetry in the Early Tudor Period* (London, 1959): chapter on 'The Humanist Heritage'.

G. Gregory Smith, *Ben Jonson* (London, 1919)

R. S. Walker, 'Ben Jonson's Lyric Poetry' in *The Criterion* XIII (London, 1933–4)

G. Walton, *Metaphysical to Augustan* (Cambridge, 1955)

KING, HENRY (1592–1669): Poet and clergyman; b. Buckinghamshire; son of bishop; Westminster School; Christ Church, Oxford; B.A., 1611; M.A. 1614; wrote elegy on Sir Walter Ralegh, 1618; wrote best poem *The Exequy* on death of wife, c. 1624; friend of Jonson and Donne and wrote elegies on both of them; bishop of Chichester, 1642; ejected, 1643, and restored at Restoration.

Life in L. Mason, 'Life and Works of Henry King' in *Transactions of the Connecticut Academy of Arts and Sciences* XVIII (1913)

Poems ed. J. Sparrow (London, 1925)

See G. Williamson, *The Donne Tradition* (Cambridge, Mass., 1930)

LILBURNE, JOHN (1615–77): Leveller leader; son of Durham squire; apprenticed to London draper; accused before Star-chamber of printing and circulating unlicensed books, 1637; imprisoned 1638–40; fought for Parliament, 1642–5; refused to take covenant, 1645, and wrote *England's Birthright Justified* while in prison; wrote pamphlets criticizing army leaders, 1648–9; imprisoned in Tower, charged with treason and acquitted, 1649; banished by special Act of 'Rump' Parliament, 1652–3; on return to England refused to promise compliance with Government and was confined in Jersey and Guernsey and at Dover Castle till 1655; became Quaker.

Life by M. A. Gibb, *John Lilburne the Leveller* (London, 1947)

England's Birthright Justified in W. Haller, *Tracts on Liberty in the Puritan Revolution* III (New York, 1934)

The Legal Fundamental Liberties of the People of England and other pamphlets in W. Haller and G. Davies, *The Leveller Tracts* (New York, 1944)

See J. Frank, *The Levellers* (Cambridge, Mass., 1955)

T. Pease, *The Leveller Movement* (London, 1916)

D. M. Wolfe, Introduction to *Leveller Manifestoes of the Puritan Revolution* (New York, 1944)

LOVELACE, RICHARD (1618–c. 1657): Poet and cavalier; b. Woolwich; member of old Kentish family; Charterhouse School; Oxford; M.A., 1636; joined court; in Scottish expedition, 1639; poems very popular with contemporary wits and poets; friends included Carew, Marvell, Henry Lawes and Charles Cotton; wrote *Stone Walls do not a Prison Make* when imprisoned, 1642, for supporting 'Kentish Petition'; joined Charles I at Oxford, 1645; fought for French king, 1646; imprisoned for seven weeks, 1648–9; while in prison wrote *Lucasta, Odes, Sonnets*, etc., died in poverty, having consumed his fortune in Cavalier cause.

Poems ed. C. H. Wilkinson (2 vols., Oxford, 1930)

See C. H. Hartmann, *The Cavalier Spirit and its Influence on the Life and Work of Richard Lovelace* (London, 1925)

MARVELL, ANDREW (1621–78): Poet and Puritan politician; b. Hull; son of clergyman of moderate Puritan sympathies; Hull Grammar School; Trinity College, Cambridge; B.A., 1638; travelled abroad, 1642–6; wrote *Horatian Ode upon Cromwell's Return from Ireland*, 1650; tutor to daughter of General Fairfax at Nun Appleton House, Yorkshire, 1651–3, when probably wrote some of most famous lyrics, including *The Garden*; tutor to William Dutton, Cromwell's ward, 1653; one of most tolerant of active Puritans; friends included James Harrington, Lovelace and Milton; Milton's colleague in Latin Secretaryship, 1657; defended Milton at his prosecution, 1660; M.P. for Hull, 1659–78; wrote much prose and some verse satires after Restoration.

Life by P. Legouis, *André Marvell, Poète, Puritain, Patriote* (Paris, 1928)

The Poems and Letters of Andrew Marvell ed. H. M. Margoliouth (2 vols., Oxford, 1927)

Andrew Marvell: Selected Poetry and Prose, ed. D. Davison (London, 1952)

The Poems of Andrew Marvell, ed. Hugh Macdonald (London, 1953)

See D. C. Allen, 'Marvell's Nymph' in *Journal of English Literary History* XXIII, No. 2 (1956)

   M. C. Bradbrook and M. G. Lloyd Thomas, *Andrew Marvell* (Cambridge, 1940)

   J. Corder, 'Marvell and Nature' in *Notes and Queries*, New Series 6, No. 2 (1959)

   D. Davison, 'Marvell's *The Definition of Love*', in *The Review of English Studies* VI, No. 22 (London, 1955)

   T. S. Eliot, 'Andrew Marvell' in *Selected Essays* (London, 1932)

   William Empson *Some Versions of Pastoral* (London, 1935): chapter on 'Marvell's Garden'; also printed in *Determinations*, ed. F. R. Leavis (London, 1934)

   F. Kermode, 'The Argument of Marvell's *Garden*' in *Essays in Criticism* II (1952)

   L. D. Lerner, 'Andrew Marvell: "An Horatian Ode Upon Cromwell's Return From Ireland"', contained in *Interpretations*, ed. John Wain (London, 1955).

John Press, *Andrew Marvell* (London, 1958)

J. H. Summers, 'Marvell's Nature' in *Journal of English Literary History* XX (1953)

Ruth Wallerstein, *Studies in Seventeenth Century Poetic* (University of Wisconsin, 1950)

G. Walton, *Metaphysical to Augustan* (Cambridge, 1955)

H. Wendell Smith, 'Cowley, Marvell and the Second Temple' in *Scrutiny* XIX (Cambridge, 1953)

G. Williamson, *The Donne Tradition* (Cambridge, Mass., 1930)

MILTON, JOHN (1608–74): Poet and Puritan administrator; b. London; son of prosperous scrivener; spent childhood in household which was Puritan, yet cultured and humanist; St Paul's School, 1620?–5?; Christ's College, Cambridge, 1625, where wrote some of earlier poems; at nineteen expressed desire to use native language 'in some graver subject'; wrote *On the Morning of Christ's Nativity*, 1629; abandoned original intention to take holy orders because could not bring himself to submit to discipline of Church; lived at Horton, Buckinghamshire, 1632–8, reading classics and studying mathematics and music and writing poems, including *L'Allegro* and *Il Penseroso*; *Comus*, produced 1634 at Ludlow Castle by one of his friends, Henry Lawes, the musician; lamented death of Cambridge friend, Edward King in *Lycidas*, 1637; travelled in Italy, France and Switzerland, 1638–9, but returned to England because of threat of Civil War; spent next twenty years teaching and pamphleteering on behalf of Puritans; married Mary Powell, member of Cavalier family, 1642; on her desertion wrote treatise on *The Doctrine and Discipline of Divorce*; published *Areopagitica*, 1644; published English and Latin poems, 1645; reunited with wife, 1645, till her death, 1652; Latin Secretaryship to Commonwealth Government, 1649; became completely blind, 1652; married Katherine Woodcock, 1656, and deplored her death in sonnet, 1658; began *Paradise Lost* probably c. 1658; prosecuted at Restoration but escaped with nominal imprisonment; married Elizabeth Minshull, 1663, and retired from public life; published *Paradise Lost*, 1667, and *Paradise Regained* and *Samson Agonistes*, 1671.

Life by D. Masson, *Life of John Milton* (7 vols., London, 1858–94; index and rev. ed. vol. I, 1881)

H. Darbishire ed., *The Early Lives of Milton* (London, 1952–6)

J. M. French ed., *Life Records* (5 vols., New Brunswick, N.J., 1949–58)

R. Graves, *Wife to Mr Milton* (London, 1942)

A. Sewell, *Study in Milton's Christian Doctrine* (London, 1939)

Works of John Milton ed. F. A. Patterson *et al.* (20 vols., Columbia, 1931–40); abr. ed. *The Student's Milton* (New York, 1933)

Poetical Works ed. H. C. Beeching (Oxford, rev. ed. 1904), ed. H. Darbishire (London, 1952–6), ed. B. A. Wright (E.L., 1956)

Paradise Lost ed. M. Y. Hughes (New York, 1935)

Paradise Regained ed. M. Y. Hughes (New York, 1937)

Complete Prose Works (Yale Edition, 7 vols., New Haven and London, 1953–)

Milton's Prose ed. M. W. Wallace (World's Classics, 1925)

Prose Selections ed. M. Y. Hughes (New York, 1947)

See R. M. Adams, *Ikon: John Milton and the Modern Critics* (Ithaca, N.Y., 1955)

A. Barker, *Milton and the Puritan Dilemma* (Toronto, 1942)

Millicent Bell, 'The Fallacy of the Fall in *Paradise Lost*' in *Publications of the Modern Language Association* LXVIII (1953)

J. B. Broadbent, *Some Graver Subject: An Essay on Paradise Lost* (London, 1960)

C. Brooks and J. E. Hardy, 'Essays in Analysis' in their ed. of *Poems of Mr John Milton, 1645* (New York, 1951)

D. Bush, *Paradise Lost in Our Time* (New York, 1945)

C. H. Collins Baker, 'Some Illustrators of Milton's *Paradise Lost*' in *The Library*, 5th Series III (1948)

H. Darbishire, ed., *Poetical Works of John Milton* (Oxford, 1958)

T. S. Eliot, essays on Milton in *T. S. Eliot: Selected Prose* ed. J. Hayward (London, 1953) and in *On Poetry and Poets* (London, 1957)

W. Empson, ' "All" in *Paradise Lost*' in *Structure of Complex Words* (London, 1951); 'Milton and Bentley' in *Some Versions of Pastoral* (London, 1935)

W. Empson, *Milton's God* (London, 1961)

J. H. Hanford, *A Milton Handbook* (4th ed., New York, 1946)

F. Kermode, ed., *The Living Milton* (London, 1960)

G. W. Knight, 'The Frozen Labyrinth: An Essay on Milton' in *The Burning Oracle* (London, 1939)

F. R. Leavis, 'Milton's Verse' in *Revaluation* (London, 1936); 'Mr Eliot and Milton' and 'In Defence of Milton' in *The Common Pursuit* (London, 1951)

C. S. Lewis, *A Preface to Paradise Lost* (London, 1942)

A. O. Lovejoy, 'Milton and the Paradox of the Fortunate Fall' in *Essays in the History of Ideas* (Baltimore, 1948)

K. Muir, *John Milton* (London, 1955)

J. Peter, *A Critique of Paradise Lost* (London, 1960)

F. T. Prince, *The Italian Element in Milton's Verse* (Oxford, 1954)

B. Rajan, *Paradise Lost and the Seventeenth-Century Reader* (London, 1947)

Sir Walter Raleigh, *Milton* (London, 1900)

J. C. Ransom, 'A Poem Nearly Anonymous' (*Lycidas*) in *The World's Body* (New York, 1938)

M. M. Ross, *Milton's Royalism: A Study of the Conflict of Symbol and Idea in the Poems* (Ithaca, N.Y., 1941)

D. Saurat, *Milton, Man and Thinker* (rev. ed., London, 1944)

A. Stein, *Answerable Style: Essays on Paradise Lost* (Minneapolis, 1953)

J. H. Summers, '"Grateful Vicissitude" in *Paradise Lost*' in *Publications of the Modern Language Association* LXIX (1954)

E. M. W. Tillyard, *Milton* (London, 1930)

E. M. W. Tillyard, *Studies in Milton* (London, 1951)

Rosemond Tuve, *Images and Themes in Five Poems by Milton* (Cambridge, Mass., and London, 1957)

A. J. A. Waldock, *Paradise Lost and Its Critics* (Cambridge, 1947)

G. Whiting, *Milton's Literary Milieu* (Chapel Hill, 1939)

B. Willey, 'The Heroic Poem in a Scientific Age' in *Seventeenth Century Background* (London, 1934)

MORE, HENRY (1614–87): Poet, philosopher and theologian; b. Lincolnshire; son of Calvinist and Cavalier family; Eton; Christ's College, Cambridge, 1631, where met Whichcote and younger Platonists; M.A. and Fellow, 1639; took orders but declined preferment and devoted life to study, writing and conversation; published *Philosophical Poems*, 1647; published *An Antidote against Atheism*, 1652, and from then wrote mainly prose; friends and other correspondents included Cudworth and other Platonists, Descartes, Jeremy Taylor, and William Penn.

Philosophical Writings of Henry More ed. F. I. Mackinnon (New York, 1925)

See F. J. Powicke, *The Cambridge Platonists* (London, 1926)

OVERBURY, SIR THOMAS (1581–1613): Character-writer; second ed. of poem, *A Wife now the widow of Sir Thomas Overbury*, included twenty-two prose characters attributed to Overbury 'and other learned gentlemen his friends'; final ed. contained eighty-three characters which are work of number of writers; two of best of these – 'A Fair and Happy Milkmaid' and 'A Franklin' – usually attributed to Webster; died in mysterious circumstances, possibly murdered.

The Overburian Characters ed. W. D. Paylor (Oxford, 1936)

See D. Nichol Smith, *Characters of the Seventeenth Century* (Oxford, 1918)

OVERTON, RICHARD (fl. 1642–63): Leveller, pamphleteer and satirist; attacked bishops in *Lambeth Fayre*, 1642; published *Man's Mortality*, 1644, which was followed by establishment of sect called 'soul sleepers' and attacked by Parliament; wrote tracts signed 'Martin Marpriest' attacking Westminster Assembly of Divines, 1646; wrote *A Remonstrance of Many Thousand Citizens* in defence of imprisoned Lilburne, 1646; imprisoned for defence of Lilburne, 1646–7; imprisoned in Tower with other Leveller leaders for contribution to second part of *England's New Chains Discovered*, 1649; escaped to Flanders with

Sexby, 1655, and obtained commission from Charles II; last Leveller to carry on struggle – imprisoned 1659 and 1663.

> *A Remonstrance of Many Thousand Citizens* in W. Haller, *Tracts on Liberty in the Puritan Revolution* III (New York, 1934)
> *An Appeal from the Degenerate Representative Body* in D. M. Wolfe, *Leveller Manifestoes of the Puritan Revolution* (New York, 1944)

PARKER, HENRY (1604–52): Political theorist; M.A., St Edmund Hall, Oxford, 1628; Lincoln's Inn, 1637; secretary to Parliamentary army, 1642; secretary to House of Commons, 1645; published numerous pamphlets advocating moderate Parliamentarism.

> *Observations upon some of his Majesty's Late Answers* (London, 1642)
> See J. W. Allen, *English Political Thought 1603–44* (London, 1938)
> W. K. Jordan, *Men of Substance* (Chicago, 1942)

RANDOLPH, THOMAS (1605–35): Poet and dramatist; b. Northamptonshire; son of steward to Edward, Lord Zouch; Westminster School; Cambridge, where won reputation as writer of English and Latin verse; great admirer of Jonson to whom wrote *Gratulatory to Mr Ben Jonson for His Adopting Him to be His Son*; friend of James Shirley and Sir Kenelm Digby; wrote pastorals, elegies and epithalamia; also wrote five plays which were performed in his lifetime.

> *Poems and Amyntas* ed. J. J. Parry (Yale, 1927)
> *Poems* ed. G. Thorn Drury (London, 1929)
> See G. C. Moore Smith, *Thomas Randolph* (Warton Lecture on English Poetry; London, 1927)

SELDEN, JOHN (1584–1644): Scholar, lawyer and politician; Inner Temple; friend of Jonson; great reputation for scholarship among his contemporaries; very active in public life; M.P. in Long Parliament; *Table Talk*, compiled by secretary during last twenty years of life, published 1689.

> *Table Talk* ed. Sir F. Pollock (Selden Society, 1927)
> See H. Paul, *Men and Letters* (London, 1901)

SUCKLING, SIR JOHN (1609–42): Poet, dramatist and courtier; b. Twickenham, Middlesex; son of important court official; Trinity College, Cambridge; travelled in France and Italy; fought in Germany under Gustavus Adolphus; returned to England, 1632, and joined court circle where acquired reputation for wit, conversation and accomplishments, and also for dissipation; took part in expedition against Scots, 1639; began writing, 1637 – poetry notable for lightness and humour rather than for depth of feeling or polish; published best poem, *Ballad upon a Wedding*, 1640; good letter-writer; wrote four plays, mainly interesting today because of their allusions to contemporary writers; took part in royalist conspiracy to free Earl of Strafford, 1641; on discovery of this plot, escaped to France where, according to Aubrey, he poisoned himself.

> Life by A. I. Suckling prefixed to his *Selections* (London, 1836)
>
> *Works* ed. A. H. Thompson (London, 1910)
>
> *Poems* ed. R. G. Howarth in *Minor Poets of the Seventeenth Century* (E.L., 1931)
>
> See F. W. Moorman in *C.H.E.L.*, VIII (1912)

TAYLOR, JEREMY (1613–67): Priest and writer; b. Cambridge; son of barber; Cambridge, 1626; B.A., 1630–1; M.A., 1633–4; Fellow of Caius College c. 1633; took orders; preaching impressed Laud who sent him to Oxford where became Fellow of All Souls, 1636; Chaplain to Laud and then Chaplain-in-ordinary to Charles II; published *Sermon upon the Anniversary of the Gunpowder Treason*, 1638; taken prisoner by Parliamentary forces, 1645; on release settled at Golden Grove, Carmarthenshire, where found occupation as teacher and as chaplain to second Earl of Carbery; wrote *The Rule and Exercises of Holy Living*, 1650, and *The Rule and Exercises of Holy Dying*, 1651; Bishop of Down and Connor, 1661.

> *Works* (including *Life*) ed. R. Heber (15 vols., London, 1822; rev. C. P. Eden, 10 vols., 1847–54)
>
> *The Golden Grove; Selected Passages from . . . Jeremy Taylor* ed. L. P. Smith (Oxford, 1930)
>
> See E. Gosse, *Jeremy Taylor* (London, 1903)
>
> W. J. Brown, *Jeremy Taylor* (London, 1925)

VAUGHAN, HENRY (c. 1622–95): Poet and physician; b. Newton-by-Usk, Brecknockshire; member of old and distinguished Welsh family; Jesus College, Oxford, 1638; studied law in London; took some part in Civil War on royalist side; practised medicine for few years at Brecknock, then settled as doctor at Newton-by-Usk c. 1650; began literary career by writing secular poetry, published 1646 and 1651; experienced religious conversion c. 1648 and in preface to 2nd part of *Silex Scintillans*, 1655, repudiated frivolous verse.

> F. E. Hutchinson, *Henry Vaughan; a Life and Interpretation* (Oxford, 1947)
>
> *The Works of Henry Vaughan* ed. L. C. Martin (2nd ed., Oxford, 1957)
>
> See J. Bennett, *Four Metaphysical Poets* (Cambridge, 1934)
>
> R. Garner, *Henry Vaughan* (Cambridge, 1959)
>
> E. Holmes, *Henry Vaughan and the Hermetic Philosophy* (Oxford, 1932)
>
> J. B. Leishman, *Metaphysical Poets* (Oxford, 1934)
>
> M. M. Mahood, *Poetry and Humanism* (London, 1950)
>
> H. C. White, *The Metaphysical Poets* (New York, 1936)

WALLER, EDMUND (1606–87): Poet; b. Hertfordshire; son of wealthy country gentleman; Eton; Cambridge; M.P. from age of sixteen; frequent visitor to Penshurst, home of Sidneys; published first collection of poems, 1645; one of best songs, 'Go Lovely Rose', first printed

in miscellany, *Ayres and Dialogues*, 1655; popular with all courts –
wrote panegyrics on Charles I, Cromwell, Charles II and Prince of
Orange; verse notable for smoothness and polish and more characteristic of Restoration era than of preceding one; greatly admired by contemporaries, who regarded him, with Denham, as one of pioneers of
new versification.

Life by Dr Johnson in *Lives of the English Poets* (1779)
Poems ed. G. Thorn Drury (2 vols., London, 1905)
See F. W. Bateson, *English Poetry: a Critical Introduction* (London, 1950)

WALTON, IZAAK (1593–1683): Bibliographer; b. London; son of shop-
keeper; self-educated; one of Donne's parishioners and describes himself as 'the poorest, the meanest of all his friends'; literary life began
when became friend of Sir Henry Wotton, who commissioned him to
collect material for life of Donne; prefixed *Life of Donne* to ed. Donne's
Sermons, 1640; published *Life of Sir Henry Wotton*, 1651; wrote *The
Compleat Angler* in retirement and published it 1653; published *Life
of George Herbert*, 1670, and *Life of Sanderson*, 1678.

Lives ed. G. Saintsbury (World's Classics, 1927)
The Compleat Angler mod. ed. A. Lang (E.L., 1906)

WALWYN, WILLIAM (fl. 1649): Leveller pamphleteer; silk-man of
London; read Montaigne and classical writers; took Parliamentary
side; published *Power of Love*, advocating religious tolerance and
practical Christianity, 1643; imprisoned, 1649, for share in *England's
New Chains Discovered*.

'The Power of Love' in W. Haller, *Tracts on Liberty in the Puritan Revo-
lution* II (New York, 1934) and *England's Lamentable Slavery* in Haller, III
'Walwyn's Just Defence' in W. Haller and G. Davies, *The Leveller Tracts*
(New York, 1944)
See W. Schenk in *The Concern for Social Justice in the Puritan Revolution*
(London, 1947)

WINSTANLEY, GERRARD (1609–after 1660): Leader of 'Diggers';
became prominent, 1649, as leader of party of men who tried to set up
model community at St George's Hill, Surrey, asserting right of common people to claim land without paying rent; published tracts on
subject of communal ownership and on religious questions; became
Quaker.

Selections from the Works of Gerrard Winstanley ed. L. D. Hamilton
(London, 1944)
See D. W. Petegorsky, *Left-Wing Democracy in the English Civil War*
(London, 1940)
E. Bernstein, *Cromwell and Communism* (London, 1930)
L. H. Berens, *The Digger Movement* (London, 1906)

INDEX

*Other Pelicans are described
on the following pages*

THE LITERARY CRITICS

GEORGE WATSON

A 553

This is the first history of English criticism by a British scholar since Saintsbury's, which is now over fifty years old. It is also highly original in approach. The author, who is a Cambridge lecturer in English, sees the development of criticism as a dynamic and uneven process. He dissociates himself from what he calls the 'Tidy School' of critical historians, which takes for granted a steady evolution of doctrine. Instead he traces a pattern broken up by sudden disturbances. The great critics refuse to accept obsolescent critical assumptions: they interrupt the commonplace literary debates of their day with their forcefully vital new ideas.

The Literary Critics forms a detailed illustration and development of this theme. It deals with English descriptive criticism – the analysis of literary works – from its origins in Dryden through the writings of the Augustans, Johnson, the Romantic critics, Arnold, and (in America) Henry James, to T. S. Eliot and the contemporary scene. The book's fresh approach to a valuable aspect of literary studies makes it equally stimulating for student or layman.

A SHORT HISTORY OF
ENGLISH LITERATURE

SIR IFOR EVANS

A 72

Here in the space of two hundred pages Sir Ifor Evans provides a panorama of English Literature from *Beowulf* to James Joyce. The precision and lucidity with which he evaluates the periods and varieties of our literature express themselves with an economy of language which enables him to cover the wide field without skimming. This well-considered and companionable book rapidly and clearly surveys the principal modes of literature – poetry, drama, and the novel – throughout twelve centuries.

'Professor Evans writes to the classical model, as brief, as lucid. He relates the arts to society instead of penning them in the study. As a judge he is tolerant and undogmatic, but never slack in his standards. He is fair to all and gushes over none. ... This justice of approach is coupled with a mastery of phrase which makes the writing lively without being exhaustingly exhibitionist in judgement or epigrammatic in style' – Ivor Brown in the *Observer*

A SHORT HISTORY OF
ITALIAN LITERATURE

J. H. WHITFIELD

A 455

It is over sixty years since Richard Garnett published in 1898 the
last History of Italian Literature to be written by an Englishman.
The time is therefore more than ripe for this firsthand account of the
whole field, from the origins and from the first great figure, Dante,
through Petrarch, Machiavelli and the Renascence, Tasso, Leopardi,
and Manzoni, down to Pirandello in our own day. In this book,
synopsis and biography have been kept at bay, to give place to a
reasoned and a personal account of the major authors and the major
trends of Italian culture. The strength of this new *History of Italian
Literature* lies especially in the fact that its author has never been
afraid to tackle in his criticism the greatest authors, and the greatest
problems, of the Italian tradition, and is in consequence one of the
few whose views on certain major authors have made their impact in
Italy itself. In this book the whole field of Italian literature, with its
unrivalled contribution to the general culture of Europe, is seen from
a new standpoint. This is not only a useful and reliable manual for
reference, but also a book to be read.

THE LITERATURE OF THE
UNITED STATES

MARCUS CUNLIFFE

A 289

The Literature of the United States is not intended as a textbook or work of reference, but as a general introduction to the main themes and figures of the American literary scene, from colonial times to the present day. Literature is to some extent treated as an expression of American character and experience. Thus, the problems faced by American writers *as Americans* are stressed throughout. However, it is suggested – especially in the concluding chapters – that the division between American and European literary qualities has been unfortunate, though understandable; and that it is a sign of American cultural maturity that the division is now less insisted upon than formerly. A table of dates in American history is appended, and the *Notes on Further Reading* are designed to lead those interested toward a fuller acquaintance with the subject.

'This most admirable book reveals many qualities in its author . . . but good sense is the first and most important of his assets . . . Mr Cunliffe is not only sensible – he is just. . . . He is very good, too, on the social side of literature. . . . In short a very good book indeed and wonderful value for the money.' – D. W. Brogan in *The Manchester Guardian*

A SHORT HISTORY
OF FRENCH LITERATURE

GEOFFREY BRERETON

A 297

This compact history deals in outline with the whole of French literature, from the *chansons de geste* to the theatre to-day. While the chief works of the Middle Ages are described briefly, the great writers since the beginning of the Renaissance receive fuller treatment, and almost half the book is devoted to the nineteenth and twentieth centuries. Over eight hundred years of rich and varied writing are treated on a scale which makes clear the great general movements of thought and taste without neglecting the characteristic qualities of individual authors and their works. These are approached primarily as literature, to be read as the personal expressions of particularly interesting minds, but they are related to the social history of their time and, on occasion, to the literatures of countries other than France. The book is intended both for the general reader and for the student who wishes to take his bearings before specializing in any one particular field. Based on modern scholarship and reflecting modern critical opinion, it is a concisely informative as well as a companionable work.

THE PELICAN
HISTORY OF ENGLAND

While each volume is complete in itself, the whole series, edited by
J. E. Morpurgo, has been planned to provide an intelligent and con-
secutive guide to the development of English society in all its aspects.
The eight volumes are:

'*As a portent in the broadening of popular culture the influence of this wonderful series has yet to receive full recognition and precise assessment. No
venture could be more enterprising or show more confidence in the public's
willingness to purchase thoughtful books. . . .*' – The Listener

THE PELICAN HISTORY OF ART

Edited by Nikolaus Pevsner

THE ART AND ARCHITECTURE OF INDIA
Benjamin Rowland
Professor of Fine Arts, Harvard University

ART AND ARCHITECTURE IN FRANCE: 1500 TO 1700
Anthony Blunt
Director of the Courtauld Institute of Art, University of London;
Surveyor of the Queen's Pictures

THE ART AND ARCHITECTURE OF RUSSIA
George Heard Hamilton
Associate Professor, Yale University

PAINTING IN BRITAIN: THE MIDDLE AGES
Margaret Rickert
Sometime Associate Professor, University of Chicago

PAINTING IN BRITAIN: 1530 TO 1790
Ellis K. Waterhouse
Director of the Barber Institute of Fine Art, Birmingham

ARCHITECTURE IN BRITAIN: 1530 TO 1830
John Summerson
Curator, Sir John Soane's Museum, London

SCULPTURE IN BRITAIN: THE MIDDLE AGES
Laurence Stone
Fellow of Wadham College, Oxford

THE ART AND ARCHITECTURE OF JAPAN
Robert Treat Paine
Assistant Curator, Museum of Fine Arts, Boston, Mass;
and Alexander Soper
Professor at Bryn Mawr College, Penn.

THE ART AND ARCHITECTURE OF THE ANCIENT ORIENT
Henri Frankfort
Late Director Warburg Institute, University of London

FIVE HUNDRED YEARS OF PRINTING

S. H. STEINBERG

A 343

Since this book first appeared in 1955 it has established itself as a standard work, been published in a hardback edition, and been translated into German and Italian. For this fully revised edition there are many new illustrations, which have now been worked into the body of the text for greater ease of reference.

Five Hundred Years of Printing traces the close interrelation between printing and culture. The author's erudite but highly readable survey takes in not only a long time-span but also particular topics like censorship, best-sellers, popular series, and the connexion between printing and education, language, and literature. Here indeed, as Beatrice Warde writes in her foreword, 'are the five hundred years of printing as a creator of changes in human lives'.

'A concise and scholarly but entertaining account of the story of the relation between printing and civilization' – *The British Printer*